Assault on Paradise

Social Change in a Brazilian Village

Assault on Paradise

Social Change in a Brazilian Village

Conrad Phillip Kottak
University of Michigan

RANDOM HOUSE NEW YORK

First Edition
98765432
Copyright © 1983 by Random House, Inc.

Library of Congress Cataloging in Publication Data

Kottak, Conrad Phillip.
  Assault on paradise.

  Bibliography: p.
  Includes index.
  1. Arembepe (Brazil)—Social conditions. I. Title.
HN290.A73K67 1983   306'.0981'42   82-25059
ISBN 0-394-33409-4

Cover photo © Emil Javorsky

Cover design by Nancy Bumpus

Manufactured in the United States of America

To Cecilia and Charles Wagley

Preface

For two decades I have been studying Arembepe, Bahia, Brazil. My research in this coastal community in the western hemisphere's second largest nation began unusually and accidentally, but it continued because of the fascinating transformation I could see occurring there. The story of change in Arembepe is interesting in its own right, particularly in terms of such issues as economic development, industrial pollution, and the spread of a "world culture" and an international political economy. Accordingly, I think that *Assault on Paradise* will be of particular interest to Latin Americanists, applied anthropologists, development specialists, and comparative economists. However, it was not just for them that I wrote the book.

Assault on Paradise was also written for the novice anthropologist. In deciding how I would make this narrative unfold I kept in mind the introductory students I have taught for fifteen years. This I did for several reasons. First, I began doing anthropological field work myself—in Arembepe—when I was a college student. *Assault on Paradise* describes my grappling with the alien nature of another culture, my fledgling attempts at ethnography, and my development as an anthropologist. I write about some of the ways in which my career and my personal life have been intertwined with Arembepe and with its transformation over two decades. I know that students appreciate books like Napoleon Chagnon's *Yanomamo: The Fierce People* because they blend descriptions of people in another culture with the anthropologist's recollection of his own attitudes, feelings, and reactions. I tried not to forget this as I wrote *Assault on Paradise*.

The second reason I decided to write for the beginning student also has to do with my introductory teaching experience. Usually I supplement a textbook with two ethnographies, the first about a "primitive" society, the second about a "peasant-type" culture or about social change. Such books as *Yanomamo: The Fierce People, Return to Laughter, The Forest People,* and *The Harmless People* are all studies of technologically simple hunter-gatherers or tribal cultivators. Arembepe, on the other hand, is a community in a state-level society, and *Assault on Paradise* is therefore intended for the second half of the introductory course.

I am pleased that my editors at Random House gave me the opportunity to tell Arembepe's story in a way that I hope will hold the attention of introductory students while also teaching them something of value about anthropology. I have tried to write a book that is both academically sound and relatively jargon free. Finally, because my main goal has been to make *Assault on Paradise* an effective teaching book, I have covered a broad range of topics normally discussed in the introductory course, including ethnographic field methods, kinship, social organization, economy, political organization, culture and personality, religion, social stratification, and such contemporary forces as mechanization, industrialization, suburbanization, and internationalization through tourism and the mass media.

C. P. K.

Acknowledgments

From a glance at the list of "Principal Characters," the reader can tell that this book introduces not just Arembepeiros, but anthropologists as well. Arembepe's first anthropological experience was as a "field-team village," visited by various members of the Columbia branch of the Columbia-Cornell-Harvard-Illinois Summer Field Studies Program in Anthropology between 1962 and 1964. I want to acknowledge my debt to all the members of those field teams who worked with me or shared their findings and impressions about Arembepe. I must single out Peter Gorlin and Niles Eldredge, but David G. Epstein, Erica Bressler, and Shepard Forman also deserve special thanks. Maxine Margolis helped with the 1982 fieldwork, as did Jerald Milanich, who carefully sketched the map of Arembepe in 1980 and then had it prepared by his staff at the Florida State Museum. Jerry also took many of the photos incorporated in this book. Thanks to Juliet Maria Kottak, Nicholas Charles Kottak, and Nara Bales Milanich for their help, too.

As *Assault on Paradise* makes obvious, Betty Wagley Kottak began studying Arembepe with me in 1962 and has been part of this story ever since. I am profoundly grateful for her companionship, assistance, insights, and analyses.

Marvin Harris encouraged and motivated the teen-aged anthropologist of 1962 to become a professional; he guided me through the doctorate, and his work continues to be an inspiration for my own. Robert Murphy and Lambros Comitas read two drafts of my doctoral dissertation and helped me develop my interpretation of Arembepe during the 1960s.

Among our Brazilian colleagues I am grateful to Dr. Thales de Azevedo, Mariá de Azevedo, Maria and Paulo Brandão, and the Azevedo family for various kinds of assistance and hospitality in Bahia.

Most obviously, this manuscript could not have been written without the friendship, help, and cooperation of hundreds of Arembepeiros. In addition to those called Alberto, Fernando, Dora, and Tomé in this book, I wish to thank Athaydes Alves de Souza, Vandice Nascimento, Aurino Alves, and Francisco dos Santos for their special help.

I am grateful to those who have read and commented on *Assault on Paradise* in manuscript form: Maxine Margolis, Niles Eldredge, Charles and Cecilia Wagley, Mariana Kottak Roberts, G. Harvey Summ, Charlotte Revilla, and several Michigan graduate students. For what he has taught me about Brazil, and for his encouragement of my research in Brazil and in anthropology generally, I am grateful to Daniel R. Gross.

It has been a pleasure working with anthropology editor David Follmer on the third editions of my textbooks *Anthropology* and *Cultural Anthropology* and now on *Assault on Paradise*. Others at Random House who merit my gratitude for their work on *Assault on Paradise* include Casimir Psujek, Fred Burns, and R. Lynn Goldberg. I am especially grateful to Jeffrey Longcope, who brought trade-publishing experience and a nonanthropologist's perspective to his evaluation of an earlier manuscript. He suggested numerous ways in which I could enliven that earlier version, encouraging me, for example, to pay more attention to letting villagers tell their own story. I believe that Jeff's input has made *Assault on Paradise* not only more readable, but also a much more effective teaching book than it would have been otherwise.

Here at Michigan, Susan Pollock has helped me meet deadlines by rapid and efficient typing and retyping, for which I am very grateful.

Several agencies and institutions have contributed to our research in Arembepe in 1962, 1964, 1965, 1973, and 1980. I acknowledge my debt to The National Institute of Mental Health for a predoctoral fellowship and later for a small grant to investigate "Local-Level Effects of Modernization," to the Foreign Area Fellowship Program for partial support, through a postdoctoral individual fellowship, of field work in Arembepe in 1973, and to the Horace H. Rackham School of Graduate Studies and the Office of the Vice President for Research of the University of Michigan.

Assault on Paradise is dedicated to Charles and Cecilia Wagley, my parents-in-law, without whom, for a variety of reasons, none of this would have happened. Cecilia Wagley has supported me in many ways; she has shared her family and her friends in Brazil and has offered me many insights about her country over the past twenty years. Chuck Wagley has always provided advice, ideas, and information when I needed them. I can only aspire to be the anthropologist and humanist that Chuck is. That humanity, coupled with the analytic and interpretive abilities of a skilled anthropologist is very obvious in his book *Welcome of Tears*. That study of the Tapirape Indians of Brazil is a work I admire tremendously, and, as much as the books mentioned in the Preface, I had *Welcome of Tears* in the back of my mind as I wrote *Assault on Paradise*. This dedication is my way of acknowledging the special place that Cecilia and Charles Wagley have occupied in my profession and in my life.

C. P. K.

Contents

Preface   vii
Acknowledgments   ix
Principal Characters   xvi

PART ONE. A STORY OF CHANGE   1

1. Before: The Sixties   3
It Began Quite by Accident   4
The Sixties   7
Malinowski and Microprojects   11
It Was an Alien Place   20

2. After: The Road to 1980   29
Obstacles to Anthropological Objectivity   40
1980: The Whole World Is Open to Arembepe   43

PART TWO. PARADISE   49

3. The Structure of Equality   51
An Open, Noncorporate Community   56
The Costs and Benefits of Kinship   61
Machismo *and Male-Female Inequality*   67
Race Relations   73

4. The Protestant Ethic and the Spirit of
Fishermen   78
The Sailor's Life   82
Excelling in an Egalitarian Society   87
The Riddle of the Spots   95

5. The Bigger Pond   101
The Patron's Shadow   105
Individuals, Not Classes   116
Experiencing the World Outside   118

PART THREE. ASSAULT ON PARADISE   125

6. The Browning of Arembepe   127
Occupational Diversity   133
Motorization and the Fishermen's Cooperative   136

From Skills to Property   140
The Dawn of Stratification   141
The Magic of Success   144
Other Changes and the Possible Danger of Overfishing   151

PART FOUR. REALITY   155

7. Another Sunrise in the Land of Dreams   157
Worlds Apart   162
Subdivisions   163
Population Growth   166
Familiar Outsiders   167
The Rental Business   169
Boxcar Apartments   170
Resident Hippies   171
The Hippie Handbook   173
Nature and Culture in the Hippie Aldeia   176
A Dimming Symbol   184

8. If You Don't Fish, You Work for Tibrás   186
Larger Boats and Long-Distance Fishing   189
Motorization and the Cooperative   192
Marketing   193
A Double Profit   195
The Genesis of Stratification: Capital and Land Time   197
New Crews: Strangers and Debtors   199
From Fellowship to Exploitation   201
Where Are the Arembepeiros?   203
The Basis of the New Order   204
Factory Work at Tibrás   208

9. The Web of Government   214
Welfare and Education   214
Public Health   218
Marriage and the State   224
The Sex Ratio and Female Status   229

10. Social Differentiation and the Origin of
    Deviance   231
The Rise of the Bourgeoisie   232
An Irrational Fear of Robbers   233
Alcoholism and Mental Illness   236
From Individual Idiosyncrasy to Group Label   240
Race Relations and Sex Roles   242
The Birth of Religion   245

11. A Community of Outsiders   254
   The Teacher   256
   The Village Prostitute: What Happens to the Deviant Once
   Deviance Disappears   263
   The Stranger   270
   The Innovator   276

Epilogue   288

Appendixes   291

Chapter Notes   299

References Cited   305

Index   309

Principal Characters

The Anthropologists

Conrad Phillip Kottak (Conrado)
> Author of this book, began fieldwork in Arembepe in 1962; returned in 1964, 1965, 1973, 1980.

Isabel Wagley Kottak (Betty)
> Began fieldwork in Arembepe in 1962; returned each time with Conrad.

David Epstein
> Member of 1962 field team, holds Ph.D. in anthropology from Columbia University.

Marvin Harris
> Leader of 1962 Brazil field team, Columbia-Cornell-Harvard-Illinois Summer Field Studies Program in Anthropology; currently graduate research professor of anthropology at the University of Florida.

Peter Gorlin
> Member of 1964 field team stationed in Jauá, helped complete interview schedule in Arembepe; holds Ph.D. in anthropology from Columbia University and M.D. from Harvard.

Thales de Azevedo
> Leader of 1964 Bahia field team, of which Conrad Kottak was assistant leader; Bahian physician and anthropologist.

Niles Eldredge
> Member of 1963 field team in Arembepe; currently curator of invertebrate paleontology at New York's American Museum of Natural History.

Shepard Forman
> Assistant field leader, stationed in Arembepe in 1963; holds Ph.D. in anthropology from Columbia University.

Raymond Rapaport
> Undergraduate field assistant to Conrad Kottak in 1973.

Maxine Margolis
> Helped out with 1980 field work in Arembepe; currently associate professor of anthropology at the University of Florida.

Jerald T. Milanich
> Graciously did mapping and photography of Arembepe in 1980; archaeologist at Florida State Museum, Gainesville.

The Villagers

Alberto
> Fisherman turned barkeeper, Conrad Kottak's best informant, and field assistant in 1973 and 1980.

Tomé
> Through the 1970s Arembepe's most successful fisherman, captain, and boat owner.

Dora
> Anthropologists' cook on several occasions; unmarried mother formerly classified as a village prostitute.

Fernando
> Moderately successful fishing captain; joined a cult and turned to alcohol in reaction to Arembepe's transformation.

Amy
> Claudia's daughter, inherited her business.

Aunt Dalia
> Businesswoman whose success rested on sales to hippies, ran juice bar in Street Down There.

Carolina
> Alberto's wife, started successful business in Street Down There in the early 1970s; cult participant.

Claudia
> Opened Arembepe's best restaurant in the early 1970s.

Dinho
> Tomé's younger brother; by 1980 owned five boats, marketed fish, and was Arembepe's richest entrepreneur.

Jaime
> Tibrás worker in 1980; water boy for 1964 and 1965 field teams.

Julia
>   Psychotic young villager with penchant for nudism.

Laurentino
>   Iconoclastic storekeeper suspected of devil worship.

Maria
>   "Saint's daughter" in local *candomblé* cult.

Roberto
>   Fish marketer from Salvador, visited Arembepe through 1964.

Prudencio
>   Agent of Arembepe's absentee landlords.

The Landlords

Jorge Camões
>   First of Arembepe's absentee landlords to obtain university education; masterminded Arembepe's real estate boom.

Francisca Ricardo
>   Last landlord to reside in Arembepe; died in 1924.

Assault on Paradise

Social Change in a Brazilian Village

Part One

A Story of Change

1 Before: The Sixties

This anthropological study of rapid change in a formerly isolated and tranquil Atlantic coastal community in Brazil covers nearly twenty years. The story of Arembepe[1] (Ah-*raim*-beppy), once just a small fishing village in Bahia state, north-central Brazil, is worth telling in its own right. But it also has a larger significance. Although far more dramatically than most, Arembepe has met the increasingly common fate of the little community in the Third World. As a result of their poverty and powerlessness, the people of Arembepe, or Arembepeiros (Ah-raim-bep-*pay*-roos), have been compelled by external forces to give up a large part of their previous autonomy, egalitarianism, and peace of mind. Like a thousand other places, Arembepe has grown increasingly dependent on, and vulnerable to, a world political economy of which its inhabitants have little understanding, and over which they have even less control. And provincial folk who once were impressed by, yet dared only gently probe, the novelty and strangeness of foreign ways have become eager initiates into a mass-mediated world culture.

This book is based on five visits to Arembepe: in 1962, 1964, 1965, 1973, and 1980. The book's structure is based on the contrast between the traditional village of the 1960s and the contemporary community of the 1980s. Chapters 3–5 give baseline information about Arembepe through 1965, before it encountered those forces of change that had modified community life so obviously by the mid-1970s: motorization of the fishing industry, tourism and the "hippie" invasion, massive industrial pollution, and suburbanization through the opening of a paved road to Salvador, the state capital. These and other trends associated with economic development had drastically altered community life by 1973, when I returned to Arembepe after an eight-year absence (Chapter 6). My 1973 fieldwork provided a picture of Arembepe in transition. Accordingly, Chapter 6, which describes Arembepe in 1973, provides a transition to Part IV (Chapters 7–11), which describes the hugely transformed community of 1980. Arembepe is being drawn ever more firmly into the web of expanding Salvador—a metropolis with more than 1 million people—and through it into a world system and toward cultural homogenization. This book tells the story of that transformation.

It Began Quite by Accident

This is a story of change, but it did not start out to be that. In fact, it began quite by accident. I first lived in Arembepe during the (North American) summer of 1962. That was between my junior and senior years at New York City's Columbia College, where I was majoring in anthropology. I went to Arembepe as a participant in a now defunct program designed to provide undergraduates with experience doing ethnography—firsthand study of an alien society's culture and social life. The program's cumbersome title, the Columbia-Cornell-Harvard-Illinois Summer Field Studies Program in Anthropology, reflected participation by four universities, each with a different field station. The others were in Peru, Mexico, and Ecuador. The area around Salvador, Brazil, had just been chosen for the Columbia field station, and that is where I was sent.

The field team leader was Professor Marvin Harris, who was later to become my adviser and doctoral dissertation committee chairman during my graduate work in anthropology at Columbia University, which began in 1963. Also in Salvador that year was Professor Charles Wagley, another Columbia anthropologist, who had worked with Harris and others to establish the program. Through their links with Bahian social scientists, Harris and Wagley chose two villages that were sufficiently remote to be anthropologically interesting but close enough to Salvador to maintain contact with the undergraduates. The two communities lay along the same road. Abrantes, the agricultural village, nearer to Salvador, was district seat for Arembepe, the more remote fishing village. Liking the coast, I expressed a preference for Arembepe, where I was assigned, along with fellow team member David Epstein. Harris arranged for us to rent the dilapidated three-bedroom summer house of a city man who sometimes vacationed in Arembepe.

In the meantime, Professor Wagley's daughter, Betty, a Barnard College student who was considering majoring in anthropology, arrived to spend the summer with her parents in Salvador. She went along with us to visit Abrantes and Arembepe and decided that she, too, would like some fieldwork experience in the latter. Betty arranged lodging with a local woman, but since David and I had hired a cook, she ate with us and shared the cost of food and supplies. Betty's mother is Brazilian, and Betty, who was herself born in Brazil, is bilingual in Portuguese, which made her more adept at fieldwork than either David or I. She was also kind enough to translate for us on many occasions.

Having taught anthropology now for fifteen years, I retrospectively realize how unusual my first field experience was. Most anthropologists begin fieldwork, which is required for the doctorate, after a few years of graduate study and not as undergraduates. Furthermore, they usually determine for themselves the part of the world they want to work in and the kind of problem they will investigate there. For example, my own most lengthy ethnographic project came at the end of graduate school. Having taken courses about several world areas, I became particularly interested in Madagascar. I read as much as I could about the cultures of Madagascar and settled on a problem—the social implications of an economic change, the expansion of irrigated agriculture—that could be investigated there.

In the case of Arembepe, however, someone else—the directors of the summer field program, for which I was chosen competitively—selected the general area, and even the specific village, for me. I did not have time to do the extensive background reading that normally precedes fieldwork, nor did I have much time to study the language that I would be using in the field. I therefore had no control over the initial choice of Arembepe, though I did decide to keep on studying it, particularly when, by 1973, it became apparent that

Arembepe was changing more rapidly in a decade than some communities have changed in centuries—which is why I decided to write this book.

Most of my preparation for my 1962 fieldwork was in a prefield seminar that Harris offered at Columbia, and in another seminar about ethnographic field techniques taught by Professor Lambros Comitas. In Harris's class, students talked about the kinds of research we planned to do when we got to Brazil, and Harris urged us to do microprojects, focusing on limited aspects of community life that we could investigate easily in three months. The program's founders did not intend for this to be traditional holistic ethnography—intensive study of all aspects of life through long-term residence and participant observation. Comitas's seminar, on the other hand, had introduced me to techniques used in long-term, in-depth ethnography. As I describe later on, one of my problems in doing fieldwork in Arembepe in 1962 was the conflict between my own desire to do a holistic study and the program's preference for a microproject.

The program's goals were limited, and I now realize that this was realistic, since we were novices. Harris and the other leaders intended for us to get our feet wet—to see if we actually liked fieldwork enough to pursue a career in cultural anthropology and to give us an experience that would help prepare us for subsequent, longer-term field research. As preparation for our microprojects, the prefield seminar assignment was to do background reading and a research paper on the topic we planned to investigate in Brazil. Harris suggested that I study race relations, which already had a large literature. Comparisons of race relations in Brazil and the United States are in order because both countries have a heritage of slavery and plantation life, and in both there has been considerable mixture of Europeans, Africans, and (to a lesser extent) Native Americans. For the seminar, I read extensively. I learned the main differences between the role of race in Brazil and the United States and wrote a research paper on my findings. Harris and I later worked out a specific microproject on Brazilian racial classification for the field, which is discussed later in this chapter.

Although I prepared myself adequately to investigate Brazilian race relations, my preparation in Brazilian Portuguese was insufficient, and language turned out to be my biggest barrier in the field. The only Romance language I had ever studied was Latin, for two years in high school. I had taken German in college, which was no help at all. I had never been abroad before and had no experience actually speaking a foreign language: high school and college had barely taught me how to read one. As a result, I spent most of the summer of 1962 asking Brazilians to repeat everything they said to me, which led Arembepeiros to call me a *papagaio* ("parrot")—because I could only echo words that someone else had originated. I discovered that it is difficult to gain profound insight into native social life when you can't converse even as well as a five-year-old.

The Sixties

In June 1962, when I first visited Arembepe, the 60 kilometer trip from Salvador was neither simple nor certain. It required about three hours in a vehicle equipped with four-wheel drive. I first arrived, and indeed have always visited,

"We always got stuck at least once." The road to Arembepe, passing through the district seat, Abrantes, in 1964. (Conrad P. Kottak)

Arembepe during the austral winter. Located some 13 degrees south of the equator and at sea level, Arembepe is never cold, but June and July are rainy months, making travel difficult. The clay-surfaced road was usually muddy, and we always got stuck at least once in any round trip. Since the field team used a large and heavy jeep station wagon, the task of getting unstuck usually required a work group of field team members and a dozen helpful onlookers. Friendly natives would do most of the work, we learned to hope, particularly when we were headed into Salvador for occasional "rest and recreation." Otherwise we would have to walk into the lobby of a city hotel covered with red mud, raising doubts about whether we should be given lodging.

On the road to Arembepe, sand, lagoons, and more sand came after the mud. Following a heavy rain, crossing the freshwater lagoons that bound Arembepe on the west made the jeep seem like a motorboat, as high water washed onto the cabin floor, and occasionally stalled the engine. After the lagoons came the dunes, with their closely planted coconut trees—posing another traffic hazard. Making it into the village required finding another vehicle's tracks, flooring the

During the 1960s, as we approached Arembepe, the clay road yielded to sand. (Conrad P. Kottak)

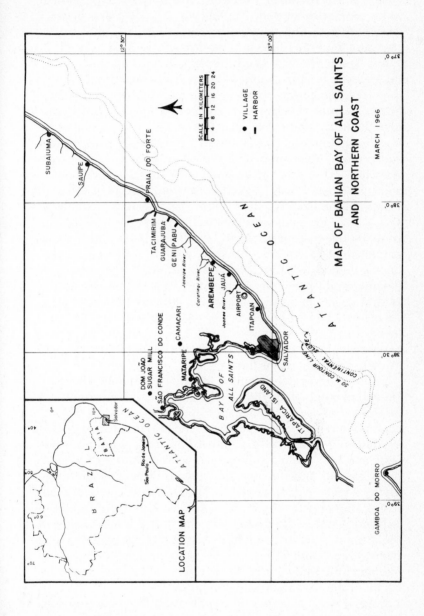

MAP OF BAHIAN BAY OF ALL SAINTS AND NORTHERN COAST

MARCH 1966

SCALE IN KILOMETERS
0 4 8 12 16 20 24

• VILLAGE
▬ HARBOR

SUBAIUMA
SAUIPE
PRAIA DO FORTE
TACIMIRIM
GUARAJUBA
GENIPABU
AREMBEPE
JAUÁ
Jacuipe River
Capivara River
Joanes River
AIRPORT
ITAPOAN
CAMACARI
SÃO FRANCISCO DO CONDE
DOM JOÃO
SUGAR MILL
MATARIPE
SALVADOR

ATLANTIC OCEAN

50 M CONTOUR LINE
CONTINENTAL SLOPE

BAY OF ALL SAINTS

ITAPARICA ISLAND

GAMBOA DO MORRO

12° 30'
13° 00'

37° 0'
38° 0'
38° 30'
39° 0'

LOCATION MAP

BRAZIL
BAHIA
Salvador
São Paulo
Rio de Janeiro
ATLANTIC OCEAN

accelerator, and for some, exhorting deities for assistance. Once, as a particularly frustrating trip from the city seemed to be coming to an end, I pulled up in front of the house I was renting to find that the brakes had failed; only frantic pumping kept me from crashing through the kitchen wall.

But Arembepe was worth the trip. I can't imagine an anthropologist finding a more stereotypically beautiful field setting. The village was strung along a narrow strip of land (less than a kilometer) between ocean and lagoons. More spectacular than any South Sea island I later visited, Arembepe's houses—many brightly painted in tones of blue, pink, peach, and orange—stood under lofty coconut palms. To the east, stretches of smooth white sand and protected swimming areas alternated with jagged rocks and churning Atlantic waves. In the heat of a clear, sunny day in August, Arembepe was alive with color: the green-blue hues of ocean and lagoon, orange-reds of bricks and roof tiles, pinks and blues of painted houses, greens of palms, and white of sand. Arembepe's colorfully painted fishing boats were anchored each evening and on Sunday in the port located just east of the central square and the small, white, attractive Roman Catholic chapel. The harbor is formed by a rugged, partially submerged reef; the boats rowed out each morning through its narrow channels, then raised their sunbleached sails to travel to their destinations for the day.

Arembepe in 1962 belonged in a movie. (In fact, a team of French photographers did use the chapel as a background for fashion advertisements that appeared in *Vogue* in 1966.) This conjunction of natural beauty with the middle-class appeal of a "quaint," remote village subsisting on a wind-powered, hook-and-line fishing industry had already attracted a handful of tourists and summer (dry season, December to February) residents to Arembepe in 1962. However, the poor quality of the road made it a lengthy and difficult trip from Salvador even in the dry season, and only a few residents of the capital—primarily middle-class and lower-middle-class people—had summer houses in Arembepe. Limited bus service began in 1965, but it attracted few visitors until the condition of the road improved around 1970.

Poverty and poor public health were the most obvious blights that made Arembepe of the 1960s—despite the title of this book—something less than paradise. In theory, Arembepeiros got their drinking water from Big Well, a tiny settlement about 2 kilometers away. An entrepreneur who resided there made money selling barrels of water in Arembepe. In fact, however, when well water was not immediately or readily available, Arembepeiros occasionally drank water from the freshwater lagoon. Some mothers even used lagoon water in the powdered milk they mixed for their children. Considering these traditional uses of water—and the fact that the bushes where Arembepeiros relieved themselves were just on the edge of the lagoon, which rises during the rainy season—it is easy to understand why most children in Arembepe in the 1960s showed symptoms of intestinal disorders and of extreme malnutrition (the latter partly caused by the presence of enervating parasites in their bodies).

Malinowski and Microprojects

I entered this romantic yet imperfect setting as a fledgling ethnographer with ambitious goals and a huge linguistic impediment. Two dimensions of the work I did in Arembepe beginning in 1962 bear discussion here. One involves my scientific and professional aims. The second has to do with my personal reactions to an alien setting. First the scientific goals.

As a conscientious anthropology major, I very much wanted to put into personal practice some of the lessons I had learned in my classes. I wanted to do the kinds of things, for example, that Bronislaw Malinowski describes as the ethnographer's work in the first chapter of his well-known book *Argonauts of the Western Pacific*, which is a study of fishermen and traders in Melanesia. We had read this classic in Comitas's seminar.

During the summer of '62 I often compared my own experiences with Malinowski's; the settings of our fieldwork struck me as similar. He had also worked in what seemed a romantic, tropical South Sea setting (the Trobriand Islands). Despite the fact that Arembepe is on the mainland, the phrase "South Sea island" kept running through my head during my 1960s field trips. As I read Malinowski's description of the moment when the ethnographer "sets foot upon a native beach, and makes his first attempts to get in touch with the natives" (Malinowski, 1961, p. 4), I imagined myself in his sandals. He had talked of trying to get to know the natives by observing them making things and writing down names of tools. Like me, Malinowski initially had trouble communicating with the natives. "I was quite unable to enter any more detailed or explicit conversation with them at first. I knew well that the best remedy for this was to collect concrete data, and accordingly I took a village census, wrote down genealogies, drew up plans and collected the terms of kinship" (Malinowski, 1961, p. 5).

I was eager to do these things that Malinowski had done, especially to census the village. However, field leader Harris discouraged me, offering another lesson: before I could hope to gather the kind of detailed and accurate data that ethnography demands, I would have to establish rapport within the community. People would have to get to know and trust me. I would have to convince them that I was not dangerous and that it would not be to their disadvantage to answer my questions. Furthermore, I did not yet know enough about village life to devise pertinent questions to ask during a census. Accordingly, but regretfully, I put the census on hold and set about "building rapport." David Epstein and Betty Wagley, my associates in the field, were doing the same thing, as did Marvin Harris, when he eventually moved in with David and me to spend the month of August in Arembepe.

How does one establish rapport? "Get to know the men," I was told. To do this I started joining the fishermen for their evening bath in the freshwater lagoon. I developed my first doubts about the wisdom of this kind of participant observation when I accidentally swatted a floating piece of donkey dung (I like to think I identified the correct mammal) during my third bath. I abandoned lagoon bathing once and for all, however, when I learned of the lagoon system's infestation by schistosomes—liver flukes. Thereafter, I was careful to avoid the lagoon and followed the advice of public health officials to rub exposed body parts with alcohol whenever I came into contact with lagoon water. Arembepeiros found these precautions laughable: Not to worry, they said—there

The beautiful, microbe-infested, freshwater lagoon that bordered Arembepe to the west, at sundown. (Courtesy Jerald T. Milanich)

were small fish in the lagoon that ate the liver flukes (and germs in general) so that there was no health threat to people.

If the lagoon was now off-limits, there was still the chapel stoop, where each evening, after the fishing fleet had returned, baths had been taken, and the day's main meal consumed, men would gather to talk. This area was male territory. Only small girls and old women dared approach. David and I would sit and try to talk. My Portuguese remained rudimentary; I resented David because he spoke and seemed to understand better than I did. Still, villagers tossed questions my way. They were curious about the United States, and their questions were scintillating: "Were there camels in the United States? . . . Elephants? . . . Monkeys?" They went through a litany of animals they had seen on the lottery tickets that people brought back from Salvador. "Look! Up in the sky. It's a jet from the United States heading for Rio," they observed every other night, reflecting the airline's schedule. Whenever, after minutes of laborious mental rehearsal, I managed to find the proper Portuguese words to ask a ques-

tion about Arembepe, I would get an incomprehensible re-
ply, followed by some such query as "Have you ever seen a
bear, Conrado?"

"Bear, bear," I parroted.

"Parrot, parrot," they guffawed.

"Yes, I have seen a bear. I have seen a bear in a zoo."

Rapport building was fascinating indeed.

Visions of Malinowski danced in my head as I came to resent this kind of activity as a waste of time. I was eager to do
something "more scientific." The microproject that Marvin
Harris and I had planned for me involved testing a difference between race relations in Brazil and the United States.
In the United States one's racial identity is determined by a
rule of descent. If an American has one black parent and one
white one, he or she is assigned, automatically at birth and
without regard for physical appearance, to "the black race."
In Brazil, it seemed that several factors determined racial
identity and that no descent rule operated. Since, however,
the absence of such a rule had never been investigated sys-
tematically, we decided that a genetically and phenotypically (physically) diverse and mixed community such as
Arembepe would be a good place to test it.

When a descent rule operates, full siblings are assigned to
the same descent group. Thus in the United States, siblings
cannot belong to different races. In Arembepe, Harris and I
set out to find full siblings who were physically very different, to see if they were assigned to different races. We soon
found three sisters with widely varying skin shades, hair
types, and facial features. After we had photographed them,
I finally got to do something that seemed more professional
than answering questions about what animals were to be
found in the United States. I chose a sample of 100 villagers
and showed the photo of the sisters to all, asking them to tell
me each girl's race. Sure enough, I found that many different
terms were employed, that full siblings could indeed belong
to different races in Brazil.

Some interesting new questions about Brazilian race relations were stimulated by that first survey, and Harris and I
devised another set of questions about drawings of individuals who contrasted phenotypically. As a result of questioning another sample of villagers, I found that Arembepeiros

used far more racial terms (over forty) than had previously been reported for a Brazilian community. More interestingly, they used them inconsistently, so that the racial term used for another person might vary from day to day, as might even self-identification. By the time my three months in Arembepe were up, I had developed a specialized linguistic proficiency in Brazilian racial terminology, and Harris and I had the basis for a couple of innovative journal articles. Although I still felt guilty that I had not managed to do a Malinowskian village census, I did think that I had accomplished something during my first field experience.

If I was ever to work again in Brazil, I knew that I would have to improve my Portuguese. I could get only so far, I realized, talking about race relations. Therefore, I spent the next summer taking an intensive course in Brazilian Portuguese at Columbia University while another field team lived in Arembepe. Also in that summer of 1963, Betty Wagley and I, whose romance had begun under Arembepe's full moon, got married; and I began graduate school in the fall.

I was delighted, in the spring, to be offered the job of assistant leader of the program's 1964 team, and I returned to Arembepe in June of that year determined finally to do my census. And not just a census. By then I had studied more anthropology and my Portuguese had improved dramatically; I felt that I was ready to do a full-fledged interview schedule. Peter Gorlin, who now holds a Ph.D. in anthropology and an M.D. degree, was an undergraduate field team member stationed in Jauá, the next fishing village south of Arembepe. Peter had read Malinowski, too, and he was as eager as I to employ Malinowski's "method of concrete, statistical documentation" (1961, p. 24), in order to satisfy the ethnographer's "fundamental obligation of giving a complete survey of the phenomena, and not of picking out the sensational [and] the singular" (1961, p. 11).

I felt ready to do a survey of all the households in Arembepe, and Peter wanted to do the same in Jauá. But we needed "an instrument." The field team leader, Bahian physician and anthropologist Thales de Azevedo, supplied us with one—an interview schedule that had been previously used in southern Bahia. We modified the schedule for the fishing villages and had it printed up.

1964 field-team members Peter Gorlin (second from left) and Erica Bressler with their host family in Jauá, the fishing village just south of Arembepe. Note the range of physical variation among the natives of this area. (Conrad P. Kottak)

An *interview schedule* contrasts with a questionnaire in that respondents fill out questionnaires, whereas with an interview schedule the interviewer, in this case the ethnographer, asks informants a set of questions and then fills in the answers on the form. Like other social scientists, many anthropologists like to gather comparable quantifiable information about people in the group they are studying, as I wanted to do in Arembepe. However, sociologists normally work with literate people, who can fill out the answer sheets or questionnaire forms themselves. Anthropologists, on the other hand, have not usually worked in places where most people are literate; so we have to record the answers ourselves. Because we are in charge of pacing, we can also choose to digress temporarily from the scheduled questions to follow up intriguing bits of information that emerge during the interview. Thus the researcher can keep the interview open-ended and exploratory while also asking all respondents the same basic set of questions. I learned as much about Arembepe through such open-ended questioning as I did from the formal queries.

Yet another difference between the research techniques of anthropologists and sociologists is illustrated by our interviews in Arembepe and Jauá. Since sociologists normally deal with large and complex societies, such as the contemporary United States, they must use *sampling techniques*, which enable them to make inferences about larger groups on the basis of a detailed study of smaller ones. However, like most anthropologists, we did not need to do sampling in Arembepe and Jauá, since both were sufficiently small for us to do total samples—that is, to complete the schedule with all the households in each community. Arembepe, it turned out, had 159 households and Jauá about 40.

A final contrast between cultural anthropology and sociology is worth mentioning. Sociologists often enjoy the luxury of distributing their questionnaires by mail or having graduate-student research assistants administer them as well as code and analyze them. But the anthropologist works right in the community and thereby faces a hundred real-world obstacles. My main problem doing the interview schedule in Arembepe was not the few villagers who slammed doors and windows in my face, or even the snot-nosed children who used my pants as a handkerchief. Rather, it was fleas. I still recall my third or fourth interview, in a sand-floored hut in northern Arembepe. As I asked the set of questions to a dozen cooperative, smiling, hospitable members of an extended family, I began to itch, particularly in the crotch. For the good of science I made it through to the end of the form, but I did not tarry for open-ended inquiry. Instead I ran home, through the house, out the back door, and right into the harbor at high tide. I quickly removed my shorts and let the salt water burn into the flea wounds. Fleas bothered most of us, particularly Betty, that summer. The remedy for the men, we discovered, was to wear pants with cuffs liberally sprinkled with flea powder. In this way we managed to interview in virtually all of Arembepe's households, despite the predatory sand fleas with their seemingly special thirst for North American blood.

Our interview schedule was eight pages long and included

questions (for each household member) about age, sex, racial identity, diet, employment, religious beliefs and practices, education, political preferences, possessions, consumption patterns, and ownership of livestock, boats, coconut trees, land, and farms. As the field leader who worked most closely with Peter, I encouraged him not to do a microproject but to follow the Malinowskian path that I had always wanted to tread. He did it with gusto; in two months he had finished the schedule with all the households in Jauá, and he hiked up the beach to spend August helping Betty and me complete the schedule in Arembepe.

There are advantages, I now realize, in both models for brief fieldwork. A microproject is easily manageable and offers the promise of a modest scientific paper. Yet the holistic Malinowskian approach is also valuable. I am convinced that my Portuguese would have gotten much better if I had done the interview schedule the first summer, rather than limiting my talk to rapport building and race relations. I later found this to be true, when I used a simple interview schedule fairly soon after I began working among the Betsileo people of Madagascar in 1966. The first interview schedule does not have to be as detailed as the one we used in Arembepe. In Madagascar I used a succession of schedules, about different subjects and of increasing complexity. All provided me with comparable information about a group of people, and all increased my ability to discuss a range of topics significant to the Betsileo. Similarly, Peter Gorlin's work with the interview schedule in Jauá and Arembepe in 1964 helped him improve his Portuguese much more quickly than I had done in 1962.

There was an added benefit from doing the interview schedule that I did not fully realize in 1964: it got at least one member of the field team into every home in Arembepe. Years later I was to hear from many villagers that they remembered these visits warmly. Our questions, asked in their homes, had communicated our personal interest and had shown villagers that we were not the kind of outsiders who disdain Arembepeiros, considering their own life style incomparably superior.

I found Arembepeiros to be open, warm, and hospitable people, much less wary of outsiders than the Betsileo I studied for fourteen months in 1966–1967. Most Arembepeiros welcomed us into their homes and gladly answered our questions. A handful, however, played hard to get, slamming windows and doors as I approached, telling neighbors that they would not answer our questions. I had to settle for sketchier information about them and could only make estimates of their incomes and consumption patterns, on the basis of public information and behavior. Fortunately, since the 1964 interview schedule data are the basis for much of this book's comparison of Arembepe of the 1960s with that community today, fewer than a dozen households, scattered throughout the village, refused to let us do the schedule.

The interview schedule was not the only thing I did in Arembepe in 1964. Soon after my arrival, I met an excellent informant, Alberto, whose name figures prominently in the story that follows. A forty-year-old fisherman, Alberto was the eldest brother of our cook. He felt free to visit our house almost every night, and he was eager to instruct me about the fishing industry. I got additional information about fishing by talking to fishermen and fish marketers on the beach, and by going out in several boats, including that of Tomé, Arembepe's most successful boat captain and owner. Tomé's name, too, is a prominent one in Arembepe's recent history.

In 1965 I had my third chance to study Arembepe. The results of analyzing the interview schedules and my information on fishing had been so promising that both Marvin Harris and I felt that I might, with one more summer, amass sufficient data to write my doctoral dissertation about Arembepe, which I did. This time Betty and I were not part of a field team but on our own. A graduate fellowship and grant supported my work, and living was still cheap in cash-poor Arembepe. That summer, I again followed the Malinowskian plan, but I already had much of the statistical and observational data needed for the "firm, clear outline" of my community's organization and the "anatomy of its culture" (Malinowski, 1961, p. 24). Now I needed flesh for the skeleton. So I spent the summer of 1965 gathering data on the "imponderabilia of actual life . . . collected through minute, detailed observations . . . made possible by close contact with native life" (Malinowski, 1961, p. 24). By this time, however, I didn't really have to harken back to Malinowski to know that although I had the bare bones, I still needed to find out more about native opinions, values, and feelings; to listen to stories, examine cases, and gather intimate, basic details about everyday life. Like Napoleon Chagnon, the principal ethnographer of the Yanomamo Indians of Venezuela, I knew "how much I enjoyed reading monographs that were sprinkled with real people, that described real events, and that had some sweat and tears, some smells and sentiments mingled with the words" (Chagnon, 1977, p. xi). I wanted to add such dimensions—feeling tones—to my ethnography of Arembepe.

It Was an Alien Place

Those were some of my professional goals and scientific procedures. The other aspect of doing ethnography is more personal. No matter how objective and scientific they fancy themselves, anthropologists are not mechanical measuring instruments. We are inevitably participant observers, taking part in—and by so doing modifying, no matter how slightly— the phenomena we are investigating and seeking to understand. Not recording machines but people, anthropologists are raised in particular cultural traditions, possess idiosyncratic personality traits and experiences, have their own motivations, impressions, values, and reactions. Nor are our informants all alike, and we come to appreciate them differently. Some we never appreciate; an occasional one we detest.

Brought up in one culture, intensely curious about others, anthropologists nevertheless experience culture shock, particularly on the first field trip. *Culture shock* refers to the whole set of feelings about being in an alien setting, and the ensuing reactions. It is a chilly, creepy feeling of alienation, of being without some of the most ordinary, trivial—and therefore basic—cues of one's culture of origin.

As I planned my departure for Brazil in 1962 I could not know just how naked I would feel without the cloak of my own language and culture. My sojourn in Arembepe would be my first trip outside the United States. I was an urban boy who had grown up in Atlanta, Georgia, and New York City. I had little experience with rural life in my own country, none with Latin America, and I had received only minimal training in the Portuguese language.

New York City direct to Salvador, Bahia, Brazil. Just a brief stopover in Rio de Janeiro; a longer visit would be a reward at the end of fieldwork. As our propjet approached tropical Salvador, I couldn't believe the whiteness of the sand. "That's not snow, is it?" I remarked to a fellow field team member. Marvin Harris had arranged our food and lodging at the Paradise Hotel, overlooking Bahia's magnificent, endlessly blue, All Saints' Bay. My first impressions of Bahia were of smells—alien odors of ripe and decaying mangoes, bananas, and passion fruit—and of swatting ubiquitous fruit flies I had never seen before, although I had read extensively about their reproductive behavior in genetics classes. There were strange concoctions of rice, black beans, and gelatinous gobs of unidentifiable meats and floating pieces of skin. Coffee was strong and sugar crude, and every table top had containers for toothpicks and manioc (cassava) flour, to sprinkle, like parmesan cheese, on anything one might eat. I remember oatmeal soup and a slimy stew of beef tongue in tomatoes. At one meal a disintegrating fish head, eyes still attached, but barely, stared up at me as the rest of its body floated in a bowl of bright orange palm oil. Bearing my culture's don't-drink-the-water complex, it took me a few days to discover that plain mineral water quenched thirst better than the gaseous variety. Downstairs was the Boite Clock, a nightclub whose rhythmic bossa nova music often kept us from sleeping.

I only vaguely remember my first day in Arembepe. Unlike ethnographers who have studied remote tribes in the tropical forests of interior South America or the highlands of New Guinea, I did not have to hike or ride a canoe for days to arrive at my field site. Arembepe was not isolated relative to such places, only relative to every other place *I* had ever been. My first contact with Arembepe was just a visit, to arrange lodging. We found the crumbling summer house of a man who lived in Salvador, and arranged to rent it and have it cleaned. We hired Dora, a twenty-five-year-old unmarried mother of two, to cook for us, and another woman to clean house and do our laundry. My first visit to Arembepe didn't

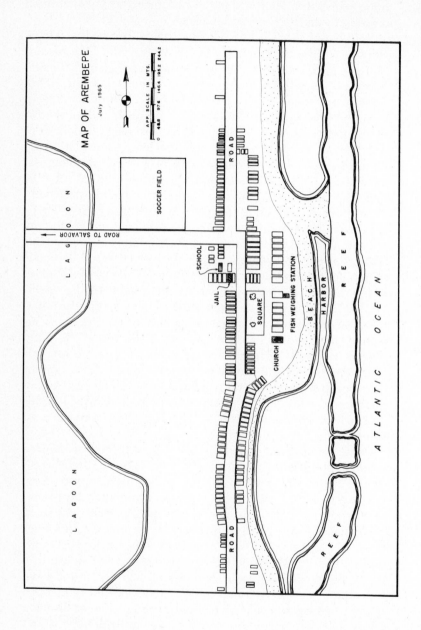

leave much of an impression because I knew I'd still have a few more days at the Paradise Hotel, with a real toilet and shower, before having to rough it "in the field."

Back in the city, using her almost native fluency in Brazilian language and culture, Betty Wagley bargained for our canvas cots, pots, pans, flashlights, and other supplies from small stores in Salvador's least expensive commercial zones. I don't remember our actual move to Arembepe or who accompanied us. There were field team members to deposit in Abrantes, on the road to Arembepe, and Harris had employed a chauffeur for the program's jeep station wagon. But I do recall what happened when we arrived. There was no formal road into the village. Entering through southern Arembepe, vehicles simply threaded their way around coconut trees, following tracks left by automobiles that had passed previously. A crowd of children had heard us coming, and they pursued our car through the village streets until we parked in front of our house, near the central square. Our first few days in Arembepe were spent with children following us everywhere. For weeks we had few moments of privacy. Children watched our every move through our living room window. Occasionally one made an incomprehensible remark. Usually they just stood there. Sometimes they would groom one another's hair, eating the lice they found.

Outcasts from an urban culture, David and I locked our doors. Once he went into Salvador and I stayed the night alone.

"Conrado's scared," said Dora. "He's afraid of the *bichos* [beasts, real and imaginary] outside." There was really nothing to be afraid of, she assured me; a dangerous *bicho* had never bothered anyone in Arembepe, and most people didn't even have locks on their doors.

Our most annoying intruders were a few drunks who occasionally paid us nighttime visits, seeking alcohol or money to buy it. Fairly late one night (around nine or ten o'clock, after most villagers were in bed) two men pounded on our door. From their slurred speech and loudness it was apparent that both had been drinking. One was a young villager, who said that he wanted to introduce us to the other man, a visitor from Camaçari, the county seat.

"Some Americans in Camaçari taught my friend how to speak English," said the villager.

"Oh, yeah," we said. "Let's hear him."

"John Wayne," said the visitor.

"Very good," observed David. "Do you know anything else?"

"Yes," the man responded. "Fucky, fucky." (My subsequent travels throughout the world have revealed several permutations of this common but stigmatized four-letter English word.)

The sounds, sensations, sights, smells, and tastes of life in northeastern Brazil, and in Arembepe, slowly grew familiar. I gradually accepted the fact that the only toilet tissue available at a reasonable price had almost the texture of sandpaper. I grew accustomed to this world without Kleenex, in which globs of mucus habitually drooped from the noses of village children whenever a cold passed through Arembepe. A world where, seemingly without effort, women with gracefully swaying hips carried 18-liter kerosene cans of water on their heads, where boys sailed kites and sported at catching houseflies in their bare hands, where old women smoked pipes, storekeepers offered *cachaça* (common rum) at nine in the morning, and men played dominoes on lazy afternoons when there was no fishing. I was visiting a world where human life was oriented toward water—the sea, where men fished, and the lagoon, where women communally washed clothing, dishes, and their own bodies.

Arembepe was a compact village, where the walls of most houses touched those of their neighbors, where, through gossip, the peccadillos of individuals and families instantaneously became community property. Privacy was one of the scarcest commodities. No wonder villagers didn't lock their doors—who could steal anything and have it stay a secret? Young lovers found what privacy they could at night.

Even more obviously than in other places without electricity, Arembepe's night life was transformed when the moon was full. Reflected everywhere by the sand and water, moonlight turned the village by night into almost day. Young people strolled through the streets and courted on the beach. Fishermen sought octopus and "lobster" (Atlantic crayfish) on the reef. Accustomed to the electrified, artificial pace of city life, I was enchanted by the moonlight and its effect on this remote village. Moonless nights impressed me, too; for the first time I could understand how the Milky Way got its name. Only in a planetarium had I previously seen a sky so crammed with stars. Looking south, Salvador's electric lights could only slightly dim the contrast of white stars against the coal-black sky, and for the first time in my life I could view the Southern Cross it all its magnificence.

Even the most devout believer in astrology would have been impressed with the extent to which human activities were governed by the phases of the moon. This was a slower and more natural epoch in Arembepe's history than the years that were to follow. People awakened near sunrise and went to bed early. Moonlight and a calm sea permitted occasional nighttime fishing, but the pattern was for the fleet to leave in the early morning and return in the late afternoon. Boats generally went out five or six days per week; as Christians, Arembepeiros took Sunday as a day of rest. But generally, life in Arembepe followed the availability of natural light and the passing of day and night.

Another force of nature, the weather, affected the rhythm of life. My visits to Arembepe came during the season of rain and rough seas. Sailboats were especially vulnerable to high winds and stormy weather; it was dangerous to negotiate the narrow channels in Arembepe's rocky reef when racing home to escape a sudden squall. Storms usually lasted no more than a week, but I remember one three-week lull, in 1964. People speculated incessantly about when the weather would improve; of course they had no access to weathercasters. Villagers lamented that they couldn't work, and eventually they began to complain of hunger. Cattle were brought in from farms to be butchered and sold in Arembepe, but many households were too poor to buy beef. Villagers complained that they were hungry for fish, for something meaty to complement a diet of coffee, sugar, and manioc flour. The weather even forced us to let up on doing our interview schedule. There was a whole section on diet—the quantities of the various foods that people bought or ate per day, week, or month. We soon felt embarrassed asking people what they ate in normal or good times when they were virtually starving for animal protein and, indeed, for all items whose purchase required cash.

The tropical rainy season meant constant high humidity, a perfect climate for the growth of molds. My black leather dress shoes turned white with mildew. Peter Gorlin had bought a navy blue drip-dry suit before his trip to Bahia in 1964. Since we attended few formal affairs in Salvador, Peter let his suit hang in a wardrobe in Jauá until he finally needed it. Discovering, a few hours before a party, that it was covered with mildew, Peter checked into a Salvador hotel, took a shower with his suit on, lathered it, and then dripped dry for the next few hours.

The tile roofs of the houses we rented in Arembepe were never completely effective in keeping the moisture (and bats) out. Whenever it rained, we had to avoid the large leaks, but there was no place where we could be completely dry. One rainy day during the three-week fishing lull, Dora told us that lately, smelling the moist walls of her wattle-and-daub (stick-and-mud) hut, she had remembered her intense desire as a child to lick, and even eat, dirt from her home's mud walls. Many Arembepeiros did sometimes eat earth, she told us. This geophagy may have been a symptom of iron deficiency during the leanest times of year.

In addition to the everyday sensations and experiences of a foreign land and culture, there were also the special occasions. A few women held prayer sessions in their homes to honor their household saints and pray for deceased relatives. July's big event was the *Chegança,* when, in the building in the central square that served as the seat of the Fishermen's Society, fishermen went through a few hours of formal dancing and singing intended to reenact some historical event— the village had forgotten exactly what! (I believe that it was the arrival of the Portuguese in Brazil.) Saint John's night, June 24, was the lesser of Arembepe's two main annual festive events. (The ceremony for Saint Francis took place in February, the time of Arembepe's most productive fishing, and because of this was much more elaborate.) In Arembepe of the 1960s, following Iberian traditions for Saint John's night, villagers lit bonfires, drank special *cachaça* (rum) concoctions, and cooked such delicious confections as *cocada* (sweetened coconut candy) and such disgusting ones as *canjica* (a manioc flour cake, whose flavor, when prepared properly, approximates that of pencil eraser.) Childbirth brought forth other barely tolerable mixtures, most notably a drink combining *cachaça*, onion, garlic, and various exotic berries and herbs.

I can summarize my feelings about living in Arembepe during the 1960s by saying that I had a profound sense of being away from everything. In those days, virtually no one other than a fish buyer from Salvador ever drove a car into Arembepe. I felt cut off from the external world. Only a few villagers owned radios, which rarely brought news of the rest of the world anyway. I remember poring over every word of *Time*'s Latin American edition on each visit to Salvador. In fact, in later years we sometimes planned our trips into Salvador to coincide with the day the new *Time* came out.

Even for Betty Wagley Kottak, who had previously lived in Brazil, Arembepe was something special, far removed from the sophistication, stratification, and style consciousness of Rio de Janeiro and São Paulo. Social class governs interpersonal relations in Brazilian cities, and urban Brazilians, with whom Betty had spent most of her previous time in Brazil, have little direct contact with even the urban poor, whom they encounter mainly as servants and menials. Betty had been exposed to much of Brazil's "Great Tradition" (to use Robert Redfield's term for the culture of literate, mainly urban, elites) but not the "little traditions" of its peasants and rural poor. For both of us, then, as for other field team members, Arembepe's relative isolation, simplicity, autonomy, tranquility, and "naturalness" contrasted with every previous setting in our lives. Such a reaction to first fieldwork is very common among cultural anthropologists.

I believe that our work in Arembepe also provided us with a more accurate understanding of rural America as recently as the 1930s and 1940s, when in many isolated pockets, especially among the poor, night life still went on by candle and lantern light—and before the twin forces of state and corporation had fully introduced backwoods folk to the modern world's vast inventory of benefits and costs.

In Arembepe we got to know firsthand about the values and habits of poor people, how they attempted to make ends meet, how they dealt with fortune and adversity. We got to know many people as individuals and as friends. Characters such as Alberto, Dora, and Tomé, whose words, stories, and experiences are laced through this chronicle of a changing Arembepe, are much more to me than informants. They are people I value as I do my friends and special colleagues in the United States. Yet they are the kind of people that few outsiders will ever have a chance to meet. The anthropologist's special obligation is to tell their story for them.

2 *After: The Road to 1980*

When I rode into Arembepe in June 1973—eleven years after my first visit—the setting was noticeably different, as was the trip out from Salvador. Although letters from Brazil and reports of colleagues who had visited Arembepe since 1965 had prepared me for the hippie invasion and for the community's development as a tourist attraction, my first bit of direct evidence for the change was still a shock. Our jet from Rio de Janeiro landed at Salvador's remodeled airport, which lies just off the road that links Arembepe to Salvador. As our taxi headed for the city, where we were to spend a few days making arrangements for our stay, I noticed that the road toward Arembepe was now paved, and the turnoff marked with a *road sign*. Perhaps no one but a fellow anthropologist can appreciate my complex feelings on seeing the name of "my" community so publicly displayed. Anthropology, after all, grew up in small-scale, relatively isolated nonindustrial societies, and anthropologists retain at least a vestige of the profession's traditional fascination with the remote, the unusual, and the exotic. But that night, as I rode along the familiar beach highway to Salvador, I became very uneasy about my coming encounter with other manifestations of the end of my community's isolation that this road sign portended.

That encounter began the next day—not in Arembepe but watching television in Salvador and reading local newspapers. I learned that a recently opened chemical factory was polluting the freshwater lagoon system that forms the western boundary of nearby Arembepe and other coastal communities. Television camera crews made regular forays to Arembepe to interview its residents about the effects of pollution. Since Arembepe was first settled around 1900 its people had used lagoon water to wash clothes and dishes and had taken daily baths in the lagoon itself. All this had changed by 1973. Once so blue-green and deceptively clear, Arembepe's lagoon was now the dead brown of water in a vase of rotting flowers. If liver flukes and other lagoon "germs" were dead, so were the fish that had "eaten them" and that had helped tide over Arembepeiros on winter days when rough seas had prevented ocean fishing. This effect of factory pollution was visible throughout the entire lagoon system, north and south of Arembepe; but it was particularly marked in the inland waters nearest the factory, which stands between Arembepe and Jauá, the next fishing village to the south.

The reporters who visited Arembepe in June 1973 were hearing complaints by Arembepeiros that the lagoon waters now ruined their clothing and burned their eyes and nasal passages. One fisherman said that he had abandoned the lagoon after experiencing intense burning of eyes and skin during an evening bath. He had rushed home to wash his face and body in well water. Women complained that waters where they had done their laundry for years now produced huge yellow spots in their clothes. As we had done ever since learning about the schistosomiasis threat, many Arembepeiros were now getting their bathing water from Big Well. The Big Well resident who had previously shipped barrels of water to Arembepe on mule-back had acquired a large truck, which he used to transport water (and in numerous other business activities). Another businessman in Arembepe itself imported water from Big Well and sold showers in a ramshackle rooming house he had opened to cater to the tourist trade. Although chemical analysis of a few local wells showed no pollutants in 1973, eventual contamination seemed likely.

Those first few days introduced me to still another dimension of the changes that had swept Arembepe—the greatly increased urban middle-class and upper-middle-class ownership of summer homes and beach houses. Because our two small children had accompanied us, Betty and I decided that for a three-month stay we needed better accommodations than we had rented in the past. We learned that several fairly comfortable vacation homes had been built on oceanfront lots south of Arembepe. A friend in Salvador had arranged for us to meet with and rent from an owner of one of these houses—for a rent that, in dollars, was about five times what we had paid on our last visit. Part of this increase reflected inflation of the U.S. dollar and our larger and more comfortable quarters. However, much of the high rental price was a measure of Arembepe's new popularity as a tourist resort for the nearby city—even though we would be residing in Arembepe during the off-season.

Our lodging proved to be further south of the fishing village than I had anticipated when agreeing to rent. This was unfortunate, since my residence half a kilometer away partially removed me from village life and discouraged some of the nighttime visits that had figured prominently in previous fieldwork.

Once house and car rentals had been arranged in Salvador, I was ready to revisit Arembepe itself. I set out for "the field" in one of the two extremely temperamental Brazilian-made Volkswagen beetles I rented successively that summer. This was to be a leisurely drive. I wanted to observe changes along the route. However, a more daring driver could have made the trip in little more than an hour. After a few miles of *autoestrada* ("superhighway") under construction, I rejoined the familiar two-lane coastal road that had been the starting stretch of all my previous journeys to Arembepe. Signs of Salvador's own expansion and of its growth as a major tourist attraction within Brazil were obvious. (It is Brazil's oldest and one of its most beautiful, colorful, and interesting cities.) I encountered several new beachfront hotels and popular restaurants, and a growing beach-focused neighborhood, Pituba, which Arembepeiros could now easily reach by bus to purchase supplies that used to require a trip into midtown Salvador.

At Itapoan, a fishing village that once had been as isolated as Arembepe was in 1962, now virtually a neighborhood of Salvador, the road leaves the coast and heads inland. Previously the paved road had yielded to clay on entering Santo Amaro, seat of the municipality just south of Camaçari, Arembepe's own municipal seat. Much more distressing than the dirt road, however, just on the other side of Portão, the next village, had stood a decaying and very hazardous bridge over the Joanes River. But the paved highway of 1973 simply skirted the periphery of Santo Amaro, Portão, Abrantes, and the other communities along the route, and I whizzed over the Joanes River barely recalling that its crossing had once meant that everyone but the driver got out and walked across—to reduce the number of fatalities that would occur when the remaining bridge planks finally went. The good condition of the road made the next part of the trip, formerly one of the muddiest, rapid and uneventful.

Before I expected it, I saw a road sign marking the turnoff to the agricultural village and district seat of Abrantes, where several field team members had done fieldwork in 1962 and 1963. Next came the turnoff to Jauá, about 3 kilometers from the paved road, the tiny, charming coastal community studied by Elizabeth Thompson in 1963 and Peter Gorlin and Erica Bressler in 1964. I was surprised to see, at the turnoff, a brightly colored sign (my first hippie artifact) informing me that Jauá was a center of "indigenous" arts and crafts. Since I knew that the only native craft practiced in either Arembepe or Jauá was straw hat making by local women, I correctly concluded that Arembepe's southern neighbor had also experienced a flower-child invasion (on a much smaller scale than Arembepe, it turned out).

I was really not prepared, however, for the Dunes of Mordor—to invoke imagery from J. R. R. Tolkien's *Lord of the Rings*. Sand was already replacing red clay as the dominant soil, and I began to see the huge dunes that, from the air, give the Bahian coast the look of a North Pole with palm trees. However, unnaturally large piles of sand—apparently excavated during the chemical factory's construction—stood on either side of the highway at the top of a steep hill. Passing through this man-made topography, I saw the titanium-dioxide factory immediately to the east—New Jersey in Bahia: black smoke and grey-green slime. All the nearby dunes were covered with sulfurous wastes produced in the manufacture of titanium dioxide (an ingredient used in paints, dyes, and other products, which, as one American television commercial has it, "whitens up our lives"). Here, on the boundaries of my South Sea paradise, Tibrás (Titanium of Brazil), a multinational corporation, had deposited giant scoops of ersatz mashed potatoes topped by generous portions of Hollywood-vomit gravy.

The Tibrás factory in 1980. (Courtesy Jerald T. Milanich)

Then—as testimony to the primacy of business—the road ended. The paved road simply stopped at the entrance to the factory's parking lot. Thereafter came a hardened clay-surfaced road that entered the northern part of Arembepe 5 kilometers farther on. Although this portion of clay road was considerably better than anything that had existed in 1965, some areas did get fairly messy; however, I never got stuck during the 1973 rainy season. Soon I passed Big Well with its new gasoline pump. Then came the brown lagoon on either side of the road. To the right was something totally new: a squalid little settlement—Caraúnas—which turned out to be Arembepe's first ghetto, spawned by the subdivision and sale of local real estate. And finally, straight ahead lay Arembepe, which the road entered just north of the central square.

Previously, variation in house placement and construction materials had provided evidence for slight differences in wealth, although all Arembepeiros had been members of the national lower class. Brick houses with red tile roofs had been concentrated in the main square and immediately to the north, in an area that had begun as a secondary square but was lengthening into an open rectangle. Moving north,

Wattle-and-daub huts like these were common in Arembepe during the 1960s. Houses began to thin out near the village's fringes. Shown here, the northern fringe. (Conrad P. Kottak)

on either side of the two parallel rows, brick houses had gradually given way to wattle and daub, and tiles to palm-frond roofs. The same change had taken place south of the central square, which opened into the narrow Street Down There, whose seaside houses were much nearer the surf than those in the north. Crude huts with palm-frond roofs had re-appeared at the southern end of this street, inhabited by the poorest Arembepeiros, including recent immigrants who had not yet found regular places in fishing crews, and odd job-bers at various menial professions. However, most of these southern household heads had been women with no stable, co-resident husband to act as father to their children, or al-coholic males who had trouble working regularly.

Numerous changes were obvious by 1973. For example, many of the people who had once lived in the wattle-and-daub huts were residing on the other side of the lagoon in Caraúnas, the new satellite village. The huts they had once inhabited at the end of Street Down There were now brightly painted. Their residents were the few hippies who had stayed on after most had left Arembepe in 1971 and

One of the substantial summer houses south of Arembepe, the area where we stayed in 1973. (Courtesy Jerald T. Milanich)

1972. The hut interiors were tidier and more attractive now. For example, in one hut, layers of clean straw mats protected a French woman and her seven-year-old Franco-Italian son from the earth floor.

Change was even more visible further south, where there had previously been just one house. Now, half a kilometer away stood several substantial vacation homes of middle-class and upper-middle-class "summer people" *(veranistas)*. They had bought the most attractive lots created by the sub-division of the estate that until recently had been held jointly by a family of absentee landowners. Four of these houses overlooked the ocean. The one we rented was desirably located nearest "Old Arembepe," a harbored area where the fishing settlement had been located until around 1900. (The fishermen moved to Arembepe's current location as part of a shift from raft to sailboat fishing, which demanded a calmer harbor and more channels in the reef.) Since the cove that our house overlooked was one of Arembepe's best swimming areas, visitors came on weekends to enjoy the beach, even during the rainy season. The neighboring house to the south was unoccupied, as ours otherwise would have been until late

August, when its owner, a businessman from an interior city, planned to begin vacationing. Beyond was the home of the only year-round residents of the neighborhood, a European-born businessman and his West Indian wife; he commuted to a job in Camaçari, the municipal seat, still a more time-consuming journey in 1973 than the trip to Salvador. The next beachfront lot was the huge property of a man who had once occupied high political office—a friend of the landowner responsible for Arembepe's development. The politician and his relatives had apparently acquired most of the seafront land further south, but they were not yet building there. New houses were still being constructed on the west side of the clay road that passed all these houses and continued south. These were much less opulent but were placed sufficiently close to the beach to give their absentee owners ready access when they vacationed in Arembepe.

This new summer people's neighborhood was reputedly alive with activity during the dry season and school vacations, but it was extremely quiet during our stay, and we often felt isolated. Our living arrangement—which required that I go up to Arembepe to do fieldwork, or that villagers visit me far from their homes—was, in retrospect, the most unsatisfactory part of my 1973 stay. Furthermore, our old village friends did little to make our isolation easier to bear, since they continually expressed concern about our safety. This was just one manifestation of a noticeably greater atmosphere of fear and insecurity among Arembepeiros. "Get a gun," several villagers told us; robbers would surely come to rob and kill "rich Americans." One evening Betty and I managed to get away from Arembepe for our wedding anniversary. Just before we left we were warned that police from Salvador had been there that day searching for two armed bandits: we'd better be careful on the road and certainly shouldn't pick up hitchhikers (our previous practice). When we returned home around midnight, having encountered no villains, we found our children sleeping soundly despite the noise of exploding firecrackers. Worried about an imminent attack, the villagers we had left in charge were tossing lighted firecrackers out of the second-story window into the back yard, to convince potential aggressors that we had guns.

A summer people area was also developing at the northern

end of Arembepe, where the main landlord, a resident of Salvador, had built a weekend and vacation domicile befitting the role of community patron that he had played ever since my first acquaintance with Arembepe. This vacation house and a few others nearby actually joined up with Arembepe.

Arembepe's increasingly substantial housing was not limited to the outsiders' homes. Throughout the village there were more brick-and-tile structures, and Arembepeiros themselves were acquiring such "modern" conveniences as bottled gas–fueled lamps and stoves, as well as toilets, showers, and refrigerators. Arembepe in 1973 still lacked electricity, that sine qua non of nighttime *movimento* ("urban excitement," which it now has). And it still lacked telephones.

Although a new, larger, and more substantial schoolhouse had been built, the qualifications of the local women who taught there in 1973 had not improved much over 1965, when neither teacher had more than a third-grade education. Literacy was still uncommon, with a third of the adult population totally unable to read or write, and another third barely able to sign their names. Arembepe's school system was simply a local manifestation of the limited educational opportunities that prevailed throughout rural Brazil. Although about half of Brazil's school-age population (seven to fourteen years old) lived in rural areas in 1970, only 47 percent attended school, compared to 88 percent of their urban peers (Hausmann and Haar, 1978). In the state of Bahia, one of the nation's poorest, things were even worse. Only 6 percent of students who entered first grade completed eighth. Like most northeastern rural schoolchildren, Arembepeiros "studied" in a one-room schoolhouse, taught by barely literate women.

Health care, too, remained woefully inadequate. The nearest pharmacies were in Itapoan and Pituba, an hour's bus trip away. Drugs were dispensed without a prescription, and few Arembepeiros had ever consulted a "real doctor," getting whatever "expert" medical advice they obtained from pharmacists. Arembepe's health situation was therefore yet another local manifestation of a more general barrier, between lower-class Brazilians and adequate health care. Shamanistic cures were sometimes used instead. Brazil's highest infant mortality rate was in the northeast—180 per thousand versus

112 nationally in 1964 (Robock, 1975). Although there was one physician for every 2,000 Brazilians in 1970, most doctors worked in urban centers and were concentrated in the industrial south (Robock, 1975). The cold statistics of poverty hit home in Arembepe. The wife of Alberto, my best informant, had lost ten out of her thirteen children to such communicable diseases as infectious diarrhea, influenza, pneumonia, tuberculosis, measles, and tetanus—all made more deadly by severe malnutrition. Despite the exotic tropical façade, Arembepe's poor public health and short life expectancy had always been obvious warps in paradise.

Although locally available education and health care had barely improved between 1965 and 1973, evidence of Arembepe's physical growth and differentiation was everywhere. What had once been a single, fairly homogeneous community had broken up along socioeconomic lines into a central village (Arembepe proper) and class-affiliated neighborhoods. The middle- and upper-middle-class people who lived south and north of Arembepe had not been there previously, and the abjectly poor inhabitants of Caraúnas had once been housed in Arembepe itself. A third satellite community had developed 2 kilometers further north, near the Caratingi River, where hippies had joined the few river fishermen who had previously maintained makeshift huts there. By 1973 this had become a small hamlet of sixteen huts.

Arembepe proper had grown through natural population increase and immigration. Outsiders had purchased some of the brick houses, mainly in the central square. These vacation homes, though more modest than those in the area where we rented, brought urban visitors into the midst of community life at certain times of year. Three houses now sold rooms and meals to visitors, and several small stores had opened to cater to the tourist industry. Arembepe had expanded not just north and south but in the only other direction possible—west (since the houses on the eastern side are very near the sea). New rows of houses had been built between Arembepe and the lagoon. Several streets perpendicular to the sea led down to the lagoon.

The village population had grown substantially in less than a decade. Compared to 159 inhabited houses and 730 people in 1964, Arembepe proper now had about 280 houses

and more than 1,000 permanent residents. Add the 44 inhabited houses and 180 people of Caraúnas and the 16 houses
and 55 people of Caratingi, for overall totals of 340 houses
and over 1,200 residents in 1973. Arembepe's population had
also grown much harder to census accurately, since it
swelled on weekends, during the dry season, and during
school vacations, and since the immigration rate had increased. Still, Arembepe's 1973 population may actually
have stood *below* its size between 1969 and 1972, when
"hundreds of hippies" reportedly rented houses and huts, or
camped out on the beach and among the coconut trees north
and south of Arembepe, as in neighboring Jauá.

Only a dozen hippies remained in 1973. Arembepeiros distinguished male hippies *(ippis)* from females *(ippas)*. I first
encountered one of them late one morning as I was transact-
ing business in a store at the northern end of Street Down
There. Clad in cut-off shorts, with long hair, he seemed distinctly nonnative; I was forcibly reminded of the appearance,
demeanor, and attire of summer school students then at the
University of Michigan. "Hey man," I heard. Lo and behold,
my first Arembepe hippie could speak my native language.
He turned out to be Richie from Rhode Island, an amiable
young man who lived a simple life on funds occasionally ca-
bled from home. Like the other hippies, he bathed in the
surf, smoked marijuana, bothered—and was bothered by—no
one.

In addition to Richie, Arembepe's 1973 hippies included a
young Englishwoman, a few southern Brazilians, and an Argentinian couple. Most cosmopolitan was the Frenchwoman
who had lived with her first husband in Zaire and Madagascar and, thereafter, in Italy with the father of her son, just before moving to Arembepe. These remnants of the "hippie invasion," Arembepeiros (and outsiders who had been there)
assured me, offered no hint of what things had been like at
its height, when Janis Joplin, Mick Jagger, and Roman Polanski had visited Arembepe; when people had lain nude, had
sex, and smoked marijuana on the beach. (When, during my
1973 visit, Arembepeiros presented this stereotypical picture
of hippie behavior, they did so with considerably more
amusement and less disapproval than that typically expressed by "straight" U.S. citizens in the late 1960s and early

1970s.) By 1973, one hippie couple was working at artisanry and seemed fairly well integrated into local life. By 1980, a few others had joined them as permanent residents.

Obstacles to Anthropological Objectivity

During my eight-year absence from Arembepe, I had not been totally shut off from my village's notoriety. Friends in Rio and São Paulo had read national magazine stories about Arembepe and the hippies, and Bahians had written me about plans to build the factory. However, seeing the changes firsthand was still a shock, and I resented them. I was infuriated by the factory—by its destruction of natural beauty and its threat to Arembepe's existence. I was irritated by the summer people and tourists who, having spent a few months, weeks, or even days in Arembepe, habitually described it to me as if *they* were the experts on community life. And I also resented the hippies, although they at least appreciated Arembepe for its beauty, its simplicity, and its isolation—attributes that had previously made it so special to me. Yet because the hippies were so unlike the old-time Arembepeiros, and so similar to the kind of people I encountered regularly in my North American university environment, I could only view them as intruders in the tropical paradise I had staked out years earlier. To Arembepe's invasion by outsiders I attributed the villagers' new fears and insecurities, their uncertainty about their future, their experimentation with alien life styles. I was distressed to discover that some of my best friends were being possessed by spirits, joining cults, drinking too much, suffering from poor health, and carrying revolvers.

Anthropologists are trained to be reasonably objective and nonjudgmental in their studies of foreign cultures, but objectivity is sometimes a difficult goal. In this case, my own biases against change, my romantic wish to recapture the unaltered past, affected my research in 1973. I did a new village census and map, which allowed me to estimate changes in Arembepe's size, occupational structure, consumption patterns, and the provenience of its population. But I found myself focusing on familiar features of community life and avoiding (though not totally ignoring) the new. For example, I examined the kinship composition of households, as I had in the past, to note the main changes. I put Raymond Rapaport, a University of Michigan undergraduate who had accompanied me as a field assistant, to work studying the fishing industry, keeping track of crew composition, catches, marketing, and the newly established fishermen's cooperative. I worked closely with Alberto, whom I hired as my local field assistant in 1973, to determine births, deaths, migration, shifts in residence, and occupational changes. I did several interviews with old informants, usually in the summer house I had rented south of Arembepe proper. I drove to the village, less than a kilometer away, protected by my car from unwanted encounters, and I found myself avoiding the central areas where I had spent so much time before. In contrast to previous visits, when we had tried to enter every house at least once, I now preferred having informants come to my house rather than going to theirs.

Ray Rapaport suggested that I might want to get to know the hippies better, as he was doing. I should have followed his advice, but in 1973 I never even visited the main hippie settlement on the Caratingi River—"the Aldeia," a fifteen-minute walk north of Arembepe. I let Ray and Alberto do the census there, and I relied mainly on Ray's reports about the hippies. I now realize that I saw the hippies as rivals. Their youth reminded me of our 1960s field teams. Their quest for the natural and the primitive was disquietingly familiar to an anthropologist. I felt my own youth and opportunities for adventure slipping away because of my new parental responsibilities and obligations to act like a professor.

Anthropologists are widely thought of as unorthodox investigators of strange places and mysterious people, willing to forgo the comforts of civilization for the romance of distant simplicity. We are rather like professional hippies. In 1973 I wanted the amateur anthropologists to leave. I wanted Arembepe preserved for the real anthropologists—myself and my field team colleagues. However, realizing that I couldn't have my wish, I avoided the hippies and tried to discount their impact on village life.

Similarly, I avoided the tourists. It made no difference whether they were urban elite summer-house owners or rude incipient alcoholics spending Sundays in local bars. I concentrated on how the old was changing, and I looked away from what was totally new. The bright spots were the successes of a few of my old friends, such as Tomé, who were making the most of Arembepe's opening up to the outside world. It appeared that through new opportunities a few Arembepeiros might eventually rise out of poverty. But on the whole it seemed to me the bad outweighed the good.

It is often asserted that the kinds of people who go into anthropology are those who feel uncomfortable in their own society, or dissatisfied with it, and who therefore seek the alien or the past. I now recognize that the nostalgia for the old Arembepe that I experienced in 1973 grew out of my own impossible wish to rediscover my first "anthropological reality." Arembepe when I first studied it had seemed as different from modern industrial America as any setting I could imagine. It became my ethnographic paradise. My wife and I had met there, had returned many times; it had been "our community." Now we had to share it with many other outsiders, whom I resented. I acted as though, by ignoring them, I might magically rid the community of their presence.

These reactions became apparent to me in 1979 when I started this book. I discovered that completion of Arembepe's story would require another trip. After all, six years had elapsed since 1973, and I wanted to see what had become of the issues that were unsettled before, particularly the pollution problem. However, the second reason for the revisit was just as compelling. I needed to get additional information on the areas of village life I had avoided in 1973: hippies, tourism, and the factory. Correctly, as it turned out, I felt that I was now ready to deal with these external forces of change more objectively than in 1973. Chapters 7–11, which are based mainly on my 1980 sojourn in Arembepe, present an ambivalent, although somewhat more cheerful portrayal of community life than that based on my 1973 observations (Chapter 6). Not only had there been some real improvements in the community's situation; there had also been a change in me, the ethnographer. In 1980 I found myself less resentful, less personally involved, and capable of being less impressionistic about a fascinating process of change, which, I now realized, could be studied but not halted.

1980: The Whole World Is Open to Arembepe

I suppose that after my depressing 1973 stay, any revisit could only have been an improvement. When I returned to Arembepe for about three weeks in August 1980, I was accompanied by an informal field team consisting of two anthropologists—Dr. Maxine Margolis and Dr. Jerald Milanich —their daughter, Nara; Betty Wagley Kottak, now a practicing social worker; and our two children, Juliet and Nicholas, aged twelve and nine. Although Maxine, Jerry, and Nara stayed only about ten days, it was pleasant and efficient to have several people involved in a common inquiry, and this reminded me a bit of my early research in Arembepe in 1962 and 1964. Maxine and Betty, both of whom had worked in Brazil previously, helped out with interviewing and other research. Jerry Milanich used his expertise as an archaeologist to map the village, and his skills with a camera to take many of the photos included in this book. The children, who spoke no Portuguese, reported their observations and counted things—including over 300 cars one Sunday afternoon.

My family had spent almost two weeks in Rio de Janeiro before flying up to Bahia. This gave us a chance to become acquainted with national trends before revisiting Arembepe, providing a useful introduction to general changes in Brazil between 1973 and 1980. National forces now affected Arembepe much more than previously; because of the spread of electricity, radio, and television, villagers were even knowledgeable about international events. I could only contrast Arembepe's information explosion with 1962, when I had spent evenings—a stranger from a distant land, sitting with the fishermen on the chapel stoop being endlessly interrogated about the animals to be found in the United States.

In 1980, as one fisherman remarked, "The whole world is open to Arembepe." Instead of "Are there elephants in America?" I was told about the fishermen's strike in France and labor unions in Poland, and was asked about the chances and merits of President Carter and Senator Kennedy, who were then competing for the 1980 Democratic presidential nomination. Arembepe's internationalization was well advanced.

My stay in Rio had been pleasant, but I had found Brazil less different from the United States than I remembered. Traffic noise and air pollution were horrendous; consumer products similar to those sold in American stores were available everywhere; supermarkets had replaced small stores in many neighborhoods. There were joggers along the beach; Tom and Jerry spoke Portuguese on Saturday morning television; and I was even able to order a *quarterão* at the Copacabana McDonald's. This impression of a world civilization eroding cultural differences followed me to Salvador and then to Arembepe, where many roofs were now adorned with "fish spines," the television antennas that betoken the replacement of local cultural events with transoceanic homogeneity. My once-isolated fishing community had become part of Marshall McLuhan's world village.

This time, however, I was not surprised by the changes I encountered on my way out to Arembepe, since friends and media accounts had kept me reasonably up-to-date and since the alterations simply continued trends that had been obvious in 1973. The road was better. And there was a gas station in Portão, only 18 kilometers from Arembepe, where I fueled my rented car on Fridays—since, in the midst of the global energy crisis of 1980, Brazilian gas stations closed for the weekend. When we reached the Tibrás factory, I was pleased to find that the dunes were now spic and span; there was a neat pile of chartreuse sand inside the factory's fences. Though the factory smokestack still fumed, there was no more Hollywood-vomit gravy to destroy the natural beauty of the sandy approach to Arembepe.

The factory is situated on a rise, from which the Atlantic can be seen for the first time—because the beach road turns inward at Itapoan, more than 20 kilometers away. On this sunny Wednesday in August, the tropical blue of the nearby sea was impressive, but I wondered about the value of the luxury houses included in the new beachfront development due east of the factory, just south of Arembepe. Although lagoon pollution had been stopped, sulfuric acid still poured into the Atlantic less than three kilometers out from these villas.

Pavement now continued on to Arembepe, and beyond. Through joint state-federal financing, an asphalted highway, known as Coconut Road, had been completed as far as 20 kilometers north of Arembepe. Planned as a coastal highway, it was eventually to link Bahia with its northern neighbor, Sergipe.

On the northeastern corner of the asphalted turnoff to Arembepe, on a ridge overlooking the lagoons, stood a new satellite, Volta do Robalo. Volta's growth was the newest manifestation of the landowning family's lotting scheme; several Arembepeiros had purchased land and built houses there. Volta looked more prosperous than Caraúnas had in 1973; it was attracting wealthier Arembepeiros. But Caraúnas, too, which we soon passed on the right, was more attractive now. It had doubled in size, to 100 houses—no longer the wattle-and-daub shacks of 1973 but brick structures with tile roofs. Of the four parallel streets in Caraúnas, only the one nearest the lagoon, where the first houses had been built, still had shabby residences. The most agreeable sight during

The asphalted road, plus electricity, went right into Arembepe by 1980. (Courtesy Jerald T. Milanich)

our approach to Arembepe was the lagoon, which had regained its aqua color. There women were washing clothes, as small children bathed, cavorted, and learned to swim.

Just before reaching Arembepe proper, a road sign proclaimed an "urban zone," and we had to slow down for raised pavement designed to reduce speeds—as hundreds of automobiles now entered the town each weekend. The road's point of entrance was the same, but there was more pavement now in the central part of the village. And at the entry point stood a newsstand where nudie and sex magazines were sold—a local manifestation of Brazil's *abertura* ("opening"), the recent relaxation after years of censorship by a hard-line military government.

Arriving around noon, our first need was lunch. We parked in front of Claudia's Restaurant, where Ray Rapaport, my field assistant, had boarded in 1973. Our first encounter with a villager, Claudia's daughter Amy, would have been more agreeable had we not learned that Claudia and her husband had both died during the past year. This surprised us, since Claudia had always been one of Arembepe's most vigorous people, and neither she nor her husband had been over sixty. Having inherited the successful business her mother had built up, Amy was one of several Arembepe women whose status had risen as the value of local property increased because of Arembepe's greater contact with the outside world. Since women were almost as influential as men in the store and restaurant business, some were now creating substantial estates to leave to their children.

There were signs of Arembepe's new sophistication, its participation in national culture patterns, in Amy's menu. We had noticed in the south and in Salvador that Brazilian common rum (*cachaça*) was enjoying a new popularity as the basis for a series of apéritifs. Arembepe's bartenders knew how to make these drinks, along with others using Bacardi rum, whisky, vodka, and gin. In a village where strong drink had once been reserved for alcoholics and festive occasions, bars now stocked Old Eight whisky and Dreher's cognac, as well as cold beer, the favorite drink of weekend visitors. Although generally a bit cheaper, the cost of eating and drinking in Arembepe was now within the range of city prices.

Arembepe in 1980 looked larger and cleaner than my memory of it in 1973; but my overall impression of Arembepe, and of the Salvador area generally, was that change was less noticeable than before. Perhaps this reflects the erosion of cultural differences mentioned previously. However, I believe that the outline of change had already been determined in 1973; in 1980 it was simply being filled in. A profusion of bars, restaurants, and rooming houses offered testimony to tourism's increasingly prominent role in Arembepe's 1980 economy. The factory managers lunching at Claudia's Restaurant suggested Tibrás's new concern with its image and with the welfare of its neighbors. From Claudia's seaview window I could see the new, larger motorboats that now typified Arembepe's fishing fleet. During August 1980 I noted many signs of a new, diversified economy and of related social changes, including the emergence of socioeconomic classes, new religious phenomena, and previously unknown forms of social deviance.

Few communities in or out of Brazil have experienced so many changes occurring so quickly, and this is what makes Arembepe so special and so worthy of anthropological study. Without even planning it at first, I had been able to observe a process of sociocultural microevolution that in some ways paralleled changes that, on the basis of the archaeological record, had taken thousands of years to unfold for the first time. In barely twenty years Arembepe had moved from a relatively isolated, egalitarian, and homogeneous community to one with occupational diversity, religious differences, high- and low-status neighborhoods, and social classes. In the ancient Middle East, once the economy shifted from hunting and gathering to plant cultivation and stockbreeding, it took 4,000 years for social stratification to develop. Yet major economic change and an analogous social transformation had taken place in Arembepe in less than two decades. Arembepe's experience also offers a speeded-up picture of the local-level effects of the "modernization" that today is affecting thousands of small communities throughout the world.

However, before the full story of Arembepe's transformation can be told and understood, we must go back to the beginning—to Arembepe's essential character, its basically egalitarian socioeconomic structure: the distinctive constellation of attitudes, values, and customary ways of thinking and acting that had managed to survive into the 1960s for me to witness as the "before" picture in this chronicle of change.

Part Two
Paradise

3 The Structure of Equality

Because it was fairly isolated and had a relatively simple social structure, even during the 1960s Arembepe had contrasted with other Brazilian communities that ethnographers had studied. With a few exceptions (e.g., Johnson, 1971), anthropologists had studied stratified Brazilian communities, usually county seats. Arembepe, however, had lacked the class-based contrasts in wealth, occupation, education, political power, and influence that existed in these communities. It had been a relatively homogeneous lower-class community, with few insurmountable obstacles to achieving success within the local society and economy, but with many impediments to rising out of the national lower class.

An Arembepeiro's lower-class status became particularly obvious when he or she left the community and came into contact, most frequently in Salvador, with a member of the middle or upper class. Manners, dress, and speech provided cues that urban Brazilians routinely use to identify lower-class people, and Arembepeiros in the city experienced discrimination as poor, powerless, "uneducated" people, and as "country bumpkins."

However, contrasts in income, inherited wealth, and life style within Arembepe itself were minuscule when compared to the large-scale wealth differences that exist in Brazil as a whole. The local ladder of success was built of closely spaced rungs, and anyone could climb it. In this respect, Arembepe contrasted with stratified communities, in which inherited wealth gives some people a headstart in terms of economic opportunities and social status. The wealth differences that did exist in Arembepe itself placed its residents in a graded—rather than stratified—hierarchy. That is, there were no sharp differences between a poor and a rich group.

Accordingly, the data on 1964 household budgets (roughly approximating yearly income) given in Appendix 1 show a very gradual increase from poorest to wealthiest household, with no large gaps. And the largest household budget reflects an income worth about $1,000 in 1964—far less than a Brazilian middle-class household earned. In other words, Arembepe of the 1960s had a social hierarchy but no social classes. In anthropological parlance, its social system was ranked rather than stratified.

No greater socioeconomic contrasts than these existed in Arembepe simply because, ever since its founding, the village had been cut off from external resources that might have brought its people greater wealth and power. Arembepeiros were poor because of their circumstances, not because they lacked ambition. Many villagers, in fact, were extremely ambitious, contradicting assumptions of the many "experts" on Third World economic development who attribute the persistence of poverty and lack of progress to such factors as "low achievement motivation" or "lack of appropriate values." Indeed, all successful Arembepeiros were self-made entrepreneurs, and achievement in this small Brazilian fishing village was based on exactly those personality characteristics that sociologist Max Weber, in his famous book, *The Protestant Ethic and the Spirit of Capitalism* (1958), attributed to the first capitalists. Weber argued that the rise of Protestantism in Europe helped capitalism's advance by teaching such values as profit making, hard work, rational planning, willingness to assume calculated risks, simple tastes, an ascetic life style, stability, trustworthiness, and sobriety. According to Weber, early Protestantism, by viewing business success as a sign of divine favor, also promoted individualism—since the individual, rather than the household or family, would be eternally graced or damned.

Nevertheless, despite the existence of appropriate values in Arembepe, economic advance by its residents was objectively limited by a combination of meager resources and certain social factors, known as leveling mechanisms, that operated to keep ambitious villagers "in their place." *Leveling mechanisms* are social devices that discourage individuals from seeking to achieve more than their peers; they punish those that do and thereby reduce them to the common level.

Such mechanisms, according to Weber, also existed in the European peasant community prior to the rise of capitalism; and anthropologist George Foster has similarly examined the prominent role of leveling mechanisms in "classic" peasant societies throughout the world.

Weber contended that peasant values (shared, he said, with the Roman Catholic church) opposed the rise of capitalism and Protestantism. Peasants, said Weber, worked just hard enough to produce for their immediate needs; then they quit, mistrusting individuals who needlessly worked more than others. Protestant-capitalist individualism had to overcome the collectivism of the peasant community, in which gossip and other forms of social pressure were used to bring deviant individuals back in line.

Weber's description of Europe before the rise of Protestantism and capitalism is similar to Foster's (1965) discussion of peasants; and like Weber's analysis, Foster's has some relevance for Arembepe, even though Arembepeiros were fishermen rather than peasants making their living off agriculture. Foster argues that peasants throughout the world share an "image of limited good," according to which all valued things are finite. They regard the total amount of health, wealth, honor, and success available to community members as limited, so that one person can excel only at the expense of others. Unless good fortune can clearly be shown to come from outside the community (for example, from external wage work or from winning a lottery) and unless the fruits of success are shared at least partly with other community members, unusually successful individuals are condemned through such ostracizing techniques (leveling mechanisms) as gossip, avoidance, insults, and sometimes physical attack.

The Arembepe of the 1960s, although neither Protestant nor peasant, included expressions both of Protestant-capitalist-individualist values and of community collectivism and the image of limited good. These values had developed among the villagers without religious support. Even though, through baptism, all Arembepeiros were nominally Roman Catholics, organized religion played little part in local life. A priest visited the village twice each year, but only women and children attended the chapel services. "The chapel is a place for women," asserted one fisherman. "They're the ones

who have the prayer meetings and cut flowers for the saints."
(The "saints" were prominently displayed household figurines.) Men had their doubts about the full sanctity of a
priestly existence, particularly about the ability of priests to
adhere to the vow of celibacy. Arembepeiros were certainly
not the devout Catholics of Mediterranean or east European
peasant communities.

Furthermore, their values had been influenced by the beliefs and world view of neighboring farm communities—that
is, of rural peasants—and by the attitudes and character traits
evoked by their own fishing economy, which distinguished
Arembepe from neighboring communities of cultivators. Like
the hunting-gathering economies that existed everywhere
until about 10,000 years ago, and that still survive in a few
marginal areas of the world today, a fishing economy is a
form of foraging, rather than food production. Arembepe's
fishermen, like hunter-gatherers generally, appropriated and
depended on what nature offered, rather than planting, tend-
ing, and harvesting plants, or stockbreeding animals. Seasonal fish runs are larger some years than others. Some days,
fishing at a given spot on the open sea is productive; others,
it is not. "Sometimes the fish get smart and move away. Or
they hide in the rocks. Fishing isn't a profession you can
count on; everything depends on your luck," remarked Alberto, the fisherman who became my best informant, as we
rocked up and down on the Atlantic one day in July 1964,
waiting for the first bite.

Food production offers more certainty; variations in crop
yields from year to year are more predictable and more subject to human control. Farmers follow an established calen-
dar of cultivation and can usually count on a harvest season.
Similarly, herders lead their animals through a well-trodden
annual trek, following seasonally available pasture. Fishing
demands less routine and more innovation than food production. If all fishermen have access to the same technology and
share the same fishing territory, as was true in Arembepe in
the 1960s, larger catches depend most clearly on harder
work. Considering a long enough time period, so that chance
differences in daily catches can be evened out, the fishing
crew that works the longest hours will catch the most fish.
However, it isn't just hard work and long hours that make

either a wealthy capitalist or a successful fisherman. The captains of Arembepe's fishing boats in the 1960s pursued varied strategies, and some had greater payoffs than others. In general, however, the most successful captains were those who innovated—by experimenting with new technology, by seeking out new fishing grounds, by traveling to familiar fishing banks out of season, by evaluating costs and benefits, and by taking carefully calculated risks.

I had trouble getting Tomé, Arembepe's most successful fisherman, to agree on a day to take me out fishing. "There's always the chance that I'll decide to sail up to Guarajuba [10 kilometers away] to look for *guaraçaim* [*Caranx latus*], and I may fish there through the night." Tomé was afraid that I might not tolerate an expedition that lasted longer than the normal eight to ten hours. His habit was to see where the other boats were going, then to try his luck in less frequently fished, usually more distant, areas, and to fish longer hours. His reward was Arembepe's largest income based on fishing.

Experimentation, risk taking, and innovation—entrepreneurial activity in general—were keys not just to profitable fishing but to overall economic success in Arembepe, and indeed throughout Brazil, during the 1960s. The inflation that continues to plague Brazil was particularly severe during the early 1960s. The exchange rate of (old) cruzeiros per U.S. dollar increased from 475 in 1962 to 620 in 1963, 1,500 in 1964, and 1,800 in 1965. (It rose to 6,500 [6.5 new cruzeiros] in 1973 and had reached 60,000 [60] by 1980.) To hoard wealth under such circumstances would have spelled economic disaster, and ambitious Arembepeiros were reinvesting in land, coconut trees, boats, new fishing equipment, and consumer goods. Arembepe's most enterprising land-based entrepreneurs, as well as its most successful fishermen, were particularly willing to experiment with new options for the reinvestment of their profits. Because of inflation, therefore, behavior and values favored on the open sea found reinforcement on the land, and this is one reason why entrepreneurial activity has been marked in Arembepe since my first visit.

During the 1960s individuals with intelligence, ambition, business sense, and some literacy could actually move from the very bottom to the very top of the community's economic hierarchy. However, to go further, to succeed in the outside world, was impossibly difficult. The volume of wealth being generated in Arembepe was insufficient to propel any native son into the national middle class. Limited educational opportunities formed another barrier. Only through study outside could Arembepe's children qualify for the relatively greater incomes offered, for example, by Petrobrás, the national oil monopoly; but only a few natives had acquired such schooling and such jobs. Furthermore, the other prominent dimension of Arembepe's value system (community collectivism and leveling mechanisms) acted as a brake on individual economic advance. As a man's wealth increased, so did his obligations to share with others. And these obligations were respected, since no one could be sure that, given old age or infirmity, he might not himself have to depend on others. No pensions or social security benefits were available to lower-class rural fishermen in Brazil in the 1960s. Kinship and community constituted Arembepe's only social security system.

An Open, Noncorporate Community

Although the scale of Arembepe's confrontation with the outside world has increased dramatically since 1965, the village had never actually been isolated from external forces. Indeed, despite its egalitarian values and unstratified social structure, Arembepe has always been an "open, noncorporate community," one of two basic types of Latin American peasant communities identified by anthropologist Eric Wolf (1955). Arembepe had all the defining features of the open community—including substantial production for cash as well as subsistence, reliance on external supplies, and participation in national culture through use of the national language. For several decades Arembepeiros have sold their fish to outside buyers—at first to small-scale mule drivers who transported fish to villages nearer Salvador and occasionally to Camaçari, the municipal seat; later to buyers who came in motor vehicles from Salvador and its suburbs. Coconuts, traditionally Arembepe's only other important export product, were also marketed in the capital.

Arembepeiros have also long depended on items raised or manufactured outside. Most of the boats in the fishing fleet in the 1960s had been made elsewhere, and only one Arembepeiro still knew how to make a sailboat from scratch. However, fishing did not yet rely on motors and fossil-fuel energy, and Arembepe's fishermen therefore lacked the worries about costs, supplies, and repairs that accompany such dependence. Traditionally Arembepeiros bought such items as kerosene, rice, sugar, beans, coffee, lard, matches, soft drinks, beer, *cachaça*, and soap from local storekeepers. There were twelve small stores in Arembepe in 1964, one for every 60 of the village's 730 inhabitants. Three of these did considerably more business than the others.

Arembepeiros' ties with the world outside were mainly economic. Some villagers had left to study or work outside. A few men were fishing on commercial trawlers out of Salvador, Rio de Janeiro, and other major ports. Some native women worked as domestics in Salvador, and others had studied *candomblé*, an Afro-Brazilian spirit-possession cult, at one of the cult houses in the capital. The family that owned the land on which Arembepe was situated all resided outside. Except for the well-educated landowner who was planning the subdivision of his family's estate, the sale of lots, and Arembepe's development as a resort, the landlords rarely visited Arembepe and had little to do with life there. They were represented locally by Prudencio, an elderly man who collected the nominal rents that Arembepeiros paid for their house sites. These rents, worth between $.50 and $1.00 per year in 1964, had been set at a given amount by law and had been tremendously reduced in value through inflation. Prudencio also granted requests to build new dwellings and oversaw the marketing of the produce of the landowners' 5,600 coconut trees.

One fishing captain summed up the role of the landlords and their agent in village life: "Prudencio's the closest thing we have to a chief *(chefe)* here in Arembepe. But that's because he stands in for the landlords. They don't bother us much. They're mainly interested in their coconuts."

Despite Arembepe's traditional economic orientation to the outside world, villagers had been shielded to a remarkable extent from the differential power relationships routinely experienced firsthand by most lower-class Brazilians. For a variety of reasons, Arembepe until the 1960s had remained relatively isolated from the national power structure. As noted, a poor, seasonally impassable road limited contacts with Salvador. Until bus service came, villagers had to walk 18 kilometers to Portão to catch a bus to the city, and the round trip took two days. There had been relatively little in Arembepe's economy or placement to attract powerful outsiders. The estate of land and coconut trees on which the village stood was inadequate to support even the middle-class life style of the landowners, and the last one had left Arembepe in 1925. All her heirs pursued careers in the city and have rarely bothered the people of Arembepe. During the 1960s, one of them, Jorge Camões, was able, for the first time, to end Arembepe's isolation by initiating its development as a tourist resort. Jorge was the first member of his family to obtain a university education. He combined this with business knowledge, political clout, and an influential position in the state division of the national highway development agency.

Previously, Arembepe's location—its shielding by sand, lagoons, and ocean—and its limited resources had prevented its being a center of anything. For example, the land's agricultural productivity is low. "Nothing grows here. Not even watermelon and peanuts." Villagers got their produce from agricultural estates located a few kilometers to the west, but sandy soils rendered even their farming potential low. Indeed, throughout the entire municipality (county) of Camaçari during the 1960s the main economic activities were charcoal extraction, small-scale subsistence cultivation, and coconut production. Arembepe's land is suited only for the last. Its only export products were fish, coconuts, and the straw hats made by local women. Coconuts brought villagers, including landowners, just $5,000 annually, and the cash receipts of the entire straw hat industry did not exceed $50 per year. Fish catches were limited by Arembepe's rudimentary technology—sailboats with small crews doing day-long hook-and-line fishing. Until a tourist industry became possible about 1970, Arembepe had little to offer outside investors.

Along with its economy, Arembepe's internal political structure was also undeveloped. It had never been the seat of a municipality, or even of a rural "district." Arembepe's official classification was "hamlet," and it was included in one of the six districts of its municipality, with Abrantes, along the route to Salvador, as its district seat. Arembepe thus lacked the roster of tax collector, justice of the peace, statistical agent, postal official, and other government officials who are present even in district seats. The infusion of these relatively well-paying positions might have brought substantial wealth contrasts to the community and might have threatened the graded hierarchy of wealth. "Abrantes has a few people who are fairly well-off because they managed to get jobs as civil servants, but there's no one like that here in Arembepe. All we've got is fishermen and storekeepers." Civil service positions would also have brought "the government"—with its contrasts in power and authority—right into Arembepe. But this had never happened.

Arembepe's relatively undifferentiated social structure included surprisingly few political figures for a community in one of the world's largest and most populous countries. As noted, there was a local caretaker for the landowners' estate and coconut crop. A municipally appointed local police officer (*subdelegado*) drew a small salary but was afraid to use the revolver that the county had provided. No arrests were ever made, and the jail stood empty, except for some of the officer's visiting friends who were allowed to sleep there. The policeman's father was the only Arembepeiro to hold a federal position. With a long history as a successful sailboat captain, this old man had fished both in Itapoan and in Arembepe. He held the post of port captain, in theory overseeing fishing operations between Itapoan and Praia do Forte, a fishing community to the north. He also theoretically granted fishing permits to all fishermen in this area, although few of them actually had such licenses.

The port captain explained: "It's hard for Arembepeiros to get to Salvador to get the papers they need for fishing licenses. Most fishermen don't even know how to read. Anyway, why do they need licenses when no one from the government ever comes here to check." No successor replaced this man on his retirement, and he continued to carry out his duties informally until his death in 1973, while receiving the only federal pension in Arembepe.

The roster of Arembepe's leadership positions ended with the officers of the Fishermen's Society and of the Saint Francis Soccer Club. The soccer club included both local fishermen and native sons employed outside Arembepe who returned on weekends to play against other communities. Tomé, Arembepe's most successful fisherman, was its captain. The Fishermen's Society organized the annual festivals for Arembepe's patron saint, Saint Francis (held on February 20), and for Saint John (on June 24). Its two officers were the treasurer and the collector of funds. Normally, Arembepe's most successful fisherman, the owner and captain of the boat with the year's largest catch, was treasurer. Tomé was elected to this position in 1965.

Very little that was collective, communal, governmental, or even political could be detected in Arembepe. Arembepe also contrasted with the typical rural Brazilian community as described by Charles Wagley (1963, p. 148), in that it was not an urban or quasi-urban nucleus for surrounding rural neighborhoods. In the 1960s Arembepe had a single satellite, Big Well, with eight houses. Residents of two agricultural estates, Açu and Coqueiros, located a few kilometers to the west, visited Arembepe to buy fish and to sell their produce. Twenty Arembepeiros rented small farm sites (usually one *tarefa*, .44 hectare) on these lands, which they worked to supplement their incomes and diets from fishing or business. Many of the coconut trees owned in 1964 by 42 percent of Arembepe's population were located in Açu and Coqueiros, and many residents of Arembepe had migrated from these western estates. After gaining their freedom in 1889, the slaves whose descendants make up a large percentage of Arembepe's population seem, from Arembepeiros' recollections about history, initially to have taken up subsistence farming on these estates. Thereafter, their children and grandchildren gradually left farming for seasonal—and then year-round—fishing and residence in Arembepe.

"I remember one of my grandmothers who had been a slave," recounted Alberto. "After she was freed she moved to Açu and took up with my grandfather. For a while they farmed; then he began to fish. Eventually they moved to Arembepe and he became a full-time fisherman."

Arembepe's relative isolation from power wielders was

also a result of the split between its economic orientation to- ward Salvador and its political orientation toward Camaçari. Rose Lee Gross (1964) has described the manner in which Salvador has always drained Camaçari, like Arembepe, of landowners, rural elites, and most natives with middle-class aspirations. Arembepe stands, therefore, as a good illustra- tion of a pattern that applies to a "suburban" zone that ra- diates out from the capital to Camaçari, 43 kilometers away— and to other rural towns within a 50- to 100-kilometer radius of Salvador.

Indeed, Camaçari's orientation toward the capital, rather than toward its own hinterland, was another reason for Arembepe's isolation from power during the 1960s. Further- more, the fact that Arembepeiros received cash from Salva- dor on the one hand and political orders from Camaçari on the other meant that political and economic power could not be used to reinforce each other. Candidates for office in Ca- maçari had no control over Arembepeiros' marketing of fish and coconuts and could do Arembepeiros no economic harm.

The Costs and Benefits of Kinship

Several factors therefore combined to keep Arembepe rel- atively isolated from the Brazilian power structure. And this is why—despite Arembepe's economic dependence on the outside world and its inclusion within a modern nation—its social relations and community life during the mid-1960s were comparable in many respects to the egalitarian, kin- ship-based societies that anthropologists have studied in other parts of the world. With no major economic gaps or marked contrasts in power and authority dividing Arem- bepe's population, they kept up the fiction that they were all relatives. The twin assertions "We're all equal here" and "We're all relatives here" were offered again and again as Arembepeiros' own summaries of the nature and basis of community life. Like members of the same clan in a nonin- dustrial society, most Arembepeiros were unable to specify genealogical links to distant kin. "What difference does it make," they asked me, "as long as we know we're relatives?"

As in most nonindustrial societies, close personal relationships among Arembepeiros were either based or modeled on kinship and marriage. A degree of village social solidarity was promoted, for example, by the myth that all Arembepeiros were kin. It is important, however, to point out that social solidarity and community were actually much *less* developed in Arembepe than in societies with clans and lineages— which use genealogy to include some people, and *exclude* others, from membership in a given descent group. Intense social solidarity demands that some people be excluded. By asserting that they all were related—that is, by excluding no one—Arembepeiros were actually weakening kinship's potential strength in creating and maintaining group solidarity.

That Arembepeiros were only half-serious when they claimed that all villagers were related was clear from their other statements about kinship. Like lower-class Brazilians generally, Arembepeiros calculated kinship more narrowly than members of the middle or upper class, who, according to Wagley (1963, pp. 196–198), frequently recognize kinship with hundreds of people. Despite this, kinship reckoning in Arembepe was more inclusive than that of typical middle-class Americans. For example, Arembepeiros normally called the first cousins of their parents "uncle" and "aunt," and the children of their own first cousins "nephew" and "niece." However, kinship calculations broke down with more remote relatives. More distant cousins were called either "third cousin" or simply "distant cousin," and this was not considered a close relationship. Arembepeiros did not share the anthropologist's delight in tracing genealogies and discovering complicated links of kinship. I exasperated Alberto with my queries about specific kinship links among fishermen. "It doesn't mean anything if people in the same crews happen to be third cousins. Only closer relatives fish together because they're related."

Nor did Arembepeiros trace kinship far into the past. Rarely did villagers remember the names of great-grandparents, and then only of those they had known. Last names were used infrequently in village life, and most Arembepeiros were known—sometimes only—by nicknames derived from, say, a physical attribute ("Little Black José"), a characteristic ability ("Coconut Breaker"), or provenience ("Sergipe," a state to the north). Few Arembepeiros knew the full names of even their close relatives, and this was another sign of their isolation from the national power structure, where full names are used in legal contexts that Arembepeiros generally avoided.

In addition to rights and obligations based on kinship, Arembepeiros acquired others through marriage. Both formal and informal ties linked husband and wife. The most common union (40 percent of the unions in Arembepe in 1964) was a stable common-law marriage. Less common (28 percent), but with more prestige, was legal (civil) marriage, performed by a justice of the peace and conferring inheritance rights. Half the estate went to the surviving spouse, the other half to the children. The union with most prestige (10 percent of all marriages) combined legal validity with a church ceremony. A few Arembepeiros (8 percent) had been married in a religious service only. A civil marriage was for life, and Arembepeiros used the multiple marriage types to cope with the difficulty of getting divorced in Brazil.

"First I lived with one woman for a few years," recounted a retired fisherman. "I got tired of her and left her for another woman that I liked better. But I still wasn't ready for a legal marriage, so we just had a church ceremony. Then, after leaving her and taking up with my wife, I finally decided I was ready for a civil marriage."

A surplus of women (54 percent) in the population between the ages of sixteen and forty-nine was one reason why some of Arembepe's women lacked co-resident husbands. Eight couples participated in visiting common-law unions. These "husbands" were formally married to other women. Their visiting unions were secondary relationships, but some were fairly stable, having lasted several years. Nevertheless, the women involved in them were severely stigmatized. They were castigated as *raparigas* ("village prostitutes"). "Those are the good-for-nothing females who live off other women's husbands" was one elderly woman's expression of a common village opinion.

For Arembepeiros there was a quantum leap in the rights and obligations that went with legal, compared to common-law, unions, even stable ones. Common-law spouses had no right to inherit; nor did their children, unless they had been registered in a parent's name. Furthermore, in-law relationships were created only by legal marriage. A man who married in a civil ceremony assumed obligations to share not just with wife and children but to contribute, if necessary, to the support of his wife's parents and siblings. However, men in common-law unions denied that they had "parents-in-law" or "brothers-in-law."

I have noted that the rights and obligations associated with kinship and marriage constituted Arembepeiros' main social security system in 1965. However, Arembepeiros had to weigh the benefits of a system of sharing with kin and in-laws against its costs. This was the most obvious cost: Arembepeiros were expected to share in proportion to their success. Thus as ambitious men climbed higher and higher on the local success ladder, they acquired ever more dependents. To maintain their standing in community opinion, and to insure that they could depend on others in their old age, they *had to share*. However, sharing was a powerful leveling mechanism, constantly draining their surplus wealth and limiting their upward mobility—keeping them firmly entrenched in the national lower class. The correlation between wealth and dependents was one of the main reasons why Arembepe of the 1960s remained an unstratified, lower-class community. The leveling effects of kin and marital obligations constituted one of the main features of social life in Arembepe through 1965.

Consider the specifics of how this leveling was accomplished. As is often true in stratified nations, Brazilian cultural norms were set by the upper classes. Middle- and upper-class Brazilians usually married legally and in the church. Even Arembepeiros knew that this was the only "proper" marriage, and the most ambitious local men—who were usually also the most successful—imitated the behavior of elite Brazilians and, by doing so, hoped to acquire some of their prestige (see Kottak, 1966, p. 101). However, legal marriage drained individual wealth. For example, the surviving spouse inherited one-half of the deceased's estate. If he or she then remarried, that half might never be passed on intact to the deceased's children. Furthermore, legal marriage meant obligations to support in-laws. Cases in Arembepe confirmed that such obligations could be regular and costly.

Obligations to children also increased with rising economic status. This was most obviously because successful people had *more living children*. During the 1960s—and even in 1973—Arembepeiros were using no form of birth control. Only a few women induced abortions, since these were dangerous, and since children were valued as companions and—Arembepeiros asserted—as eventual sources of economic help to their parents. Boys were especially valued, since their economic prospects were so much brighter than those of girls.

The average married woman in Arembepe in 1964 had given birth to 5.6 live children, of whom only 3.2 survived—just 57 percent. Infant and childhood mortality was the main check on population growth, but children's chances of survival surged dramatically in wealthier households with better diets. The normal household diet included fish—usually prepared in a stew with tomatoes, onions, palm oil, vinegar, and lemon. Dried beef replaced fish once a week. Sawdust-like roasted manioc floor *(farinha)* was the main source of calories and was eaten at all meals. Other daily staples included coffee, sugar, and salt. Bananas, mangoes, and other fruits and vegetables were eaten in season. Diet was one of the main contrasts between households. The poorest villagers had no reliable supply of fish; these families often subsisted on manioc floor, coffee, and sugar. Only the wealthiest Arembepeiros could regularly afford the rice and beans that middle- and upper-class Brazilians view as the basis of "the Brazilian diet." Better-off households supplemented the staples mentioned above with milk, butter, eggs, rice, beans, and more ample portions of fresh fish, fruits, and vegetables.

Children's distended bellies and reddish hair were among the clinical signs of malnutrition and intestinal parasites. Poorer children were especially susceptible to infectious diseases, which appeared to be the main cause of death. Malnutrition and its consequences also affected fetuses; most Arembepe women had had a miscarriage or given birth to a stillborn baby. Like other fishermen, Alberto had lost children to malnutrition and disease, but his losses were extreme. I witnessed an especially painful one. In June 1964 Alberto asked me to drive him and his severely ill two-and-a-half-year-old son to a doctor in Itapoan. The boy had been vomiting and had had diarrhea for days, was running a fever, and had not been able to sleep. The child's nonstop screams unnerved me during the long drive over the muddy road to Itapoan. We arrived to find that the doctor had not come in that day, but the pharmacist prescribed medication, telling Alberto that the doctor always used those pills when confronted with the boy's symptoms. I tried to persuade Alberto that we should drive on to a clinic in Salvador, but he refused, and I still regret that I did not push harder. The boy slept during most of our return trip to Arembepe, but he died that night, and Alberto, whose surplus cash had been used for the medicine, reluctantly accepted my offer of a few dollars to help pay for a bare cardboard coffin.

Adequate incomes bought better diets and medicines, and provided the means and the confidence to seek out better medical attention than was locally available. Thus most of the children born in Arembepe's wealthiest households survived. But this meant more mouths to feed, and—since the heads of such households usually wanted better education for their children—it meant increased expenditures on outside schooling. In the absence of birth control, the correlation between economic success and large families was another siphoner of wealth that braked individual economic advance. Tomé, a fishing entrepreneur, envisioned a life of constant hard work if he was to feed, clothe, and educate his growing family. With an income three times that of Alberto, Tomé and his wife had never lost a child. But he recognized that his growing family would, in the short run, be a drain on his resources. "But in the end, I'll have successful sons to help their mother and me, if we need it, in old age."

Arembepeiros knew who could best afford to share with others, since success cannot be concealed in a small community. Villagers based their expectations of others on this knowledge. Successful people had to share with more kin and in-laws, and with more distant kin, than did poorer people. Successful captains and boat owners were expected to buy beer for ordinary fishermen; storeowners had to sell on credit. Any relatively well-off person was expected to exhibit a corresponding generosity. With increasing wealth, Arembepeiros were also more frequently asked to enter into ritual kin relationships. Through baptism—which took place twice a year when a priest visited or could be done outside—a child acquired two godparents, who became the parents' co-parents *(compadres)*.

In contrast to other parts of Latin America, where the co-parent relationship is more important than godparenthood per se (Mintz and Wolf, 1950), the two types of kin relationship were equally important in Arembepe. Children asked their godparents for a blessing the first time they saw them each day. Godparents occasionally gave cookies, candy, and money, and larger presents on special occasions. Later in life one could acquire another godparent (just one) by being confirmed by a bishop of the Catholic church. Through formal marriage, a couple could acquire four more godparents, couples chosen respectively by the groom and bride.

In ritual kinship we reach the same conclusion as in kinship and marriage: ritual kinship obligations increased with wealth, and this limited individual economic advance. Thus kinship, marriage, and ritual kinship as they operated in Arembepe in the 1960s had costs and benefits. The costs were limits on the economic advance of individuals. The primary benefit was social security—guaranteed help from kin, in-laws, or ritual kin in times of need. Benefits, however, came only after costs had been paid—that is, only to those who had lived "proper" lives, not deviating too noticeably from community norms.

Machismo *and Male-Female Inequality*

We have seen that the main requirements for success in Arembepe during the 1960s were ambition, hard work, and good business and investment strategy. Another must be added: being male. It is no exaggeration to say that virtually all the wealth held by Arembepeiros in 1965—through inheritance or income—had been created, ultimately, by the entrepreneurial activity of some male. I divided Arembepe's population in 1964 into three groups, based on the proportion that individuals contributed to their household's cash income or food supply. Most primary producers were adult males. The secondary producers included a few adult males, about half the adult women, and a few teen-age boys. The dependent population included half the adult women and most of the children. The income-earning options available to females were distinctly limited. The manufacture of straw hats from palm fibers generated a *total* of just about $50 annually. A few women were the sole proprietors of successful stores, and others ran businesses or did some farming with their husbands, sometimes as fairly equal partners. Ten married women functioned as co–household heads—making major economic decisions, planning their children's lives, openly bossing their husbands.

But the behavior of these women stood out as unusual only because of the general pattern of male dominance. Of Arembepe's 159 household heads, for example, 83 percent were males. Reflecting the male's easier access to wealth were household incomes and budgets. For example, in a sample of 118 household budgets for 1964 (Appendix 1), the female-headed households ranked at the bottom: 118, 116–111, 108, 103, 101, 97, and 67. None of the households headed by women were in the wealthier half. Their average annual expenditures were equivalent to $109, compared to $314 for the male-headed households.

But there is more to the story. Only two of the 28 female-headed households in Arembepe were economically self-sufficient. One was headed by an unmarried storekeeper, the other by a woman who had inherited coconut trees. Four other women depended on partial support from other households, and the remaining 22 relied on other households for most of their support. Eight of these 22 were the secondary wives of polygynous males, and their economic situation was most precarious. The prevailing morality viewed polygyny as improper, and secondary wives were often scorned as village prostitutes. (See Dora's case in Chapter 11.) Typically, the main wife and her relatives enlisted community pressure to end the husband's philandering. When a secondary union broke up, the woman had to rely on her kin until she managed to attract another man. Arembepe included a group of such women—seen as deviants by the community, as the lowest of the low—who were forced into a succession of unions and breakups. The woman's responsibility to support her children left her with few options but to continue the pattern, and—since there was no contraception—responsibilities increased as new children were born.

A pathetic aspect of daily life in Arembepe during the 1960s was the sight of children from female-headed households on the beach, meeting the fishing boats as they returned in the early evening. When Dora, our cook in 1962, had no access to another kitchen through domestic employment, she customarily sent her oldest son each afternoon to wander from boat to boat seeking a piece of fish for their dinner. The four-year-old boy, who suffered from a congenital heart defect that killed him at age thirteen, was often successful with one of his mother's brothers, a captain. If not, he went to other maternal relatives, since his father lived in distant Camaçari, the county seat. When the boy tired, which he did easily because of the heart condition, he would squat until his energy returned for another try at getting a fisherman's attention. One of the most vivid recollections of my early years in Arembepe involves this boy's panting and squatting on the beach, and the joy on his face when he was successful in his quest for fish.

Illegitimate boys were sometimes able to get their fathers to recognize them with a fish. But often these children went from boat to boat, relying on other kin connections, a good day's fishing, or a fisherman's pity to provide animal protein and cut the monotony of a diet otherwise limited to manioc flour, coffee, and sugar.

Although there was no formal enforcement of the restriction, the beach was off-limits to "proper" Arembepe women; so women had to send their children to beg. The psychological results of asking for food and for recognition of kinship—and of often being rejected, particularly by fathers who had never legitimized their out-of-wedlock children—have been varied. Some children have grown up to be alcoholics. Others, determined never to relive such childhood experiences, have developed tremendous ambition.

"The thing I hated most during my childhood," said Arembepe's most successful businessman, "was having to beg on the beach. My father was married to another woman, and he was stingy with my mother. Then she took up with another man and my brother was born. After that man left her, it was my job to get fish for them both. I'll make sure my own sons never have to beg."

I have noted that although Arembepeiros asserted their mutual kinship, the village lacked the clans and lineages of many nonindustrial societies. It also lacked the formal patrilineal or matrilineal rules that determine descent-group membership in such societies. In theory, the kinship system in Arembepe stressed neither the father's nor the mother's side but viewed them as equal. In fact, however—and reflecting another dimension of male dominance in the community—kin links through males were more important. This was partially attributable to a long-term pattern of greater female migration to Arembepe. In fact, 60 percent of all migrants to Arembepe in 1964 were females. Most of these were between the ages of sixteen and forty-nine, the only age group in which females outnumbered males (54 percent to 46 percent). The pattern was for immigrant women—mostly from nearby agricultural estates—to seek husbands in Arembepe. As a result, 42 percent of all wives had been born outside of the village, compared to only 31 percent of the husbands.

Arembepeiros have always distinguished between natives and outsiders. However, this did not appear to be a particularly significant contrast in the 1960s, since two-thirds of the population had at least one parent who had been born outside, and since just a third of the marriages in 1964 involved two Arembepe natives. There were, however, differences in male and female strategies for entering Arembepe society. Many females came to visit relatives and stayed on. Men, too, might come because of some kin relationship. They might take up residence near a relative or friend—for example, an Arembepeiro who had farmed near the immigrant's home. Males who wanted to settle tried to find positions in crews. Usually they started fishing with less successful captains, eventually asking to fish temporarily with other crews when their regular captains missed fishing because of drunkenness or laziness. As an immigrant's reputation for reliability grew, he could graduate to one of the more successful boats. In some cases immigrants became well-to-do captains and boat owners.

Two residents of Arembepe's northern rectangle, 1964. (Conrad P. Kottak)

Male immigrants also had many more opportunities than women to join in community life. They could meet other fishermen on the beach, bathe with other men in the lagoon, and congregate in bars and on the chapel stoop, where most fishermen gathered for conversation each evening. Following a general Mediterranean and Latin American pattern, men's access to public space was much wider than women's (cf. Harding, 1975; Reiter, 1975). Adult women left home to wash, fetch water, bathe, shop, or visit neighbors and kin, but women usually associated in smaller groups and spent more time indoors.

To stay in Arembepe, immigrant women eventually had to find husbands. However, such a woman's position was even more precarious than a native woman's. Without the native's local kinship network, the immigrant faced destitution should her husband desert. Without her own family close at hand to offer at least moral support, the immigrant wife often had to tolerate more abusive treatment than a wife born in Arembepe. Nor were immigrants' children as familiar with their nonresident kin as with their native parent's family. This was

The chapel and the eastern part of Arembepe's central square, look-ing north, in 1963. Most village men are out fishing and the women are busy with chores at home or washing in the lagoon. (Courtesy Niles Eldredge)

the main reason that kin links through males showed up more often in local life—for example, among members of a boat crew.

Thus the different opportunities of men and women showed up in the economy, in access to public space, and in networks of kin-based support. They also showed up in po-litical life. Arembepe had few authority positions, and all were held by males. Most household heads and all boat cap-tains were males. These were just some of the many manifes-tations of the lower value that Arembepeiros assigned to fe-males. Parents valued boys more than girls; unhappy was the man who had not sired a *macho*. Boys got better food and generally better treatment than girls. Discrimination against girls showed up in childhood mortality—girls, because they were more likely to be neglected, were less likely to survive than boys. Thus in 1964 there were 113 boys for every 100 girls aged ten or under. No one admitted that this neglect was actually covert female infanticide, one expression of an economic devaluation of females that ramified throughout

Arembepe's social system and ideology. But villagers did recognize that boys received better care than girls. "Boys need to eat more if they're to grow up strong."

From infancy, male freedom was encouraged; girls were fettered. Girls wore dresses from their third month of life, but many boys had no shame about walking around naked until they were near adolescence. During a baby boy's first year, mothers commented on, fondled, and kissed his genitals. Fathers publicly grabbed the penises of older boys, stimulating them to erection, laughing at the child's reaction. Boys were encouraged to masturbate, to engage in homosexual play, and to have sexual relations with willing girls and women, and with livestock—from chickens (that's right) to mares.

The freedom and sexuality of maleness contrasted with the confinement and denial of being female. Arembepeiros viewed virginity as a commodity. They believed that girls had to be virgins if they hoped to marry legally. In 1965 two women had preserved their virginity until their late twenties. One eventually accomplished her long-term plan to marry a fairly successful man from outside and move closer to the city. Only as a virgin, Arembepeiros supposed, could a local woman obtain such a match. Legal marriage meant proposal, formal engagement, and a long courting period. Common-law couples, on the other hand, eloped, usually after sexual activity on the beaches or in the bush. Arembepeiros thus viewed virginity as a commodity that could be exchanged for the inheritance rights that came from legal marriage. And except for those women with inherited estates, virginity was just about all that Arembepe's women thought they had to offer prospective husbands.

Race Relations

Although Arembepe's sex roles were unequal, the general community pattern of egalitarianism did extend to race relations. Despite marked phenotypical (physical) variation in the village population, all Arembepeiros had at least some slave ancestry, and most would have been considered "black" in the United States. To investigate relationships be-

These teenagers illustrate the range of physical variation in Arembepe's mid-60s population. (Conrad P. Kottak)

tween "race" and socioeconomic variables in Arembepe, I had to work out (for reasons that will become obvious) a (five-part) scale to measure racial variation. Only 5 percent of Arembepe's population was classified as "white" (3 percent) or "black" (2 percent). Most (45 percent) were classified as intermediate *(mulato)*, dark *mulato* (24 percent), or light *mulato* (26 percent). This scheme was my own simplification, for statistical analysis, of Arembepeiros' own far more varied and detailed treatment of racial variation.

Previous studies of Brazil had clarified certain important contrasts between race relations there and in the United States. The main difference is that the United States has a dual system of stratification, in which both "race" and class divide the population, whereas in Brazil there is a single stratified order in which race, or phenotype, is simply one factor in determining a person's class affiliation. Other determinants are education, wealth, occupation, and family connections. A second fundamental contrast is the rule of hypodescent that has operated in the United States to assign—unambiguously and for life—anyone with any "black" ancestry to membership in that group (the socioeconomically

disadvantaged group, or lower category in the stratified order). In Brazil no such rule operates. My 1962 research in
Arembepe (Harris and Kottak, 1963) showed that even full
siblings could belong to different races—an impossibility if a
descent rule operates. A third contrast is that Brazilians use
many more terms than Americans to deal with racial differences. These general differences between the Brazilian and
North American racial systems applied to Arembepe.

Arembepeiros shared with other Brazilians an extensive
vocabulary of terms to describe phenotypical differences
among people. In answering questions about someone's race
(qualidade), they paid attention not simply to skin color—
which North Americans focus on by using such terms as
"black" and "white"—but also to nose length and form, lip
thickness, eye color and shape, hair type and color, and a
host of other outward traits. Just by asking 100 Arembepeiros
the race of drawings of nine phenotypically contrasting individuals, I discovered that villagers used more than forty racial terms. My research on racial terminology (Kottak, 1967b)
showed, however, that Arembepeiros were curiously incon-
sistent in their use of the terms. Presented with the drawings, which varied skin color, facial features, and hair, there
was substantial disagreement about the race of the pictured
individual. For one drawing, villagers offered nineteen different racial terms, and the least number of terms for any
drawing was nine.

Arembepeiros also disagreed about the racial classification
of real people, including themselves. I sometimes asked the
same people to tell me again what their race was, explaining
that I had forgotten their previous answer; often they would
give me a different term. When I queried them about my
race, some Arembepeiros called me a *branco* ("white"), some
a *mulato claro* ("light *mulato*"), some simply a *mulato,* and
some a *sarará* (a term considered funny, used for someone
with red skin, as I often had when sunburned, and light curly
hair). (In the United States, I am considered "white.") Some
villagers called me one term one day and another the next.
There was a similar variation in their choice of terms for
other villagers. How did this behavior compare with that of
other Brazilians, and what was its significance?

In contrast to stratified Brazilian communities, where light skin color tends to correlate with economic status, the only significant association between light skin color and wealth in Arembepe involved land ownership. As more recent descendants of slaves, Arembepe's darker people were less likely to own land than lighter covillagers. Remember, however, that land ownership played little role in Arembepe's economy. Fishing, and reinvestment of fishing profits in such areas as coconut trees, were the economic mainstays during the 1960s, and there was no correlation between skin color and success in these activities.[1] Thus there was no significant association between phenotypical variation and Arembepe's graded hierarchy of wealth differences.

And this is why my informants, although sharing extensive racial terminology with other Brazilians, used such terminology ambiguously and inconsistently: racial differences had absolutely no significance in the social world of the Arembepeiros. Two equally successful boat captains, one a light *mulato*, the other a dark *mulato*, were the best of friends, as well as *compadres*. They spent most of their leisure time together. Two poor widows, one "white," the other "black," often sat in front of their adjoining houses and made straw hats together. Officers of the Fishermen's Society and the soccer club had been men of all shades. Nor did differences in skin shade provide obstacles to marriage. None of the "whites" or "blacks" in Arembepe was married to another "white" or "black"; all were married to individuals from the intermediate categories. Prudencio, the landlord's agent and a former assemblyman in the municipal seat, was a light *mulato*. His wife, the local schoolteacher, was very dark. The two most successful businessmen were medium and dark *mulatos*. Furthermore, the kinship network of any Arembepeiro spanned a wide range of racial categories.

Both social behavior and the fluid use of racial terms demonstrated the lack of racial discrimination in egalitarian Arembepe. In communities where people are sensitive to racial differences, and where phenotypical variation is correlated with access to wealth and power, there is more concurrence about racial terms. There are strong indications that this is so in stratified Brazilian communities (see Wagley, 1952). Without substantial agreement about definitions of terms, about relationships among terms, and about the classification of actual individuals, the minimal requirements for converting racial awareness into racial discrimination are absent, as they certainly were in Arembepe during the 1960s. And this was just one more expression of the community's egalitarian social structure.

4 The Protestant Ethic and the Spirit of Fishermen

Imprisoned in the lower class for life, Arembepeiros of the 1960s confronted miserable public health, malnutrition, and high infant mortality. How then can I possibly liken Arembepe to paradise? The reason is that Arembepeiros were, in my judgment, much luckier than other lower-class Brazilians I have seen and read about—people who must contend with at least as many of the disadvantages of poverty while lacking the benefits of full employment (for males, at least), isolation from state demands, production for subsistence as well as cash, and egalitarian social relations.

We have seen that Arembepeiros were fairly free from outside interference in their lives. Powerful outsiders didn't care much about these remote villagers. There was no one to tell Arembepeiros that they should pay taxes, join the army, or fill out government forms. Disputes were settled informally, and no one ever got arrested. Rarely did a priest arrive to tell Arembepeiros that they were sinners and would burn in hell. Arembepeiros relied only minimally on supplies produced outside their municipality. They caught their own animal protein, and their manioc flour and most of the rest of what they consumed came from nearby farms. One man could still make a sailboat from start to finish. Arembepeiros did not face the chronic unemployment and still poorer public health conditions of northeast Brazilian cities. And Arembepe had neither pollution nor crime.

Most striking was economic freedom. To be sure, Arembepeiros could not aspire to more than working-class occupations. Nevertheless, no one stopped them from fishing as much as they wanted on the open sea, no one set artificially low prices for the fish they sold, and they were able to sell their produce on an open competitive market. It was in such

an open economy that the entrepreneurial, Weberian personality type described in Chapter 3 could flourish and that a
graded socioeconomic hierarchy based on individual
achievement could take shape. Such an open economy is not
universally encountered in fishing societies. Indeed we shall
see that closure of fishing opportunities figured prominently
in Arembepe's own transformation between 1965 and 1980.

A brief comparative look at technologically simple fishing
communities in other parts of the world shows that Arembepeiros were as fortunate in comparison to other fishermen as
they were relative to other lower-class Brazilians. Reviewing
the literature on fishing in several societies, anthropologist
Lambros Comitas (1962) generalized that people will rarely
select fishing as an occupation when they have the choice of
doing agriculture or wage work instead. Finding fishing less
attractive and lucrative than these other jobs, people must be
forced into fishing through economic necessity. The residents of Coqueiral, a Brazilian fishing community some 300
kilometers north of Arembepe, which Shepard Forman
(1967, 1970) studied at about the same time that I was first
working in Arembepe, provides much more support for Comitas's generalization than Arembepe. Only about 50 percent
of the men in Coqueiral were active or retired fishermen,
whereas in 1964, 74 percent of the Arembepe male work
force (180 men) fished as their main job, and another 8 percent as a secondary occupation.

Compared to other fishing communities, then, Arembepe
presented a paradox. Because it was *more of* a fishing community, it was a *less typical* fishing community. To understand why, we must consider a number of features of Arembepe's fish production and marketing that gave its fishermen
advantages absent in most other small-scale fishing industries—and thus made the choice of a fishing career an attractive one. Although the employment opportunities of Arembepeiros were limited to working-class occupations, villagers
did have some choice about how they made their living. The
occupations available to men during the 1960s included fishing (primary occupation of 74 percent of the male work
force), business (11 percent), artisanry (5 percent), local wage
work (4 percent), outside employment (4 percent), and agriculture (2 percent). Women made straw hats, ran stores,

made nets for casting in the harbor, prepared food for visitors, and washed clothes or fetched water for better-off households.

The most attractive jobs during the mid-1960s were outside Arembepe. In particular, a few young men were well enough educated to find work with Petrobrás—the federally owned oil monopoly. Some of them maintained their principal residence in Arembepe, coming home to parents, wife, and children on weekends. When I filled out a short interview schedule in August 1965 about Arembepeiros' economic aspirations and their evaluation of different jobs, most cited Petrobrás worker as the most desirable occupation. Because my respondents' economic horizons did not extend beyond working-class employment, none of them even mentioned such middle-class professions as physician, lawyer, or even druggist or bank teller. Although Salvador's proximity and growth provided Arembepeiros with better job prospects than were available to more isolated communities, most native sons eventually worked in Arembepe. For example, only 26 percent of the oldest sons of Arembepeiros were working outside in 1964.

Within Arembepe, fishing and business offered the best chance for economic success. Although the highest cash income of an ordinary fisherman (noncaptain) was just over $400 in 1964, Tomé, the captain and owner of Arembepe's most successful sailboat, made about $1,000 that year—almost as much as each of the three most successful businessmen. Note, however, that Tomé actually had the largest *effective income* in Arembepe, since his occupation—like that of all fishermen—provided food. The concept of effective income—the amount of cash remaining after food expenses are deducted—is necessary to evaluate relative economic success in Arembepe, since some occupations provide food, and others don't. Tomé's situation was particularly good since he also had a small plot where he grew vegetables and fruits.

In the mid-1960s the top rungs of Arembepe's economic success ladder were occupied by successful businessmen and captain-owners. Next came less successful business people and captain-owners, and ordinary crew members of the most successful boats. At the very bottom were women with no co-resident males. Just above them were people who

worked at odd jobs and in agriculture and the least successful fishermen, including a few unreliable captains. Any ambitious Arembepeiro chose fishing, business, or outside employment over agriculture or locally available wage work.
Bricklayers and house carpenters earned about a dollar a day.
Work as a coconut picker, husker, or collector paid even less
and was available only seasonally. Alcoholics made a pit-
tance, generally to buy rum, by running errands.

All successful Arembepeiros had more than one occupation. In 1965 Tomé, for example, fished as captain, owned his
boat, farmed a small plot, and sold coconuts. (Eventually his
inventory of money-making activities expanded to fish marketing and long-distance fishing.) Partly compensating for
the fact that fishing provides food while business does not,
Arembepe's nonfishermen had more time available to farm
and to pursue various money-making schemes. One land-
based entrepreneur, for instance, ran two stores, transported
drinking water, marketed fish and coconuts, farmed, sold his
own coconuts, and owned shares in three boats. Only 38 percent of the fishermen had multiple occupations in 1964, compared to 74 percent of the businessmen.

I must stress again the openness of Arembepe's economic
hierarchy in the 1960s, the possibility of rising from the very
bottom to the very top, through ambition, hard work, and
good business sense. Arembepe's relative good fortune compared to other fishing communities has to do with Salvador's
expansion and its seemingly inexhaustible demand for
Arembepe's fish. During the 1960s Arembepeiros saw the
cost of their fish rise faster than the general inflation rate;
and some of them profited, reinvested, and experimented at
a frantic rate. Arembepe's relative good fortune stands out
especially sharply in comparison with Forman's (1970) Coqueiral, where, during the 1960s, the mayor of the municipality and the president of the local fishing guild conspired
to block any increase in the price that fishermen received,
and prohibited fishermen from marketing their own fish.
Lacking Arembepe's proximity to a major city, Coqueiral was
economically as well as politically dependent on its municipality. The Coqueiral situation highlights Arembepe's luck
in having its market relations with one place and its political
ties with another. In Arembepe, at least through 1973, fish-

ermen were gaining more control over the production and marketing of their product. This pattern can be understood and illustrated through a more detailed description of Arembepe's fishing industry.

The Sailor's Life

For many years most Arembepeiros made their living from marine fishing. During the mid-1960s most fishing was done in small (6 meters long and 2 across at the widest point) plank launches—hull sailboats powered only by wind or rowing. (These boats were all motorized by 1973.) The number of active boats stabilized at thirty-one in 1959, after years of increase, probably because space was limited in Arembepe's small natural harbor, formed by a partially submerged sandstone reef just east of the beach. Boats entered and left the harbor through five breaks in the reef.

All fishing on the open sea was with hook and handline, but nearer shore a few other techniques were used. One old

Arembepe's small natural harbor, protected by a sandstone reef. Shown here, boats sail out to sea on a day with very low tide, accompanying a full moon. (Conrad P. Kottak)

man owned a canoe and large dragnet that was set in the harbor, particularly during the summer. Arembepeiros started experimenting with trammel nets, which float vertically in the water, in 1965. Trammel nets ultimately proved most useful in lobster fishing, and during a short-lived lobster boom, the amount of trammel netting shot up from 250 meters in 1965 to 4,300 meters in 1973. Women and children used dip nets to catch small fish in the lagoon in the 1960s, but industrial pollution had removed this option by 1973. A few men set traps for shrimp in rivers north and south of Arembepe. At low tide, boys fished with poles from the reef, and women and children gathered mollusks and sea urchins on the reef.

But the mainstay of the economy has always been hook-and-line fishing on the open sea. Through the 1960s Arembepe's most productive fishing took place right above the continental slope, the rapid fall in ocean depth that begins at the end of the continental shelf—the gradually sloping coastal plain that extends only 11 kilometers offshore from Arembepe, compared to a world-wide average of just under 50 kilometers. Here is another major factor in Arembepe's favor. Because *the slope is near shore*, Arembepeiros have ready access to several varieties of fish that are found at a range of between 35 and 200 fathoms. In particular, Arembepeiros can fish for the horse-eyed bonito (*olho de boi*), a large migratory species with an annual run.

Arembepeiros distinguished three fishing seasons, as one fisherman explained. "June, July, August, into September, that's the winter. That's when fishing's usually bad, when we have to stick close to shore because of the weather. In the summer, between October and January, the ocean is as smooth as glass, and it's easy to sail and row, and visit the distant banks. In February we start the harvest of the bonito. We leave early in the morning for The Wall, and we fish all day, sometimes until the boat is full. We fish like that throughout the fall, from February to May."

In summer and fall, Arembepeiros sailed three or four hours to the slope, where most fish were caught in rocky cliff areas at depths of 60 fathoms or more. During the winter rainy season, when sudden squalls and rough seas are common, boats did most of their fishing close to shore, sailing for less than an hour to station themselves over the rocky parts of the rock and sand bottoms that occur between 8 and 20 fathoms. Fear of adverse weather was the main reason that most winter fishing took place near shore.

Although there were five seats, and named positions, in a fishing boat, the average crew size in the mid-1960s was only four men, reflecting a labor shortage. Most fishermen had set places in four- or five-man crews. Some had regular second choices, crews they fished in if their usual boat stayed in.

The main distinction in the boat was between the captain and the ordinary fishermen. During the mid-1960s captains might own all, half, or no part of their boats. At the end of each day's fishing, "the boat"—that is, the owner(s)—received about 25 percent of the proceeds from marketing the crew's total catch. The four- or five-man crew divided the remaining 75 percent equally. Captains who independently owned their boats received 25 percent as "the boat's" share and another 15 percent as crew members. After deducting maintenance expenses (usually amounting to less than $100), the average captain-owner cleared about $500 annually, plus fish for his table. The most successful ones made at least twice that much. Captains who co-owned their boats, usually with a local businessman, split "the boat's" share and expenses equally.

In 1965 access to Arembepe's fishing technology was open to any ambitious man. Although the cost of a new, fully equipped boat was almost equal to the annual income of an ordinary fisherman, money could be made in commercial fishing outside, or one could acquire a half-share by working as captain for a year or two and applying the captain's commission (25 percent of "the boat's" share) to pay off half the cost of the boat. The combination of half-ownership and hard work could thereafter produce enough money to buy a sailboat of one's own. Fishermen were using all these strategies in the mid-1960s.

Arembepe's fishermen were also benefiting from the spiraling price of fish. In 1965 the selling price of a kilogram of fish was 500 percent of the 1962 figure, whereas a new, fully equipped boat stood at just 250 percent of its 1962 value. From another angle, a fully equipped boat had cost 800 kilograms of fish in 1962, compared to only 400 kilograms in

1965. As the value of their product increased, more and more fishermen began to order boats of their own. Whereas the owners of Arembepe's three largest stores had all owned boat shares in 1964, by 1965 they had sold their shares, been deserted by their captains, or retired their boats. "I've owned a boat ever since I took over my father's business," a middle-aged storekeeper told me in 1965. "But I can't find anyone to be my captain. Now all the good captains want to own boats of their own. They forget that people like me helped them get their start by letting them fish for a half-share."

The main nonfishing owners in 1965 were people who were somehow active in the fishing economy—one man in naval carpentry and two others in fish marketing. By 1965 twenty-one captains (out of a total of thirty-one) owned all (five) or half (sixteen) of their boats, and three more were about to complete payments for half shares. Since the value of a fully equipped boat had fallen by then to about $150, the average captain-half-owner, receiving about 28 percent of his boat's annual marketed catch, cleared almost $400, permitting him fairly easily to buy the second half-share with the proceeds of a year's fishing, or to dissolve the relationship with the nonfishing owner by making a down payment on a new boat.

The pattern that was emerging in 1965 expressed the resentment of fishermen—and especially of hardworking captains—about sharing the fruits of their labor with nonfishermen. This was another leveling mechanism, a powerful check on the profits that nonfishing owners could draw from the fishing industry. "Who wants to share profits with someone who sits on shore and does nothing. Nothing, while I do all the work," said the captain whose former partner was the storekeeper quoted previously. Captains shared ownership with, or worked for, nonfishing owners only because of (1) economic necessity, (2) kinship, or (3) the captain's lack of ambition or regular work habits. However, once profits permitted captains to withdraw from these relationships, the only captains that nonfishing owners were able to attract were the least successful. Since unreliable captains tended to attract unreliable crew members, there was a real limit to the profits of the nonfishing owner. In the context of Arembepe's shortage of both captains and ordinary fishermen, the nonfishing owner of the 1960s was therefore as dependent on the capricious activities of his captain and crew as the ambitious fisherman had once been on the nonfisherman's willingness to provide capital.

Arembepe's hull sailboats were never particularly valuable or durable craft. The average boat in Arembepe in 1965 was about ten years old. All boats required minor repairs each year and substantial repairs after about seven years. "Nowadays," reported a man who in 1965 had just ordered his own boat, "it costs just as much to do a major overhaul as it does to buy a new boat. Even when you add in the cost of equipment for the new boat—things like sails and masts, water barrels, and a mooring in the harbor—it still would cost half as much to do thorough repairs on an old boat as it does to get a new one. This is why people are selling their old boats [to buyers in fishing villages to the north] and buying new ones. The new ones last longer than a boat that's been repaired."

Inheritance of sailboats was rare and did not perpetuate wealth contrasts across the generations. A boat's value was not as a commodity but as a means of production for an enthusiastic captain and crew. Without proper personnel, a boat's value could fall to nothing, as this story about Laurentino, a one-time nonfishing owner, illustrates. Laurentino, who ran a store that he had inherited from his father and another that he had started on his own, at one time held shares in four fishing boats. However, even more than most villagers, Laurentino had trouble finding captains and crew who would work for him, because he had become a very unpopular man. Unlike other storekeepers, Laurentino refused to extend credit. He was also reputed to practice *candomblé*, the Afro-Brazilian cult that barely existed in Arembepe during the mid-1960s. "They say he's got a demon (*cão*), a devil dog he keeps in a cage in his shop," said our cook, as she asked me to walk her home late one dark night. "I've never seen it, but last night I saw his door partway open, and there was a strange light coming from inside. I'm not walking by there by myself." Laurentino's antisocial behavior led to his isolation, through gossip, avoidance, and other leveling mechanisms that eventually ended his profits from the fishing industry. By 1965, Laurentino had given up trying to find captains and crews. He had managed to sell just one of his boats. The others he had chopped up and used for firewood—an excellent illustration of the limitations on nonfishing owners' profits within Arembepe's fishing industry.

Even in the early 1970s after motors had been introduced (financed by government loans to successful captains), there were limitations to the control of Arembepe's fishing industry by nonfishermen. Arembepe's rudimentary fishing technology had a low value and short lifespan, and anyone could gain access to the means of production through hard work. The nature of the fishing economy, particularly its technology, is another reason why Arembepe's mid-1960s socioeconomic hierarchy remained graded rather than stratified. (We shall see in Chapter 8, however, that all of this had changed dramatically by 1980, when it cost 5,500 kilograms of fish, rather than the 400 kilograms of 1964, to buy a boat.)

Excelling in an Egalitarian Society

The social and economic checks that kept owners who did not fish from obtaining substantial profits from marine fishing during the 1960s did not operate against captains. However, the difference in the roles of captain and ordinary fisherman was critical, since, in an egalitarian community, it offered the only significant contrast in the main unit of daily production—the boat crew. A captain's duties included fishing and, for most captains, ownership responsibilities, which were either sole or shared. One ordinary fisherman described the main features of the captain's role.

"When the weather's been bad, or looks like it could be, the captain makes the decision about whether the boat should go out. The boat leaves when the captain's ready. Once we're on the other side of the reef, he'll tell us where he thinks we should start fishing. If we don't catch much, he decides when we should try a different spot. The captain says when the fishing day ends and we head home. He's in charge of navigation. He knows where we are by reading the landmarks, and he gives the orders to raise or lower the masts and anchor."

My own observations of the behavior of several captains

confirmed the outlines of this fisherman's summary. However, the captain's special role ended when fishing began—after a spot had been determined, a rocky bottom established by dropping a plumbline, the boat properly positioned, and the anchor let down. Until the captain issued the order to set sail for home, or to move to another spot, he fished like everyone else. Although his lines were sometimes nylon rather than the cheaper cord used by ordinary fishermen, the captain's fishing was no more skillful than that of any other crew member. Captain and crew alike sat for hours in the sun—as I did several times—rocked up and down on Atlantic waters, felt the sting of sudden rain, and shared the danger of negotiating the channels during rough weather.

However, even churning seas rarely produced seasickness in an experienced sailor. "Are you going to be sick, Conrado?" I was asked at fifteen-minute intervals each time I went out with a crew for the first time. A few village men told me that they had tried fishing but chosen another occupation because they got seasick. Everyone expected me to do the same. I found seasickness hardest to resist one especially hot afternoon as the stench of rotting *manjuba* (sardinelike bait fish), next to which I had been thoughtfully positioned, wafted in my direction. "Now this is participant observation," I thought, as I imagined the tiny, glassy-eyed cadavers turning from silver to brownish green.

There was a distinct fellowship of the sea, a camaraderie born of those hours of shared waiting punctuated by an occasional flurry of activity, as luck brought hooks and fish together over a rocky feeding ground. In general, if fishing at a given spot was good for one, it was good for all. Because of this, all boats used the "joint line" system of dividing the day's catch of small fish. Larger fish, which were rarer catches, were also pooled in some boats, but in others they were sold independently by the man who had caught them.

The captain's special role resumed when he gave the orders to lift the anchor and set sail for home. He made the decision to beach the boat during rough weather, when it seemed likely that fishing would be postponed for a few days, or when there was danger that boats, crowded in the small harbor and jostled by large waves, would collide and be damaged. Beaching the fleet was a rapid, arduous, communal task, undertaken as threatening weather brought boats home earlier than usual on a winter afternoon. Every man on the beach—whether or not his boat had fished that day, whether or not his boat was already beached, even whether or not he was a fisherman—was expected to help: laying out and positioning the massive wooden rollers, pushing and pulling the vessel up to the dunes, to safety beyond the highest waves of inclement weather.

Like any other owner, the captain turned over his boat's contribution to the Fishermen's Society for the February festival. Boat owners were supposed to contribute 5 percent of their annual marketed catch for the patron saint's festival. But "Nobody really gives more than 2 percent," one captain-owner confided to me, "and most don't even do that." Owners decided when boats needed to be caulked, painted, or otherwise repaired. Captain-owners faced loss of livelihood if their boat was damaged, but accidents were rare. The worst one I ever heard about happened in 1961. The sole survivor told me how he had held on to the wreckage of his boat. "A fish, a barracuda, stayed with me all those hours, until I washed up on shore. That must have been my guardian angel. I know I would have drowned if he hadn't been there." Owners always paid for repairs and maintenance expenses. Captain–half-owners, of course, shared both risks and benefits with their nonfishing partners; but the duties of captains who fished purely on a commission basis ended with the day's fishing.

The average crew in 1965 marketed about 3,500 kilograms of fish annually. Add to this 1,000 to 1,500 kilograms more that fishermen and their families ate, for a yearly catch of about 5,000 kilograms. However, this is an average. Some crews regularly caught much more fish than others.

How was the *fact* of differential production, which was translated into observable life-style differences within Arembepe's graded socioeconomic hierarchy, explained in a basically egalitarian community? How did Arembepeiros square their frequent assertion, "We are all equal here," with the obvious fact that they were not? Since much of the differential wealth in Arembepe was based on profits from fishing, villagers' explanations for success at sea are particularly important. They were generalized, in part at least, to land-based success and to the entire economy.

I soon found, however, that Arembepeiros held different opinions about two key questions: (1) What enabled some boats to catch more fish than others? and (2) What distinguished captains from ordinary fishermen? The answers that I got to these questions reflected the respondent's reference group. Four such groups were distinguishable: (1) successful captains, who were men ranging in age from the twenties to the mid-forties; (2) older captains who had once belonged to the first group; (3) the least successful captains, of various ages, who fished less regularly, primarily because of alcoholism; and (4) ordinary fishermen, who included retired captains and captains-to-be.

By 1965 I recognized that the opinions held by some of these groups were misconceptions that interfered with their understanding of what actually determined fishing success. However, I had come to realize that such confusion and misunderstanding were essential, since the fact that people *could* through concerted effort raise the level of production, had it been given widespread recognition, would have

Zuca, one of Arembepe's most successful captains. (Jerald T. Milanich)

threatened Arembepe's fundamental egalitarian ethos—the insistence that, despite current appearances and temporary contrasts in fortune, all villagers were really equal. What, then, were the divergent opinions?

Ordinary fishermen and unsuccessful captains usually said that *luck* enabled some captains at times to catch more fish than others. "Some captains go in luck, so that wherever they drop anchor, they catch fish," remarked one ordinary fisherman who held this opinion. However, the men who shared this view were actually reluctant to admit that specific captains regularly did better than others and to recognize the differential success that was visible in catches, life styles, and contributions to the Fishermen's Society. Ordinary fishermen and unsuccessful captains typically recognized few distinctions among captains, insisting that although some captains seemed to be having better luck than others right now, all were really equal.

By attributing success to luck and by refusing to acknowledge evidence for differential success, these people were thinking very differently from Arembepe's most successful captains. Among the better captains, those who belonged to group 1, there was a totally different emphasis—on the value of individual achievement, business success, and the rewards of hard work, planning, management, and reinvestment. Yet for *most* Arembepeiros there was no need to try harder, since success rested on luck, which was, after all, beyond human control.

The successful captains, when asked what determined success in fishing, always mentioned attributes that recalled Max Weber's Protestant ethic. Although they did not boast about their own success, they readily admitted that some captains were better than others. One explained, "The boats that catch the most fish are simply those that fish most regularly. Those captains stay out longest, and their crews work hardest." He divided captains into three groups, as I have done. The "first-class captains" that he named were the young, hard-working captain-owners or co-owners who made the largest contributions to the Fishermen's Society. Yet even this captain's opinions about what determined success revealed another theme, the importance of good vision for landmarking (discussed in the next section of this chapter),

Francisco, a fairly successful captain in 1964. (Conrad P. Kottak)

which contributed to confusion about the skills that were needed in Arembepe's fishing industry.

The element of confusion turned up in his discussion of the "second-class captains," those with "failing vision," who made lower contributions to the Fishermen's Society than the first group of captains. In this category he placed formerly successful captains who were "no longer able to see the landmarks of fishing spots." Most of these were respected older men who had belonged in the first group fifteen or twenty years earlier.

As "third-class captains," my informant mentioned men of all ages who never had been and never would be successful, primarily because they drank too much *cachaça*. Most were nonowners, the men who fished on a commission basis, who shifted from one boat to another, who commanded weak allegiance from crew members, and who sometimes worked as ordinary fishermen in other boats. They often missed fishing because of drunkenness or illness, and typically their crews shared the captain's maladies. Except for this informant's statement about the "failing vision" of the captains in group 2, his beliefs about determinants of differential success and his classification of his colleagues accorded with my own.

The opinions of the unsuccessful captains and ordinary fishermen did not. In fact the luck, or chance, to which they attributed fishing success could explain only *short-term* variations. In the long run it should have evened out for crews that spent the same amount of time fishing. Objective analysis supports the opinions of the successful captains. The factors that actually determined long-run differences in fishing production were several physical and personality traits that made certain captains good fishermen. Because they were in their twenties and thirties, they enjoyed good health, which permitted them to take their boats out regularly. Because they were dependable, they attracted hard-working crews. Their physical strength allowed them to tolerate longer hours at sea, to work harder, and to have less fear of unpleasant weather. Like Weber's Protestant-capitalists, they took calculated risks. They tried to maximize yields by straying from the dominant pattern in a given fishing season. Even during the winter, for example, they went to the continental slope, where several fish species are concentrated in a rocky cliff area. Sometimes they traveled to the north to fish in grounds that Arembepeiros normally did not use. In some cases their risks paid off in larger catches.

Also like Weber's Protestant-capitalists, although to a lesser degree, they valued sobriety. Successful captains drank less, preferred beer to rum, and imbibed only on festive occasions. More expensive in relation to alcohol content than crude rum, beer was a status symbol, and it was less intoxicating than *cachaça*. Successful captains could drink more without getting drunk. They never missed fishing because of insobriety. Like Weber's entrepreneur, who commanded the confidence of customers and workers, Arembepe's successful captains enjoyed greater crew allegiance and attracted better crew members, people who were willing and able to work longer and harder at fishing.

As rewards for their traits and activities, successful captains had better homes and diets, more material possessions, and a generally more comfortable life style than other villagers. On weekends they walked around the village, and visited bars, with short-wave radios they had purchased with their profits. Notice that such demonstration of life-style differences and conspicuous consumption partly violated both of the world views that have been attributed to people like Arembepeiros and that were discussed in Chapter 3: Weber's Protestant-capitalist ethic and Foster's image of limited good. Thus in valuing consumer goods and "the good life," Arembepeiros contrasted with Weber's early Protestants, who hid their success behind the simplicity and asceticism of the middle-class home. And in tolerating some life-style contrasts, Arembepeiros presented a *partial* contrast with the characteristic image of limited good, which Foster argues leads peasants to regard life-style differences as evidence that certain members of the community are profiting at the expense of others, and to respond with leveling mechanisms to reduce "upstarts" back to the common level.

The nature of its fishing economy was one of the main reasons why Arembepe stood between the image of limited good that Foster attributed to peasant societies and the Protestant ethic that Weber linked to early capitalism. Under favorable circumstances—such as those prevailing in Arembepe in the mid-1960s—successful fishing demands certain personality traits. Surveying data on personality structure from several societies, Barry, Bacon, and Child (1959) found that foragers[1] emphasized achievement, competition, self-reliance, and independence. These personality traits are particularly important among open-sea fishermen, mainly because it is difficult to demarcate property at sea, to control marine resources, to supervise production, and to store the product. Most important, within the constraints of the technology, labor, and marketing available to them, Arembepeiros could increase open-sea fish production without endangering the species they relied on.[2] To Arembepe's fishermen the sea itself was a virtually limitless frontier; the main impediments to increasing fishing territory were technological, for one thing, reliance on wind power. In contrast, as Foster has noted, *peasants'* resources are usually limited and their payoffs often come all at once, at harvest time. But for Arembepeiros, as for many open-sea fishermen, chance and hard work governed the level of production, given existing technology and marketing possibilities. To use Foster's terms, good was therefore not limited; it could be increased without harming others.

Thus because of the values and behavior that governed

success in an open, marine fishing economy in the context of favorable marketing opportunities, the most successful Arembepeiros were independent and achievement-oriented. Nevertheless, since Arembepe simultaneously shared cultural and structural traits with nearby peasant communities, and also because of its general poverty, it also exhibited some of the features of Foster's image of limited good—for example, the ideology of equality, obligations to share, and leveling mechanisms. Consider now one of the most curious arenas in which aspects of these world views met.

The Riddle of the Spots

I have mentioned that most Arembepeiros *erroneously* believed that a particular physical attribute—good eyesight—explained why some people were captains whereas others were not, and why—aside from luck—some captains were more successful than others. Specifically, this attribute was said to permit a captain to locate and remember discrete fishing spots through a visual triangulation system of landmarking.

Fishermen recognized and named both broad zones of the ocean floor and smaller spots within them; both were called *pesqueiros*. They correctly believed that most fish were caught in rocky areas, where smaller fish fed on vegetation, and larger fish species on smaller ones. The fishermen of Arembepe thought that some rocky areas had more fish than others, and they used landmarks to identify them. Most of Arembepe's winter fishing (using landmarks) was done within four kilometers of the shore in four zones of rock and sand bottoms. Most summer and fall fishing (without landmarks) was done over the continental slope, where boats lined up and fished within sight of one another. Plumbing was always used to locate these slope fishing grounds.

Although I do not question either the existence or the usefulness of landmarking in Arembepe, I believe that Arembepeiros had an exaggerated belief in the precision, scale, and significance of their landmarking system. It is not unusual for ethnographers to find, after careful investigation, striking contrasts between their own conclusions and the beliefs of some, or even most, informants. What might account for such a difference between the native's account (the *emic* explanation) and the anthropologist's (the *etic* account)? One possibility, of course, is that the anthropologist is wrong. Another is that informants are consciously lying. Or it may be that natives consider the matter in question too trivial for careful thought or lack the scientific knowledge necessary for an accurate explanation. Often, however, an exaggerated or inaccurate belief that is widely shared by community members turns out to have a definite function, which the anthropologist discovers is of critical importance to the social system.

Frequently that function is to block full understanding of, or to *mystify*, native recognition of what is actually going on, since full understanding might pose a threat to the system's smooth functioning. Some examples of mystification in our own society include politicians' frequent statements that our national defense budget is intended to ensure peace, or that the "laziness" of welfare recipients is the reason for their joblessness. These American mystifications have the function or effect of diverting our attention away from true causes— the lobbying and clout of giant military-industrial institutions, and an insufficiency of jobs that makes unemployment inevitable. By interfering with people's knowledge of the status quo, mystification helps discourage actions that might act to change it. This was exactly the case with Arembepeiros' beliefs concerning the role of landmarking and the spots in determining differential fishing success.

Arembepeiros' beliefs stood in the way of their complete recognition of much more important determinants of fishing success (i.e., entrepreneurial behavior and values). However, this mystification was fully compatible with, and indeed was expectable within, a classless, achievement-oriented community, which like Morton Fried's (1960) "egalitarian society," attributed all differences in accomplishment by people of roughly the same age and sex to personal characteristics over which individuals have little conscious control. In Arembepe as in the egalitarian society, people thought that some individuals excelled because they happened to have certain talents, abilities, or personal characteristics—physical, spiritual, or psychological. The egalitarian society poses a sharp contrast to the stratified society, in which people's class background always affects their status and opportunities as adults.

In accordance with Arembepeiros' ideology, most villagers viewed luck and good vision as the criteria for fishing success. These were appropriate ideas for an egalitarian community. Luck, after all, is impersonal and beyond human control. Sharpness of vision is a personal physical characteristic over which individuals (in the absence of eyeglasses) also lack control. Making these the criteria of success helped resolve the contradiction to egalitarian structure and ethos posed by the *fact* that individuals *could,* through hard work—over which they obviously did have control—raise the level of production.

As noted, the only significant contrast in the Arembepe crew was between captain and ordinary crew member. Accordingly, villagers had to view the captain as endowed with certain special skills that justified his larger share of the catch. The ability to locate and remember fishing spots became the primary test of what it took to be a captain. Ordinary fishermen then had a ready excuse for not being captains. It was not that they were lazy, stupid, or unreliable; it was just that their eyesight was too poor to permit them to see and to line up landmarks.

The exaggeration of landmarking's significance becomes clear when we focus on what actually happened when a boat reached a fishing spot. When returning to a spot that had previously been marked, the boat sailed until the captain lined up one set of markers, then sailed on line with the first set until he saw the second set come into line. However, before lowering anchor and dropping sail, someone always dropped a plumbline to determine whether the bottom was rocky—and thus whether the crew had actually reached their destination. Sometimes plumbing continued for more than half an hour. When many plumbings were required, the markers were usually forgotten and positioning was done solely on the basis of plumbline results.

I eventually discovered that the exaggerated impression of the precision of the location system was being created mainly by older captains, some of whom claimed to know how to find very small spots—for example, the size of a boat. Younger captains denied that spots could be so small. So did an expert on fishing and navigation techniques I consulted in Salvador, who asserted that landmarking techniques used by Brazilian coastal fishermen could differentiate no spots smaller than 8 meters by 8 meters—about five times the figure offered by the older captains.

I interpret older captains' statements about the landmarking system as comparable to the privileged information (often of a supernatural nature) that older men claim, and are believed to have, in many egalitarian hunting and gathering societies. In Arembepe, too, old men were perpetuating, and many young men accepting, a myth about what led to success. In a community where male supremacy and masculine vitality were highly valued, captains could not offer their failing overall strength as a reason for their declining catches. However, they *could* gracefully mention one definite and uncontrollable physical attribute—good eyesight—believed to fail inexorably, and they had a culturally acceptable way of explaining their impending or actual retirement as captain. Failing vision was therefore a convenient excuse for the older captain's declining productivity, the real cause of which lay in a general loss of vitality that the community's emphasis on *machismo* made it necessary to disguise.

The physical infirmities of old age, which limited regular fishing and exertion in general, could actually include failing vision; but they were certainly not confined to it. (In fact, by 1965 a number of former captains had obtained prescription glasses, but they had not resumed the captain's role.) By citing failing vision as the reason for their retirement, older captains could maintain the respect of younger men for a physical attribute that supposedly had once granted them large catches. By insisting that loss of accurate vision was the inevitable outcome of a life at sea, older captains held out to their younger colleagues the prospect of a similar fate. Ordinary fishermen, too, believed that success was fleeting and fickle, and that the life-style differences that existed at one moment, founded on luck and eyesight, might be leveled out the next.

The older captains' mystification concerned not just the landmarking system's precision but also its scale. Captains claimed to have marked and memorized between 5 and 200 spots. Older captains always claimed to know the most. "I could mark about 100 spots," remarked one fifty-five-year-old captain. "But that is nothing. There are captains who know between 200 and 300." However, Tomé, Arembepe's most successful captain, claimed to have marked just 20 spots, and another young entrepreneur gave a similar number. "Twenty's the average," said the latter. "No one could remember 100 spots; even 50 would be remarkable."

Despite Arembepeiros' statements that captains needed the ability to locate spots, I must stress now that most fishing in Arembepe did not entail marking spots at all. Only the zones that were fished during winter, the ones nearest shore, had spot landmarks. Plumbing rather than landmarks was used to identify rocky bottoms in the more distant summer and fall fishing zones. "There are landmarks for The Wall [the slope], but even captains with a hawk's eyes have trouble seeing them from way out there," asserted a fisherman. "That's why plumbing is always done."

If the spots were fewer, less precise, and generally of less significance than most Arembepeiros believed, did they have *any* economic utility? Niles Eldredge (1963, p. 27), a 1963 field team member who also studied Arembepe's fishing industry, has reasonably argued that spots were marked and memorized because a landmarking system eliminated much time-consuming plumbing activity. This utilitarian reason, along with the function of locating *general* areas of the ocean floor (zones and large rocky areas), may adequately explain the widespread use of landmarking through visual triangulation among coastal fishermen throughout the world.

It should also be remembered, in assessing the relevance of spots to the captain's role in Arembepe, that even the valued attributes of the captain were defined by technological and economic constraints in the mid-1960s. As Alberto, an ordinary fisherman who said that his poor eyesight and memory had always kept him from being a captain, put it, "If I had enough money to buy a small motorboat, I could go out to The Wall any time I wanted. That way I could easily catch more fish than even the best captain fishing close to shore. Even with a small boat and a motor, I could become the most successful fisherman in Arembepe." Confirming some of Alberto's points are certain changes that took place between 1965 and 1973. With motorization in the early 1970s came year-round fishing in summer and fall zones as well as entry into the captain's role by former noncaptains—and even former nonfishermen. These changes are examined in Chapter 6.

A combination of local and regional factors granted Arembepe rare good fortune. I have discussed the local factors here and in Chapter 3. Chapter 5 is about the regional ones. The combination of circumstances made the personalities of many Arembepeiros similar to the Weberian Protestant-capitalist type. And this is why—despite erroneous opinions held by numerous Arembepeiros about what determined success in their community—the real determinants were neither the "luck" nor the "good eyesight" that were compatible with an egalitarian, male-supremacist ideology, but rather the individualistic, achievement-oriented personality attributes of the Weberian entrepreneur. A major point of Chapters 4 and 5 should not be overlooked, however: the entrepreneurial personality types of Arembepeiros *did not cause* the community's greater fortune. Just the reverse: Arembepe's favorable local and regional conditions created and nourished these personality traits—despite a simultaneous and countervailing ideology of equality, sharing, and leveling. The "riddle of the spots" bridged the opposition between these ideologies; that is, the riddle helped make it possible to maintain both doctrines in the same community. We shall see later on, however, that these traditional beliefs in efficacious spots, once so critical in Arembepe's fishing economy, are now virtually defunct because of technological changes.

5 The Bigger Pond

Along with productive continental slope fishing, marketing opportunities that rewarded increased productivity nourished the entrepreneurial personality type in Arembepe during the 1960s. And in terms of marketing, the fishermen of Arembepe were again unusually fortunate, posing an exception to Forman's (1970, p. 13) generalization that most of the world's fishermen have limited access to marketing and limited control over the prices they receive. Some of the reasons for Arembepe's good fortune have been mentioned previously; but fish marketing deserves more attention here, since it was Arembepe's prime link with the outside world, generating about two-thirds of the village's cash income in 1965.

Arembepe's marketing opportunities have steadily improved throughout its history, particularly since the 1950s, when jeeps with four-wheel drive first came to the village to buy fish. Previously, several middlemen had used mules, donkeys, and burros to transport fish to Portão, 18 kilometers away, where it could be trucked to Salvador. This pattern did not end suddenly. When I first studied Arembepe in 1962, rainy season access was still difficult, and many fishermen continued to sell to mule drivers. Only about half the boats sold to a motorized agent, Roberto, who despite his vehicle's four-wheel drive, sometimes did not make it to Arembepe during the winter. Many people maintained their long-term arrangements with the traditional mule drivers, since they could be counted on to reach Arembepe and collect its perishable fish in good weather and bad.

But the days of the old marketing system were clearly numbered. By 1964 improvements in the road had brought two new motorized buyers to Arembepe. The owner of a wholesale fish store in Itapoan, who sold large quantities of fish to the nearby air force base and to restaurants along the road to Salvador, sent his godson. A second wholesaler transported his share of the daily catch all the way into Salvador. By 1965 both of these men had established purchasing agreements with the owners of several boats. They had weaned customers away from former buyers by offering more money.

Arembepeiros' links with the mule drivers had been both social and economic; ties of coparenthood (*compadresco*) often added social cement to the economic bond. Even Roberto, the motorized agent who was buying half of Arembepe's fish in 1962, had maintained close social relationships with his customers. He had acquired two godchildren, and he took his obligations to them seriously, eventually providing food and lodging while they attended school in Salvador. Roberto had made an arrangement with a captain-owner and his wife for room and board on nights when there were no fish to transport to Salvador. During the rainy season it was often difficult for Roberto to determine, in Salvador, whether weather conditions in Arembepe had permitted fishing. However, since a dozen boats relied on his being there to get their fish to market before they spoiled, he had to err in the fishermen's favor. So close did Roberto's social relationship with Arembepe become that in August 1962 he brought his bride there for a second wedding party and a brief honeymoon.

By 1965, however, Roberto had completely severed his economic relationship with Arembepe and was spending his time on varied business interests in Salvador. But his withdrawal had been gradual. In 1964 he still maintained his buying rights in seven boats, with whose owners he had worked out an arrangement whereby the fish would be transported and sold to the fish store in Itapoan, whose owner paid Roberto a commission.[1]

Although steady improvements in access to Salvador were decreasing the dependence of fishermen on particular buyers and raising the price of fish, Arembepeiros had always enjoyed some degree of choice about who received their fish. The traditional pattern—before motorized marketing—was for each boat to have its own mule driver, someone who could be counted on to show up when the boat went out and, on its return, to transport the fish to Portão. The number of these middlemen had swelled as fish quantity increased during summer and the bonito "harvest." Arembepeiros never needed to rely on a single buyer for their fish, since there were always several middlemen. These men, like Arembepeiros themselves, were lower-class people who had found a small niche in, and eked a meager living out of, the technologically simple distribution system that linked town and countryside.

One of these mule drivers was instrumental in the original decision of our field team to settle in Arembepe in 1962 and in arranging lodging there. The man's home was in Abrantes, the district seat, where he had become acquainted with Maria Brandão, a sociologist at the University of Bahia. He told Maria about Arembepe, which was then a remote fishing village scarcely known in Salvador, and she suggested to field leader Marvin Harris that it would be an interesting place for some of the student anthropologists to study. Maria's mule driver friend also arranged lodging for Betty Wagley with his common-law consort, an Arembepe businesswoman. By 1965, however, the mule driver had aban-

Betty converses with a nonfishing boat owner as the fleet returns one afternoon in 1964. The men on the beach are owners, marketers, and middlemen. (Conrad P. Kottak)

doned both his business and his lover in Arembepe—part of the general pattern of change in the fish marketing system.

Arembepe's marketing advantages are well illustrated in events between 1962 and 1965, the period during which the role of the external middleman was gradually eliminated and replaced by direct sale to wholesalers. Like that of the mule drivers, even Roberto's withdrawal from fish marketing expressed this shift. Despite his jeep, Roberto had been a middleman like all the rest; he had always resold to wholesalers in the city. Although Roberto is by far the most popular buyer who has ever worked in Arembepe, he too was eventually forced out because he could not offer fishermen as high a price as the wholesalers were paying. While Roberto was phasing out his involvement in Arembepe's economy, a series of new agents arrived. The particular wholesalers from Itapoan and Salvador mentioned earlier were merely the most successful out of five motorized buyers of Arembepe's fish between 1962 and 1965.

The entry of these two into local life warrants further discussion here, since it provides an excellent illustration of how Arembepe's ideology of equality affected the way that villagers interacted with outsiders. Of particular interest is the fact that the motorized fish agents, as members of the lower middle class and inhabitants of an urban environment where class contrasts were obvious in daily living, brought to Arembepe their own set of expectations about how they should treat, and be treated by, lower-class people. However, the outsiders soon learned not only that *their* expectations contrasted sharply with those of Arembepeiros, but that business success in Arembepe demanded that outsiders adopt Arembepe's values and expectations.

When in Arembepe Roberto had become an Arembepeiro. Subsequent outsiders never immersed themselves as deeply in the local social system; they didn't have to because as wholesalers they could offer better prices and service. However, their behavior did evolve noticeably as they worked their way into the economy. Thus the wholesaler from Salvador had acquired his first customers by offering higher prices, but he began to lose them because of his aloofness. Unlike previous buyers, he refused to give villagers emergency rides in his jeep, and he never engaged in repartee with locals. Most damaging to his reputation were two accidents. One killed an old-time middleman from Portão. In the other, his son ran over a village child. Trying to correct his damaged image, the wholesaler hired a driver-agent who felt more comfortable dealing with villagers, and he tried to curb his own aloofness. Nevertheless, his role in Arembepe was already being eyed by a local businessman, who knew exactly how Arembepeiros expected marketers to behave. The local man had replaced the man from Salvador by 1973.

As mentioned earlier, the Itapoan fish-shop owner was a wealthy man who did not visit Arembepe himself but sent a godson. Both of these men had roots in Itapoan's lower class, but the godson lacked his godfather's wealth (land, coconut trees, eight boats in Itapoan, and a very successful fish store) and his middle-class aspirations. They offered a good price for Arembepe's fish, and the godson knew more about getting along with fishermen than did the wholesaler from Salvador. Here again, however, different expectations led to the external buyer's eventual failure. In February 1965, during Arembepe's Saint Francis celebration, the visiting Itapoan fish shop owner got drunk and, trying to teach his wife how to drive, plowed through a fence into a back yard, injuring a fisherman. He offered to pay the victim's medical expenses. Later, however, when asked for compensation for four months of lost work time, the fish buyer refused. Someone claimed to have overheard his wife remark, "How dare he ask you for that. The fishermen here rely on you. You don't have to depend on them." This comment, retold frequently during the winter of 1965, stirred up resentment among the fishermen, who had a very different opinion about who depended on whom. Villagers considered the Itapoan businessman and his wife "uppity." They acted like *gráfinos* (elegant people), even though their roots obviously lay in the lower class. Here again, however, ambitious villagers were planning to take over the outsider's role. Arembepeiros' own fish marketing had displaced the two from Itapoan by 1973.

The Patron's Shadow

These encounters between Arembepeiros and outsiders, along with those considered later, contrasted with the relations between social classes and between patrons and clients that have been described for most of Brazil. For example, most Arembepeiros would have been unfamiliar and uncomfortable with the following stereotype.

> When addressing a member of the upper class, a Brazilian peasant will invariably lower his gaze, hat in hand, and shuffle his feet in an embarrassed mockery of his own humility. He will defer to the landowner, the shopkeeper, and the tax collector in countless ways, accepting that it is right and proper for him to do so, as long as proper behavior is reciprocated in turn. (Forman, 1975, p. 76)

Arembepeiros have been involved in unequal social relationships with outsiders, but these have exemplified what Forman calls "patron-clientship" as opposed to "patron-dependency." With patron-dependency the rural Brazilian is *forced* to continue a set of exchanges with a social superior, whereas with patron-clientship the lower-class person has some choice among potential "benefactors" who offer him differential rewards for his services and loyalty (Forman, 1975, p. 69). Forman (1975, p. 85) regards the change to patron-clientship as the most significant transformation now occurring in the Brazilian rural social system, as competition increases among the rural masses for patrons, and among patrons for clients. Forman (1975, p. 83) attributes this breakdown of patron-dependency to growing commercialism. The rural population, rather than staying put on the land, is in flux, which means that patrons are losing followings once fixed on their land.

Arembepe's weak patronage system and its similarity to patron-clientship rather than patron-dependency are not surprising. Arembepe's economy, after all, has never been based on land or permanent agriculture. The state capital's nearness has also meant that Arembepe has experienced earlier than most rural areas the commercialism that radiates out from the cities. To be sure, Arembepeiros have needed to enhance their access to capital, income, credit, information, and other benefits available from outsiders (see Gross, 1973, p. 134). However, there is a critical difference: Arembepeiros have never had their movements restricted, nor have they ever been stopped from making a living by more powerful people. The patronage relationships that *have* affected Arembepe, despite its long-term shielding from the national power structure, will now be examined.

Historically, the most likely candidates for the role of patron (and oppressor) were the owners of the land on which Arembepe is situated. However, as noted in Chapter 3, the landlords, until the mid-1960s, had sought their fortunes in Salvador and had little to do with Arembepeiros. The estate's last unitary landlord was Francisca Ricardo, who resided in Arembepe between 1875 and 1924, when she died. Francisca was a slaveowner and a member of a landed rural aristocracy. During the 1880s, just before abolition, she had her slaves plant more than 5,000 coconut trees, whose fruits were providing her heirs with more than $1,000 annually in the 1960s. Francisca was the last of Arembepe's landlords to extract her principal livelihood from this estate, which ran for six kilometers along the coast and extended two kilometers inland. On Francisca's death, the estate and trees were divided into three equal shares, for her three daughters or their heirs. All three daughters had already joined in the trek of Camaçari's rural gentry to Salvador. Thereafter until the late 1960s, when Jorge Camões, Francisca's great-grandson, began to subdivide the estate into lots, all the land was held jointly by Francisca's (fourteen) adult heirs. The landlords recognized an informal division into three parts, stemming from Francisca's daughters—one south and one north of Arembepe, and one that included the village.

One of Francisca's daughters, the heir to the estate south of Arembepe, never participated in village life, maintaining only an economic interest in her land and coconuts. Francisca's other two daughters both predeceased their mother, but *their* daughters, Emily (Jorge Camões's mother) and Nora—particularly the latter—played larger roles in Arembepe's history. The orphaned Nora (now dead) was raised in Arembepe by her grandmother, Francisca. Older Arembepeiros, recalling the tricks that village boys used to play on the crotchety old woman during her last years, expressed pity for Nora, who had to tolerate Francisca's increasing testiness as she grew older. Still, Nora became something of a romantic figure for Arembepeiros, following her marriage to a former priest, a German who left the church for love of Nora. The couple and their three children had maintained a vacation home in Arembepe, and many villagers felt that they had grown up with Nora's two sons and daughter.

From my earliest visit I had been struck by Arembepeiros' directness in dealing with outsiders, by the villagers' lack of the exaggerated deference and politeness I observed elsewhere among lower-class Brazilians. Many villagers did show respect to well-educated outsiders and to people who held professional or managerial jobs, or high political office. However, Arembepeiros refused to defer to outsiders on the basis of money alone, and they strongly resented an outsider's expectation that they do so. I was particularly interested in seeing if the pattern held up when Arembepeiros interacted with their landlords. Sure enough, I discovered that most of the landlords who resided in Arembepe after Francisca's death had been incorporated within the local social system. With the exception of Jorge Camões, who has been Arembepe's most obvious and most socially distant patron, they were treated in about the same way as Arembepeiros of similar age, sex, and personality type.

Nora's German husband, for example, always received respect—as a well-educated man, a scholar, a university professor, and a speaker of seven languages. Arembepeiros spoke of him with affection. They bragged about his accomplishments, just as they expressed pride in Jorge's university degree (the first one obtained by a member of the landowning family) and in a female landowner's certification as a secondary school teacher. Informants also joked that any man who would leave the priesthood deserved their admiration. In 1964 I accompanied a few Arembepeiros on a visit to the former priest and his sons in their suburban Salvador apartment. Although villagers treated the old man with somewhat greater deference than they would have shown toward an old man in Arembepe, they joked and used familiar language (the informal "you," for example) with his sons, who were their age peers.

In the mid-1960s Francisca's other granddaughter, Jorge's mother, shared the central third of the estate, which included Arembepe, with her two brothers. The three siblings, who were interested mainly in their yearly coconut harvest, had abandoned their concern in their land to Jorge, letting him make all the arrangements for subdivision, from which they eventually profited. Jorge's mother had never lived in Arembepe. She was born, grew up, and married in a suburb of Salvador where her father, Francisca's son-in-law Miguel Camões, held a middle-class job.

Widower Miguel retired with a comfortable pension and moved to Arembepe around 1920. Following his mother-in-law's death (soon after his arrival), he served as "chief" of Arembepe for two decades, until 1942. Miguel replaced Francisca as landlord-in-residence and became Arembepe's last landowner chief. He supervised the harvest and sale of his coconuts and granted permission to build houses and huts. He co-owned a sailboat and headed a local fishermen's cooperative that had a brief existence around 1940. Arembepeiros' recollection of Miguel's impact on village life does not suggest that he limited villagers' freedoms or interfered in their economic activities. Despite Miguel's middle-class status, he was remembered as a fairly benevolent figure who participated in local social and economic life.

Miguel's two sons, both retired civil servants like their father, resided temporarily in Arembepe after his death. One lived there for almost a decade with his second wife, a woman thirty years his junior. Miguel's other son participated more in village life. He opened a store, and as part-owner of a boat, he contributed to the fishermen's association. However, unlike his father, he never played a leadership role. Both brothers eventually moved back to the Salvador suburb where they had been born and raised, but because the second brother still visited Arembepe during my fieldwork, I was able to observe his interactions with villagers. In general this landlord was treated like, and acted like, an older Arembepeiro. He had learned how to modify, when in Arembepe, whatever cultural rules he observed in the stratified town where he resided. His "style shift"—to borrow a term from sociolinguistics (see Labov, 1972)—was obvious in what he did and said. For example, he offered certain Arembepeiros the warm hug *(abraço)* that socially equal men use in the Brazilian greeting ritual. He also knew how to use the familiar and formal "you" forms as Arembepeiros employed them. He used familiar terms with people his own age and younger, and formal terms *(o senhor, a senhora, Seu, Dona)* with much older people. Villagers reciprocated, using either formal or familiar terms with this landlord just as they did for other villagers. For example, Prudencio, who in the landlord's absence took care of his coconut trees, treated him with the familiarity reserved for good friends.

These cases of Arembepeiros' interactions with their landlords and of the estate owners' participation in village life illustrate the weakness of the patronage relationships in which Arembepeiros have participated. For landlords, just as for wholesalers seeking fish, success in the local economy demanded behavior appropriate to Arembepe, guided by an ideology of equality. Arembepeiros befriended, respected, or ridiculed landowners on the basis of their behavior and accomplishments, not merely because they happened to be landlords. This is part of a lack of class consciousness that was another prominent characteristic of Arembepe's ideology, discussed in more detail in the next section of this chapter. The openness and directness of villagers' behavior with landlords was also a direct reflection of the fact that the latter had themselves downplayed the patron's role, never seeking to limit tenants' freedom or mobility.

In 1965, although villagers were somewhat uneasy about Jorge Camões's plans for the estate's subdivision, I heard frequent favorable comparison of Arembepe's landlords with those of other fishing villages. Residents of a fishing village to the north had just won a partial victory in protracted litigation against their landlords. A fisherman told me the story. "Those awful landowners tried to evict people who had lived there all their lives. They wanted to tear down their houses so they could turn the village into a large coconut plantation. One of the sons of the family had studied agriculture at the university. He wanted to try new ways of growing coconuts, at the fishermen's expense." The court eventually ruled that villagers could remain, but their freedoms were curtailed. Marketers could not enter the village, which was surrounded with a barbed-wire fence; fishermen had to take their catch outside to be sold. Villagers were prohibited from roofing their homes with tile, nor could they even repair their houses. Despite the residents' nominal victory in court, badgering by landlords continued and that village's days as a fishing community were numbered.

Arembepeiros were therefore well aware of the differences between the landlords of other fishing villages and their own, whom they labeled "the best." Still, they were a bit uneasy about Jorge's plans for subdivision. Jorge told me that there would be three groups of lots: beachfront property, lots between the village and the lagoon, and lots west of the lagoon system. (This division was evident in Arembepe in 1973; the last group of lots formed the site of Caraúnas, Arembepe's new, extremely poor satellite.) For the first time Arembepeiros would be able to own their house sites. Previously only the dwellings themselves had been owned. Nominal rents had been paid to the landlords, via Prudencio, for the land where the houses stood. Most of Arembepe's more valuable houses—those with brick walls, tile roofs, and cement floors—had been assessed by municipal officials, and their owners paid an annual tax. This arrangement helped guarantee their investments, since a landlord desiring to evict a householder was required by law to pay the assessed value as recompense. This, of course, was only partial protection, since house values were spiraling with runaway inflation.

Jorge assured me that he had no plans to dispossess those villagers who had substantial investments in their houses. He said that he planned to give them their present lots, unless the transferral fee proved more costly than a minimal sales price, which he would then accept. Jorge also planned to (and actually did) "encourage" poorer villagers, those with wattle-and-daub shacks, to move west of the lagoon, where he would give them lots in what was to become Caraúnas.

In 1980, with much of the subdivision accomplished, only a few villagers felt cheated. Many Arembepeiros had bought their traditional house sites. Others had been persuaded to trade their desirably placed beachfront houses for larger houses and lots located between Arembepe and the lagoon, made from equivalent construction materials. Thus here again, an Arembepe landlord did not attempt to ride roughshod over his tenants, although he did look out for his own economic interests. And notice once more the contrast with the general condition of the Brazilian peasantry. In discussing conditions that led to the formation of the revolution-minded peasant leagues in northeastern Brazil in the 1960s, Forman stresses tenants'

> constant threat of summary eviction.... Peasants have little recourse when they are ordered off the land by the hired guns of the rich, who emphasize the immediacy of their demand by de-

> stroying crops and sometimes houses. In no case does a land-
> owner allow a tenant to remain on the land for any length of time
> approximating ten years, when laws of usufruct would give the
> tenant permanent rights. (Forman, 1975, p. 55)

Arembepeiros had been remarkably well shielded from such threats and actions.

Jorge and Prudencio, his agent, were only shadows of the *coroneis* (colonels or local oligarchs) whose careers in rural Brazilian politics have been well described by Daniel Gross (1973). Jorge supported Prudencio's candidates in municipal politics, and Prudencio made sure that Arembepeiros voted "along with Jorge" for state and national candidates.

Several considerations led Jorge to guide his actions so as to minimize Arembepeiros' resentment. Even after the 1964 military coup, which reduced national party politics to a government "party" and a token opposition, Jorge held on to his hopes for a role in state politics. No matter how small, Arembepe was Jorge's base, and the patron's "most important asset is his reputation, and therefore, in some sense the most important task his dependents can perform is to enhance his reputation by spreading the word of his 'goodness' throughout the countryside" (Forman, 1975, p. 77). Since Jorge could not predict the future of Brazilian politics, he tried to retain his loyal following despite the stifling effects of a dictatorship on elective politics.

Furthermore, Jorge knew from the outset of his scheme that prospective buyers of lots in Arembepe would value a resident lower-class population to supply cheap labor (as servants and menials) and products (e.g., fish and coconuts). Jorge also recognized Arembepe's charm and beauty and correctly foretold that city people would extol its quaintness and seemingly untainted isolation.

Unfortunately, Jorge could *not* predict that heirs of Francisca's cousins—fallen gentry like his own ancestors, but with more need for money—would agree to sell their interior land just south of Arembepe to a multinational corporation that would devastate the countryside by constructing a chemical factory. Yet this sad happening also sheds light on the conditions that have governed Arembepe's relationships with outsiders and that have underlain its weak patronage system. The German-based corporation in question had been seeking land for the factory site up and down the Bahian coast. Repeatedly, however, learning of the factory's potential for pollution, would-be sellers had been blocked by neighboring landed interests and their agents in government. However, Jorge's own political clout proved insufficient to halt a sale by his distant cousins that threatens to devaluate his own investment.

Readers who are familiar with sharper class contrasts may now understand more clearly just how narrow the gap has been between Arembepeiros and their landlords. Francisca's heirs have achieved varying degrees of success within the Bahian middle class, but Jorge holds the family's first university degree. He alone warrants the title of "Doctor," which enhances the status of an aspiring patron. Neither Jorge's uncles nor his mother studied beyond primary school, and some Arembepeiros have received a better education. No wonder Arembepeiros have treated most of their landlords as equals. Villagers have no conception of landownership's historic role in Brazil as a criterion—in itself—of high social status. No obvious contrast in education, behavior, or even life style has compelled Arembepeiros to defer to such people.

With Jorge, however, there is a tremendous difference, and here we find Arembepe's closest approximation to classical patronage relationships. Unlike the other landlords, unlike fish buyers, and unlike virtually all outsiders who have sought to profit from the local economy, Jorge never learned Arembepe's social system. He never adopted the villagers' ideology of equality. He did not shift style—behaving one way to lower-class people outside Arembepe and another way to Arembepeiros. Jorge acted like a patron, and villagers had to shift *their* style. They deferred to Jorge. Although Arembepeiros had relatively little practice in acting out patron-clientship, in this case they were fast learners.

A few Arembepeiros tried to make Jorge a more active participant in their social lives, without much success. Although by 1965 he had acquired five godchildren in the village, he was unable to remember any of their names. When I asked him for this information, he turned to Prudencio, who supplied it. In contrast to the relationship between Jorge's uncle and Prudencio, in which both used familiar terms and treated each other as equals, Jorge improperly used familiar

terms with Prudencio—a man twenty-five years his senior—
and received formal terms in return. Jorge treated Arembepeiros in that oblivious way that high-status Brazilians often
employ when dealing with social "inferiors"—although in
this case it was done unconsciously and unmaliciously. Jorge
simply had no interest in learning to act like a local; he had
no plans ever to participate in village life as an Arembepeiro.

Although Jorge had mastered his own role as patron, he
was unaware that villagers needed coaching as supporting
actors. As Jorge's agent, Prudencio took over the job of teaching, through the example of his own behavior, how one acted
toward a patron. Prudencio could also demonstrate the rewards of patronage. Jorge allowed him to oversee and profit
from the marketing of the fish from the two boats that he
bought between 1964 and 1965. Although Prudencio never
admitted to receiving a salary, he may have extracted a portion of the land rents he collected, and he certainly made
money supervising the marketing of the landlords' coconuts.
Prudencio's wife, though hardly more qualified than certain
other village women, had been the municipally appointed
and salaried schoolteacher ever since 1946. Even more significantly, their sons had used the patronage of Jorge and his
uncles to find relatively lucrative salaried outside employment. Arembepeiros knew that they got to Jorge through Prudencio and that to do so they must act, give, and receive like
Prudencio.

Prudencio therefore provided a critical link in Arembepe's
relationship with the outside world. In addition to economic
benefits, Jorge's backing permitted Prudencio to pursue his
ambitions in county politics. However, despite these advantages, Prudencio's wealth, income, and life style never raised
him out of the lower class. Like successful fishermen,
he merely stood at the top of a *local* success ladder. However, his ambitions were mainly political; his sons, more obviously than Prudencio himself, benefited economically.
Villagers respected Prudencio for his own accomplishments
and his role as landowners' agent. However, although other
Arembepeiros granted Prudencio special prestige, and although he acquired a reputation and influence in municipal
politics, he was always careful to observe Arembepe's cultural rules. He took his social obligations seriously. Not sur-

prisingly, in 1965 he had more godchildren than any other villager. Despite his external activities and advantages, Prudencio was always careful to respect the ideology of equality. In life style and behavior he remained firmly in the local social system.

Prudencio was one of those rarely talented individuals whose particular abilities can stand out clearly in an egalitarian community—where each man has a chance to "make it on his own" in each generation. Prudencio made it in politics and as a mediator between Arembepeiros and the landed interests that helped shape their destinies. However, Prudencio did not simply link Arembepe to the landowners and to outside politics; he also served as a model for one of the success paths available to villagers. Other Arembepeiros have been models for different paths, for example, that of the aspiring captain-owner or the businessman. Such men have all mediated and promoted social change in Arembepe.

Although many Arembepeiros sought Jorge's assistance through Prudencio, they knew that they could not expect the same benefits that Prudencio and his family received. Thus, as is generally the case with patron-clientship (as previously distinguished from patron-dependency), Arembepeiros tried to find their own patrons. Villagers attempted to establish individual personal links with outsiders. For example, all the people who own vacation homes in Arembepe have maintained patronage relationships with particular villagers.

During the 1960s, middle-class outsiders injected small amounts of cash into the village economy by offering menial employment to villagers, either in Arembepe itself or as domestics in Salvador. Unmarried women and female household heads usually preferred domestic service in Arembepe to similar employment in Salvador, for although wages were less, they had access to an improved diet for their families. The lower-middle-class owner of the house we rented in 1964 and 1965 insisted that we hire two local women as cook and washerwoman. She had employed our cook's sister as seamstress and felt that our wages should go to a family that she knew. The homeowner also wanted someone she could trust, to ensure that her house and possessions received proper care. However, our landlord's request created problems for us, since I had previously employed two other local women whose patron was the absentee owner of the house I had rented in 1962. As a result of that stay they had come to regard *me* as their patron as well and, on my return, expected to be reemployed. The solution was to split various tasks among three of the women and the adolescent son of the fourth. This arrangement provided cash and food for several households.

During our work in Arembepe many villagers befriended me and other field team members and acted as our informants. Each anthropologist established especially close relationships with certain villagers, and others, recognizing these bonds, concentrated on different field team members. In varying degrees, these Arembepeiros were all seeking the patronage of particular outsiders. Thus on my return to Arembepe in 1973, when for the first time my research grant included money for a local field assistant, it was natural for me to hire Alberto, my most reliable informant. And Betty was asked by Dora, our 1962 cook and a woman with whom she had previously established a close relationship, if she could again cook for us.

Individuals, Not Classes

With this chapter's discussion of Arembepe's links to the outside world in mind, comparison with Coqueiral, a coastal community in the state of Alagoas some 300 kilometers north of Arembepe, which anthropologist Shepard Forman studied at about the same time (mid-1960s) that I was working in Arembepe, will illustrate some additional reasons for variation among rural Brazilians. And again, it will help to show why—despite Arembepe's traditional poverty, illiteracy, powerlessness, and poor public health—I have dared to call it paradise. In contrast to Arembepe, Coqueiral had the bad, but much more typical, luck of being linked both politically and economically to its municipal seat. Most of its residents constituted the bottom layer of the county's stratified hierarchy, which was headed by owners of large nearby sugar plantations. Below the plantation owners, but with privileged access to the county elite, was the group that Forman (1970) called Coqueiral's "local bigwigs," the people who formed the top layer in Coqueiral's own stratified hierarchy. They included the president of the fishermen's guild and large-scale coconut-tree owners. The fishermen themselves occupied a degraded position, with an income below the (then) minimum wage of $20 a month. Rewards easily available in Arembepe were lacking in Coqueiral.

The crucial difference was Coqueiral's much greater poverty, Arembepe's steadily improving fortunes. Reflecting this contrast, many *fewer* leveling mechanisms operated in Coqueiral than in Arembepe. The previously described witchcraft accusations, intense gossip, social ostracism, and crew desertion that operated against "upstart" Arembepeiros—people who ignored community obligations and violated the ideology of equality—had no parallels in Coqueiral. This was because the external support of Coqueiral's bigwigs was too powerful for such mechanisms to be effective. Other villagers, furthermore, were too poor for leveling to be necessary.

Expressing these critical contrasts was the presence of class consciousness in Coqueiral, its absence in Arembepe. Thus according to Forman (1970, pp. 137–138), Coqueiral's fishermen are

> well aware of the nature of the bonds which tie them to the dominant segments of society and which clearly limit their mobility. They think in terms of "We and they" and "everything for them, nothing for us." They contrast themselves to the rich and the powerful and fear that they themselves are "nothing in the world." When queried as to why they do not try to improve their situation, they correctly cite lack of opportunity.

Since Coqueiral's fishermen were confronted each day with the glaring contrast between their own deprived life styles and those of local and municipal elites, they had developed a class consciousness. However, Arembepe's local economy, for whatever perceived reason, offered many rewards to lower-class people, and this situation hindered the emergence of class consciousness—and even of group consciousness—in Arembepe. With a local ladder of success, with differential achievement possible within the community, Arembepeiros viewed contrasts in wealth, income, prestige, and overall status in terms of individuals rather than classes.

Precisely because Arembepeiros knew that individual villagers could improve their lot, their view of their own place in Brazilian society was an imperfect one, constituting yet another socially significant mystification—like the riddle of the spots discussed in Chapter 4. Since Arembepeiros viewed differential success and upward mobility purely in local terms, most of them remained unaware of the implications of local leveling mechanisms (e.g., expected sharing in proportion to success). Nor were they fully cognizant of the larger-scale limitations that constrained them: their lower-class background, limited education and employment skills, and ultimate powerlessness against external interests—from hippies to multinational corporations—that might intrude on community life.

Arembepeiros were deluded into seeing local success as true success; local achievement was as satisfying as upward mobility in the national class structure. Hidden, therefore, behind the local ladder of wealth and social status were larger social and economic forces that blocked meaningful mobility and kept all Arembepeiros in the national lower class. In other words, Arembepeiros never developed a consciousness of themselves as belonging to a national class because they were too busy competing with each other in entrepreneurial activities within their own community.

Experiencing the World Outside

Although fully familiar with poverty, someone who never left Arembepe might, therefore, never have discovered that he or she was a member of a national lower class. As we have seen previously, a requirement for outsiders' entrance to and success in Arembepe's economy in the 1960s was that their behavior be modified to accord with the ideology of equality. This hindered the introduction of external social patterns, such as those based on class differences.[2] The main way to learn about the national class structure was to reside outside Arembepe. Of course, Arembepeiros who left the village initially took along their ideology of equality. How long and how tightly they retained it depended on how often they journeyed outside, where they went, and how long they stayed. People who made occasional trips to Salvador's commercial districts, houses of prostitution, or supermarkets might complain of the rudeness of city folk without realizing that they had experienced patterns in a national stratification system. Women who worked as domestics learned about the "politeness" that city people expected; but many of the middle-class families who vacationed in Arembepe complained that Arembepeiros made poor servants and usually quit. During the 1960s most Arembepeiros were content to live out most of their lives at home. Although at least one resident in half the households had worked outside, most had done so only temporarily in order to bring cash, the means to a more comfortable life, back home.

Because they rarely visited the city during the 1960s, Arembepeiros had trouble finding their way around when they did go. The trip took at least two days and one night. There was the 18-kilometer walk to Portão, followed by a long, always crowded bus ride. The city voyager was a resource to be tapped. Arembepeiros asked their relatives and neighbors to do errands for them in the city—to buy, for example, a piece of cloth for a new dress that would be made on one of the few (manual) sewing machines in Arembepe. Once in Salvador, villagers did not stray far from the stores and vendors near the bus station.

One expression of Arembepe's lack of formality and ignorance of external norms concerning interclass behavior was particularly irritating. During our first stay in Arembepe, village children, fascinated with the young strangers who had come to study them, saw no reason why we should not be just as closely scrutinized. During our first month in Arembepe, our privacy was shattered, each time we opened our window, by a dozen children leaning in to watch our every move. If we asked them whether they wanted something, they usually said no. The most tenacious girl, we discovered, did have designs on our chocolate bars (they kept disappearing when we left the room). The rest were there, however, simply to observe the domestic behavior of these strange young men with pale skins and typewriters. "Good manners" go along with a well-developed class structure. Poor people, in particular, are expected to know how to act when they deal with members of the more privileged classes. But Arembepe's adults didn't tell their children not to bother the Americans, because in a homogeneous community where

Betty strolls past a row of houses in northern Arembepe in 1962, accompanied, as usual, by a horde of children. (Conrad P. Kottak)

everyone had had years to learn about everyone else, what could be wrong with sizing up the new arrivals as quickly as possible?

Those who had learned most about the outside world were the Arembepeiros who had fished on commercial trawlers operating out of Salvador or Rio de Janeiro. Men who had lived in Rio complained about crime, overcrowding, and particularly about the cost of food and lodging. They talked of their longing for wife, parents, children, and the small Bahian fishing village of their birth. These men had actually experienced the plight of the urban poor, the inconvenience, impersonality, and squalor of Rio's *favelas*, the slums of nearby Niteroi, the tenements and shanty towns of Salvador's inner city and suburbs.

They had witnessed the huge contrasts between the life styles of unskilled laborers and those of the middle and upper classes. Some local women had worked in comfortable apartments and homes in Salvador. In Rio, Arembepeiros had walked along the magnificent beaches of Copacabana and Ipanema, past the high-rise luxury apartments—their ornate lobbies replete with jungle plants, marble tables, and abstract paintings—each building heavily guarded against potentially criminal intruders. Tomé, who had fished out of Rio for seven years, told of having his clothes and watch stolen when he left them unguarded on the beach while he took a dip in the ocean. Even those native sons who were doing very well, in villagers' estimation, working for the national oil company on the outskirts of Salvador, were learning what it meant to be a member of the lower class, albeit of its upper segment.

Havinghurst and Moreira (1965, p. 100) divide Brazilian society into five classes: upper, upper middle, lower middle, upper working, and lower working. As rural fishermen, virtually all Arembepeiros belonged to the lower working class, which also includes farm laborers, unskilled urban workers, and peasants. The upper working class—in which Arembepeiros working in oil might be placed—includes people with various skilled and semi-skilled jobs in factories, public service, railroads, transportation, and communication. Fifteen native sons were working for the national oil company in the mid-1960s, drawing an average annual salary worth about $1,700. Compared to even the most successful local captain-owners and businessmen, this was a large and regular salary—about ten times the cash income of the ordinary fisherman. Their incomes supported the village's most opulent life styles. One had a three-year old jeep, the only locally owned motor vehicle in 1965. Another was planning to buy a car. Both were among the rare villagers with kerosene refrigerators and stoves powered by bottled gas, transported to Arembepe by automobile.

During the 1960s most villagers agreed that Petrobrás employment was the best occupation that Arembepeiros could aspire to. Requirements for work in oil were not stringent. A good word from landlord Jorge, coupled with a third-grade education, permitted the applicant to take an exam. Natives who had passed were making between $500 and $2,500 annually. Their work took these native sons to Salvador and its suburbs and to drilling sites in adjacent municipalities. However, through their mobility and their work in stratified communities, these men were learning that despite their success relative to virtually all Arembepeiros, they still experienced the disadvantages of being lower-class Brazilians. Although they could afford certain material possessions that most Arembepeiros lacked, their salaries could not support middle-class life styles. Nor did their manners, conduct, way of speaking, or education distinguish them noticeably from members of the lower working class. Thus, although Petrobrás employment was Arembepeiros' highest ambition, the actual experiences of oil workers outside made it clear that they had become small fish in a mammoth pond.

Arembepe's relations with the outside world during the mid-1960s may now be summarized. Villagers' ties to larger-scale systems were generally favorable compared to other rural communities in northeastern Brazil. Improving access to Salvador and favorable marketing opportunities meant that the distribution of Arembepe's fish was never monopolistically controlled. Nor had outsiders ever derived substantial profits from Arembepe or its population. The separation of Arembepe's economic and political affairs, which contrasted strongly with the situation in rural Brazil generally (Gross, 1973, p. 141), was another reason why entrepreneurial activity had flourished in Arembepe. Generally advantageous material conditions supported more prosperous life styles than those prevalent among other Brazilian peasants and fishermen. Yet a world view that evaluated success in individual terms, and mainly in a local context, prevented Arembepeiros from fully recognizing and confronting the leveling mechanisms that operated in the community and the larger-scale obstacles to their rise from poverty.

The relatively egalitarian and isolated lower-class community I left in 1965 has been described in Chapters 3–5. In Chapter 5's discussion of motorized fish buyers and Jorge's plan to sell real estate there is ample evidence, however, that Arembepe's isolation, which of course had never been total, was about to end. Even the arrival of our field team in 1962 can be seen as part of the first phase of what was rapidly to become a dramatic process of internationalization. After all, who is more likely than an anthropologist, a missionary, or a trader to make earliest sustained contact with a remote community? And these were precisely the professions of most of the strangers who had come to Arembepe through the mid-1960s.

During the late 1960s and early 1970s, as I was busy investigating and writing about cultural diversity in an even more remote part of the world—the island of Madagascar—a wave of new outsiders, many foreign, were repeating my discovery of Arembepe. Many of them had moved on by the time I next returned, in 1973; but others, and their creations—most notably the titanium dioxide factory—had stayed on, and as I perceived it, this band of outsiders had managed to devastate my community in less than a decade. Chapter 6, based on my encounter with Arembepe in 1973, sets the stage for the description of today's radically altered community.

Part Three
Assault on Paradise

6 The Browning of Arembepe

This chapter delves beneath the surface changes mentioned in Chapter 2 to examine specific ways in which increased contact with the outside world and alterations in the local economy had affected social relations and attitudes in Arembepe between 1965 and 1973. Because of its nearness to a large city, it was expectable that Arembepe would experience, sooner than villages in more remote areas, the effects of the "Brazilian economic miracle." Centrally planned and directed by the military government that had ousted a popularly elected president in the "Revolution of 1964," the "economic miracle" produced a spectacular average annual real growth rate of 11 percent in Brazil's gross national product between 1968 and 1974.

The major movers in recent Brazilian economic development have been the government and the multinational corporation, and both have powerfully affected life in Arembepe. Development strategy has emphasized highway expansion and improvement. The road that since 1970 has linked the multinationally owned chemical factory near Arembepe to Salvador was a local expression of the fact that Brazil's paved highway network had more than doubled during my eight-year absence. Brazilian automobile production (controlled almost totally by multinationals) had increased even more dramatically—fivefold, to almost 1 million cars annually by 1975.

The most fundamental contrasts in Arembepe itself were that the community's population was swelling, particularly through immigration, and its economy was becoming increasingly diverse. There were signs of growth everywhere, and the stage had been set for all the major transformations that were obvious by 1980.

Wealthy summer people, members of Brazil's rapidly growing middle class, had built houses north and south of the village proper. A new settlement, Caraúnas, with fifty houses and 200 people, lay just west of the brown lagoon. Construction was booming in Arembepe itself. Since there was little space to the east, the seaward side, most of the new houses were being built between Arembepe and the lagoon, extending the village to the west. Even lower-middle-class people from the capital were doing well enough economically to buy up many of Arembepeiros' houses in the central square and the northern rectangle. Usually they tore down the old structures—even those with brick walls, cement floors, and tile roofs—to erect more durable, comfortable, and ostentatious quarters. As access to the city improved, a flood of newly prosperous Salvadorians were seeking beach property for use during weekends, school holidays, and summer vacations. Arembepe, reachable over a mostly asphalted road in just an hour, seemed a good place to invest.

Most Arembepeiros also felt that they were benefiting from a booming economy, and many were now investing their surplus cash in rental property, rather than in agricultural land or coconut trees as in the past. Several villagers were converting their houses into duplexes, extending them backward, on lots they now owned, having purchased them from Jorge and his relatives as his lotting scheme was carried out. A new living pattern showed the importance of rentals: villagers with completed duplexes would temporarily vacate their usual quarters in front, more accessible to the sea breezes, and live in back while summer people rented their homes. Although only 10 percent of Arembepe's houses were rented during our winter 1973 stay, a third had been rented—and most of these would be again—in December and January.

Improved bus service and automobiles also brought a weekly influx of nonrenters—city people who visited Arembepe for weekend picnics, bathing, and revelry. Sunday was the main tourist day. As it is throughout Brazil, Sunday is the family's day to eat out. (For Brazilians who can afford maids, Sunday is the usual maid's "day off.") The picnickers who were coming to Arembepe were primarily *farofeiros*, lower-middle-class and working-class people who brought along plastic containers of *farofa,* refried manioc flour mixed with egg or meat. Among more elite Brazilians, the term *farofeiro* is a disparaging one; when city folk told me that Arembepe had become a resort for *farofeiros,* they were saying that it had become a honky-tonk beach, like New York's Coney Island.

But many weekend visitors also journeyed to Arembepe for a meal of fresh fish, either fried or served as *muqueca* (a delicious fish stew made with tomatoes, onions, coconut, and palm oil). Arembepe now had ice chests and bottled gas–fueled refrigerators, so that fresh fish could be preserved for direct retail sale to tourists. Several villagers had opened restaurants and bars catering to the weekend and summer trade. Refrigeration also meant adequate supplies of cold beer, and the start of a pattern of heavy weekend drinking was detectable in the winter of 1973. Stores, bars, and restaurants were springing up throughout the village—responses to Arembepe's quantum leap from isolated fishing village to internationally known tourist attraction.

The more notorious side of Arembepe's transformation involves industrial pollution and hippies. These two multinational intrusions were linked together. As early as the mid-1960s, the German-Brazilian corporation that would eventually build Tibrás (Titanium of Brazil) just 5 kilometers from Arembepe was evaluating potential factory sites in Bahia. The original plan was to construct Tibrás in southern Bahia, near the city of Ilhéus. However, a combination of political pressure and difficult access to water, roads, and electricity there led Tibrás to choose the Arembepe area instead.

In manufacturing titanium dioxide, a basic ingredient in paints and dyes, Tibrás uses no local resources. The principal raw materials are a black sand imported from Australia, and sulfur, most of which comes from Mexico and Venezuela. In contrast to southern Bahia, water, roads, electricity, and especially politics (for reasons spelled out in Chapters 3 and 5) posed no insurmountable barriers in the area between the fishing villages of Arembepe and Jauá. The freshwater lagoon system offered abundant water, and preparations for a paved highway were already in progress, as were plans to open Arembepe and neighboring areas to tourism. Tibrás sped up road construction by financing 80 percent of the paving cost between the factory site and Portão, 13 kilometers away. The factory was electrified by 1970, even though electricity from a different source, the state power department, did not reach Arembepe until 1977.

The local social system was a final factor in the decision to locate in the Arembepe-Jauá area. The "fallen gentry" of the municipality of Camaçari could muster neither clout nor coalition to block an industry whose potential for pollution had already been exposed in the national media. Tibrás amassed its land by purchasing many parcels from small-scale local landowners, most of whom thought themselves lucky to obtain higher prices than they had ever imagined for their non-beachfront property. Arembepe's landowners owned none of the land where the factory was constructed.

A curious dialectic between the positive and negative effects of Tibrás on tourism and local life in general has dominated Arembepe's history since 1967, when Tibrás began to hasten road work between Portão and its newly chosen site. On the one hand, tourism in Arembepe would have lagged for several years had not Tibrás intervened to pave the highway. On the other, industrial pollution subsequently posed a severe threat to Arembepe's reputation as a tourist site. The initial agreement had been that Tibrás and the state road department would share equally in the costs of asphalting the road, which would eventually reach Arembepe. Ultimately, however, Tibrás paid most, since state funding could not keep up with Tibrás's schedule for completion. Thus Tibrás was mainly responsible for the paved road that became Arembepe's principal link with the outside world and that made it more accessible to tourists, including the hippies, whose heyday in Arembepe (1970–1971) followed completion of the highway to the factory site.

Yet Tibrás also caused the pollution that was attracting so much media attention in 1973. Tibrás wastes (ferrous sulfate and sulfuric acid) had not just permeated the lagoons but were also being dumped offshore, where they seemed likely to destroy the fishery that had sustained Arembepe for so many years. Although Arembepeiros acknowledged that the Tibrás-supported road had been good for business, although a dozen local men had found well-paying jobs at the factory, and although Tibrás personnel ate meals, rented rooms, bought fish, and brought other business to Arembepe, community opinion had turned against the factory by 1973. Arembepeiros were particularly vexed about the lagoons where they had washed and bathed for so many years.

The ensuing media coverage provided Arembepeiros with a new kind of clout, which eventually brought a halt to the most obvious pollution. Throughout the state and the nation, the public was hearing about the senseless destruction of a "natural," "simple" fishing community by a multinational corporation. I heard a man joke that Bayer, the German company that owned 38 percent of Tibrás, had deliberately planned the pollution in order to increase suffering, thus spurring demand for Bayer aspirin in Bahia. In reality, Arembepeiros were complaining more about burns than headaches, but with state and national opinion mustered against the factory, it was apparent that something would have to be done. (It had been—through more effective pollution controls—by 1980.)

The Tibrás pollution scandal was Arembepe's second encounter with the mass media; its post-Woodstock invasion by international hippies had already brought it national recognition—stories in the Brazilian equivalents of *Time* and *Newsweek*. There had been hippies in Arembepe as early as 1966–1967. At first they came during the summer and were mainly Brazilians. But as the hippie movement itself became international, and as flower children dispersed after the 1969 gathering at Woodstock, New York, young people from all over the world, including many from the United States, began to trickle into Arembepe. By 1970–1971 the trickle had become a flood. Although many hippies took up residence in Arembepe proper, the real hippie enclave became the Aldeia, a settlement on the banks of the Caratingi River, whose waters, prevented by sandstone formations from finding an immediate outlet to the Atlantic, back up and wash south to form the area's distinctive freshwater lagoon system. Adoption of the term *aldeia*, otherwise applied to small settlements of Brazil's interior Native American (Indian) tribes, symbolized the hippies' attempt to rediscover nature and to recreate a simple, communal, and "primitive" life style.

There were also economic reasons for the hippies to like Arembepe. As the vanguard of the outsiders who would eventually choose Arembepe as a vacation spot, hippies appreciated not just the natural beauty but the cheapness of food and rents. The small wattle-and-daub and palm-frond huts on the northern and southern fringes of the village could be rented for next to nothing, and local women could be found to prepare food and do washing. Most of the hippies were urbanites who did not wish to work. They were able to eke out a pleasant and relaxed existence on the money they had brought along, and occasional contributions from relatives. The hippie migration away from Arembepe to the Aldeia was not just a search for isolation; it was an economic necessity coinciding with the arrival of the lower-middle-class tourists from Salvador, who were willing to pay higher rents than the hippies. The cost of housing, food, and living generally rose in Arembepe as tourism increased.

There had always been a small village where the Aldeia grew up, a fifteen- to thirty-minute walk along beach or lagoons north of Arembepe. In summer, as the lagoons dried up, Arembepeiros had always gone to the Caratingi to wash and bathe. The combination of isolation, year-round water, cheap supplies, and spectacular setting was sufficient to attract international hippies as well as the Brazilian students who joined them during summer vacations in December and January. Just twenty hippies were living in Arembepe proper and in the Aldeia in the winter of 1973, although more probably came during the summer. There is no way of knowing for sure just how many hippies had visited Arembepe at the height of the movement, but informants spoke of "hundreds" and even "thousands." A municipal official remembered concerts in the Aldeia by Brazilian rock superstars, and a visit by Mick Jagger has become part of the settlement's quasi-mythological past for the few stragglers who have stayed on. In 1980 I was shown the ruins of the "House of the Sun," where Mick Jagger and Janis Joplin are reputed to have slept; and the ritualized retelling of the Jagger-Joplin story by hippie after hippie reminded me of the creation myths and mythological charters that anthropologists have encountered in other societies. In the fragmented social system that is all that remains of a once-populous Aldeia, Mick and Janis had become the structural analogues of Adam and Eve.

Despite the fact that I have overcome much of the resentment toward the hippies that I felt in 1973, I still believe that media accounts of the hippie invasion have overestimated their impact on Arembepe. The hippies should be seen simply as part of (although for the media the most sensational part of) Arembepe's overall tourist boom. Tourism has been as instrumental as industrialization in transforming village life. Joining hundreds of other temporary, seasonal, and more permanent residents, the hippies have helped introduce the culture patterns of the outside world into Arembepe, along with new fears, aspirations, and insecurities.

Occupational Diversity

It seemed fairly obvious in 1973 that Arembepe's days as a primarily fishing economy were numbered. It was on its way to becoming one of those more typical, occupationally diverse fishing villages mentioned in Chapter 4. Fishing did remain the most common occupation, with 53 percent of the men making their living in this way. However, the percentage was down sharply from 1964, when 74 percent claimed

"Aunt Dalia," who by 1973 had built up a good business catering to the hippies of southern Arembepe. (Courtesy, Jerald T. Milanich)

fishing as a primary occupation. The number of local business establishments had increased. Women, it seemed, had responded most quickly to the new prospects of business success (see Appendix 6). Business had always been one of the few areas where women could do well, and some of Arembepe's most successful commercial ventures in 1973 were run by such women as "Aunt Dalia" (so named by the hippies), who catered to the flower children of southern Arembepe, and Claudia, who had opened the village's most successful tourist restaurant. A quarter of the women who worked for cash in 1973 were business people, and almost as many women (sixteen) as men (twenty) ran businesses.

Arembepe was on the verge of a tourism and business florescence. However, men were reluctant at first to abandon other professions because of pollution and its chilling effect on tourism. Once this problem was solved, and the tourist trade returned, it became possible for several village men to support their families through business activities alone. But during the 1970s, it was Arembepe's women who were doing most of the innovating directed toward the tourist trade. (Appendixes 2 and 6 contain data on Arembepe's occupations in 1964, 1973, and 1980.)

Like the number of stores and bars, building-related employment increased dramatically between 1964 and 1973—from 5 percent to 15 percent of males' principal occupations. Masons, carpenters, and bricklayers moved to Arembepe from outside, and several villagers began to learn these trades. Other villagers found employment as caretakers for the summer people who owned and rented houses throughout the settlement. Villagers prosperous enough to expand their homes supplemented their ordinary cash with rental incomes. Factory employment had also increased significantly by 1973, ranking just below building as the third most common occupation among Arembepe's males (11 percent). A dozen villagers had found employment at Tibrás; others still worked for the national oil company.

Investments in rental units were replacing farm plots and coconut trees as means of protecting surplus cash from inflation and supplementing primary income. By 1973 most of Arembepe's fishermen had sold the farm plots that more than a dozen of them had worked a decade earlier. They used their gains to improve and expand their houses in order to rent to tourists and immigrants. In the fishermen's analysis, the costs (three hours of walking per round trip plus the manual labor required) of a farm plot on one of the western estates were no longer worth the benefits (fresh fruits and vegetables for household consumption and sale). Cash was now available from tourists right in Arembepe, and, villagers reasoned, once the summer people returned to Salvador, the rental-unit owners could spend most of the year themselves enjoying the better quarters they had built to suit the outsiders' city tastes. Furthermore, fresh produce was now as close as a direct bus ride to the supermarket in Pituba. Local business people also continued to sell fruits and vegetables. Since they spent more of their time on land than fishermen, business people had always had an easier time running a farm. Along with the farmers who lived on the estates, they simply increased the produce supply as Arembepe's demand increased.

Two familiar features of the village economy were disappearing in the mid-1970s. Previously, most families had raised chickens; and those who farmed occasionally owned cattle, donkeys, and other livestock. By 1973, however, most of the chickens consumed in Arembepe, like most of the meat, came from the supermarket. The second change involved ownership of coconut trees. About 40 percent of Arembepe's households had owned coconut trees in 1964, but the number dwindled throughout the 1970s, as Jorge bought up the villagers' trees in order to clear house sites and to sell coconut trees along with the land.

To be sure, Arembepe had never had a fully isolated subsistence economy. However, the decline of livestock and coconut-tree ownership are additional, if minor, illustrations that Arembepe was giving up its ability to supply its own subsistence needs as its reliance on external products and cash increased. The pattern of increasing dependence on the outside world was obvious in many areas of the economy in 1973. To summarize: I have noted the increasing prominence of tourism, business, construction, and factory employment; and the declining significance of farming, livestock, and tree ownership. The web being spun out of multiple strands of external dependence was also enveloping fishing, which even in the mid-1970s continued to be Arembepe's economic mainstay. And certain changes in fishing patterns and technology ramified throughout community social life.

Motorization and the Fishermen's Cooperative

In the 1960s the most expensive item in Arembepe's fishing industry had been the fully equipped sailboat; and as noted in Chapter 4, there were several ways in which enterprising fishermen could become boat owners. An older pattern, whereby a boat was co-owned by its captain and a nonfisherman, was changing to full ownership by the fishing captain-owner. In part this shift reflected a marketing advantage: in the context of severe inflation, the price of fish had been rising faster than the cost of a new boat. By 1973 it cost $1700 to buy a fully equipped motorized sailboat. There were also gas, oil, and maintenance expenses. (But fishermen still used wind power for part of their daily voyage.)

However, although the first motors were purchased by land-based entrepreneurs, impediments to nonfishermen's control over the fishing industry remained. First, the price of fish had continued to rise more rapidly than the general inflation rate. This reflected growing demand for fish by Salvador, a rapidly expanding metropolis and tourist center, and increased competition among potential buyers as access to Arembepe improved. A second reason for fishermen's continuing control over the fishing industry was the availability of low-interest loans from SUDEPE (Superintendência do Desenvolvimento da Pesca), the government agency charged with "developing" Brazilian fishing industries.

In 1970 SUDEPE employees had begun a series of visits designed to persuade Arembepeiros to establish a fishermen's cooperative. Villagers were told of successful cooperatives in other fishing communities, and they learned of motorization loans and other benefits. Previous efforts to build such an organization in Arembepe had failed, but this one succeeded initially because the cooperative offered several incentives to join: loans, refrigeration, bait, gasoline, oil, and other supplies. Fishermen were encouraged to keep up their membership—and thus to sell all their marketed fish to the cooperative—by competitive prices (at least until 1973) and by the debts they contracted to motorize their boats. Members were not supposed to withdraw until their installment loans were repaid. The cooperative bought members' daily catches, stored the fish in an ice vault, and arranged either its local sale or its transport to urban fish markets. The cooperative and ice vault were housed in a small building just south of the chapel and very near the harbor and the beach where the fishermen unloaded their catch. Local men were paid to conduct the daily business of recording marketed catches, dispensing cash and supplies, and deducting loan payments. A SUDEPE agent from Salvador monitored operations on a monthly basis and made sure that loan payments were on schedule. He also compiled daily data into monthly statistics that provided me with useful data (used in Appendix 3) on the year-round productivity of Arembepe's fishing industry.

Several changes accompanying the cooperative had the immediate effect of improving the time- and labor-effectiveness of local fishing. For example, the easy availability of ice, which permitted preservation of fresh fish, encouraged increased production. The example of the cooperative also spurred local innovation. One entrepreneur constructed a massive ice vault. Another businessman, longtime boat owner, and local fish marketer followed the example, while serving some of his refrigerated fish to tourists in a small restaurant and hotel that he added onto his store, favorably located at the entrance of the Salvador road into Arembepe. Formerly many boats had remained beached or in the harbor for several days during the rainy season, or they had only fished near shore for family meals. There had been no point in doing a full day's work, captains reasoned, since no one could be sure that buyers would be making the trip out from Salvador in bad weather. Now, with ice vaults in Arembepe, fish could be sought, caught, and stored anytime.

Ice and motors combined to broaden fishing opportunities, in time and space. Motorization substantially reduced the time it took to reach familiar, productive fishing grounds once used only during the calmest months—December through April. A quick return to harbor was now possible in the event of a sudden storm. Motorization also brought a tremendous expansion of the range of Arembepe's fishing industry. Tomé, who since my first visit had been Arembepe's most daring, innovative, and enterprising fisherman, and who was now its most successful by far, had bought a larger, enclosed, motorized vessel, in which he captained his crew as far away as the coast of Sergipe—150 kilometers north. Tomé took along a load of ice and sometimes stayed away for four days. (This pattern, called "ice fishing," dominated Arembepe's fishing industry in 1980.) However, even the traditional boats, once motors were added, had started fishing in banks that Arembepeiros' had only heard about in their conversations with residents of other fishing communities.

The combination of motors and ice therefore meant more distant fishing trips, fresher catches, and effective storage. The ice vaults also provided ready access to bait—one of the cooperative's most popular products. Formerly, on each fishing day, local experts in cast-net fishing had caught sardines and other small fish near shore. However, local bait fishing had been time-consuming and uncertain. Here again, the cooperative and refrigeration removed a fetter on the fishing industry. Now villagers could draw on a ready refrigerated supply of local and imported bait.

Data gathered in 1973 (Appendix 3) suggest that as a result of these and other changes, the productivity of Arembepe's fishing industry had increased significantly since 1965, and that the old seasonal constraints were of reduced importance. The rainy season seemed no longer to pose a barrier to productive fishing. The average monthly catch for June through August 1972 almost equaled the monthly average for the whole year. The most significant change was that the average *annual* marketed catch had grown by about 60 percent—from 3,500 kilograms to 5,500 kilograms.

To summarize: motorization, ice, and purchased bait (along with other changes in production and distribution discussed in the next section of this chapter) had extended the range of Arembepe's fishing industry in time and space, and the immediate effect was to increase production. This meant that by 1973 Arembepe's most enterprising fishermen were wielding greater buying power than ever before (although by June 1973 the cooperative's price for fish was finally lagging behind inflation). Larger catches and incomes, which in the long run had outpaced inflation, were enabling captain-owners to pay off their motorization loans and in other ways to decrease any residue of dependence on nonfishermen.

During a long interview with Tomé in 1973, for example, I found out that he not only owned Arembepe's largest boat (as well as an ordinary motorboat used by his two youngest brothers), but also had bought a Volkswagen van that he used to transport his fish to a fish store on the outskirts of Salvador. There he received almost half again as much for his fish (5 cruzeiros per kilogram) as the cooperative was paying (3.4 cruzeiros) at the end of March 1973, when he withdrew from it. Once Tomé perceived that he could do much better by marketing his fish himself, he rapidly repaid his SUDEPE loan and ended his fish-selling relationship with the cooperative. After deducting gasoline and other marketing costs, Tomé could now increase his annual income by about $2,000.

Tomé's confidence and success in dealing with the world outside were increasing dramatically. He had obtained financing for his van from a Salvador bank, where he had also been assured of financial help with future enterprises. By August 1973, his annual income—which had been barely $1,000 in 1964—now surpassed my salary as an associate professor at the University of Michigan.

Tomé merely led the way. Given increased opportunities to profit from fishing, other captain-owners were following his example, rapidly repaying their loans so as to increase the price they received for their fish by severing their relationship with the cooperative. The Weberian Protestant-capitalist values that I have described previously could still spell success in Arembepe's economy in 1973. Tomé and other entrepreneurs were reaping the advantages of easier access to Salvador. As they displaced fish buyers from Salvador and Itapoan, these sons of Arembepe were themselves becoming large-scale suppliers, delivering fish to wholesalers at central delivery points (Salvador's suburbs). They, and many other captain-owners, could also sell a substantial part of their catch retail to the tourists, vacationers, and other outsiders who had become a regular feature of the local scene, especially on weekends and during the summer.

From Skills to Property

Although the socioeconomic contrast between land-based
entrepreneurs and enterprising captain-owners was continuing to decrease, *overall* socioeconomic differentiation within
Arembepe was sharpening. Part of this had to do with the effects of changes in fishing technology on the relationship between captain and crew. Specifically, the link between ordinary crew member and captain-owner was becoming
decreasingly social and increasingly economic. Because of
the costs of motorization, the economic gap between captain-
owner and crew was widening. As more captains became full
owners of their boats, more of them were receiving "the
boat's" share of the daily catch. "The boat" had previously
received one-quarter of the crew's daily catch. By 1973, reflecting the cost of motor, interest payments, gas, and oil, this
had increased to one-third. (Another of Arembepe's mystifications: some fishermen were not really sure how much of
their product went to the boat owner. "The boat's" share had
always been called *o quinto*, "the fifth," of the catch, suggesting a lower contribution than fishermen were actually
giving. But now, instead of giving 25 percent when they paid
"the boat's fifth," the crew members were handing over one
fish out of three for the privilege of fishing.) The captain-
owner who fished with three other crew members, for example, now received one-third of their total catch (for "the
boat") plus his own quarter (on the average) of all fish
caught, for a total of about 50 percent of the boat's total
catch.[1] The ordinary crew member's share was only 17 percent, down from about 20 percent in the 1960s. To state the
change more dramatically, the captain-owner now received
about 3 times the ordinary crew member's share for the same
day's fishing, whereas in 1964 he had received only 2.3 times
a crew member's share. The gap was larger still by 1980.

Consider another aspect of the widening separation between captain and ordinary crew member. Previously, like
the population of Arembepe itself, captains could be placed
in a graded socioeconomic hierarchy, with the enterprising
younger captains at the top; older, less vital men below
them; and "slouches" and alcoholics at the bottom. As has
been discussed in Chapter 4, the best captains had the most

stable crews, caught the most fish, and owned all or part of their boats. Ordinary fishermen in the most successful crews received what they regarded as a fair share of the prosperity of their boats and had higher incomes and better diets than the poorer captains. By 1973, however, wealth from the fishing industry was going disproportionately to two clearly separate groups: (1) entrepreneurs (captain-owners and nonfishing owners of motorized boats) and (2) other fishermen (ordinary crew and captains who worked on a commission basis for nonfishing owners). Thus the hierarchy of gradual contrasts was dividing and congealing into discrete groups. Social ranking was being transformed into social stratification. (And as is discussed in the next two sections, considerable tension was being generated by these changes.)

Motorization also meant that the personal skills (eyesight and landmark memory) once believed to distinguish among captains, and between captains and crew, were no longer very important, since most fishing now proceeded in summer and fall zones where refined landmarking skills had never been used. So unnecessary had the captain's traditional skills become that even men who had never fished at all had now bought motorboats and were serving as their captains. However, what obviously *did* distinguish between members of some crews in 1973 was differential access to the means of production. Many of the captains had substantial investments in motors and boats, whereas the ordinary fishermen did not. These captains were now drawing a higher income mainly because of their *property* rather than because of their special skills.

The Dawn of Stratification

Social distinctions that in the past would, in the course of events, have been leveled out, had served as the raw material out of which more permanent contrasts were being constructed—given the changes in technology and marketing. Socioeconomic differentiation among fishermen increased markedly as access to the means of production grew more restricted. Those who either could afford the costs of motorization themselves or were considered sufficiently reliable to be offered loans were (1) land-based entrepreneurs—who, however, still had trouble keeping good captains and regular crews; and (2) successful fishing owners—those who had well-maintained boats, good local reputations, and possessions to back up the likelihood that their loans would be repaid.

Those who benefited most from the changes in fishing production and distribution were precisely those men who happened to be at the top of the hierarchy at a time of major economic and social change. Previously, their differential success would eventually have been subjected to those leveling mechanisms that have been described in earlier chapters. Their estates and other advantages would not have survived their deaths intact, and Arembepe would have remained hierarchical but unstratified. Now, however, it seemed that a few Arembepeiros could look forward to rising out of the national lower class.

What was happening in Arembepe in the 1970s has probably happened many times before as communities have been swept from egalitarian to stratified social relations. That is, contrasts that would eventually have been evened out under the old socioeconomic conditions were being frozen into discrete categories of privileged and underprivileged people.

As we have seen, the basis of the captain-crew distinction was shifting from skills to property, and the rewards of fishing were becoming increasingly unequal. Distinctions among captains based mainly on age and personality had always been perceptible. Now, however, the contrast between successful captain and slouch ramified throughout ordinary social life. Just as had been true in the 1960s, the men who were the most willing to sell their services as captains to nonfishing owners were neither ambitious nor particularly dependable. Some of the old alcoholic captains still worked for a commission; but several of the hired captains, like an increasing number of ordinary fishermen, were part of Arembepe's growing immigrant community—housed by and large not in Arembepe proper but in less-favored Caraúnas. These men lacked the social ties based on kinship, marriage, and ritual kinship that had always provided social support in the community. Lacking such relationships and residentially isolated, immigrants had trouble finding places in the best

Caraúnas, photographed from across a restored lagoon in 1980.
(Courtesy Jerald T. Milanich)

crews, and thus in forging social links with those Arembepeiros who could help them most. The graded hierarchy was
turning into different social worlds.

The least fortunate villagers were being physically dis-
tanced from community social life and gradually deprived of
full participation in the fellowship of the parent community.
Economic contrasts between owners and workers were increasing. Poor immigrants continued to arrive to tap the resources of a booming economy, but they faced previously absent obstacles to full integration in community life. There
were strong contrasts in life style. Tomé and other entrepreneurs could afford good brick houses with such modern conveniences as indoor plumbing, refrigerators, and gas lights.
But the emerging underclass of hired captains and ordinary
fishermen spent their evenings in the new settlement of
Caraúnas, with the fetor and mosquitoes that surrounded the
spoiled lagoon—in a prototype of the first urban ghetto.

Although many ordinary fishermen still held places in successful boats and thus could afford to stay in, and gradually
renovate, their houses in Arembepe, even they were noting
the growing contrast between captain-owner and ordinary

crew member. Fishing people who had always valued their independence from land-based entrepreneurs had grown more dependent on wealthier fishermen—the captain-owners who granted their livelihood. Social relations in the boat were becoming more like employer-employee relationships. "Things aren't the same since the owner began to take every third fish," asserted one fisherman. And another change in the division of the catch—the extension of the "separate line" principle to small fish and not just large ones, as formerly—offered further confirmation of the decreasingly social, increasingly personalistic, nature of Arembepe's fishing industry. Previously crew members had used a joint line system—pooling their day's catch of small fish and dividing them equally in the evening. The fisherman just quoted went on about changes: "Now each man marks every fish he catches with his own brand. He puts aside one out of three for 'the boat.' The rest are weighed and sold separately."

Compared to clan- and lineage-based societies in Africa or Oceania, Arembepe had never been a particularly "community-spirited" place. Villages I studied in Madagascar (Kottak, 1980) had a much better developed social sense—an idea of an ongoing community of past, present, and future members, of a social collectivity independent of its individual members. Even the Arembepe of the 1960s would surely have scored low on whatever "social solidarity" test might have been devised. Kin-based obligations had then encompassed only close kin—mainly parents, siblings, and children. By 1973, however, the tendency toward atomistic individualism and the decline of community "wholeness" was becoming much more marked. Ordinary fishermen were accusing successful captain-owners of being "interested only in money" and—to obtain it—of consulting "spirit mothers" (*mães de santo*), figures in the *candomblé* cult that had flowered in Arembepe between 1965 and 1973.

The Magic of Success

By 1973 there was unmistakable evidence that *candomblé*, an Afro-Brazilian medico-religious system, which previously had been undeveloped in Arembepe, was attracting more and more villagers. Its spread to Arembepe was yet another dimension of the community's suburbanization, as Arembepeiros spent more time outside and as outsiders flocked to Arembepe, so that urban and regional culture patterns were being quickly adopted. During the 1960s Arembepeiros had consulted a curer on a nearby agricultural estate. With malady or without, most villagers had made the trip to see the revival meeting type of pavilion where the curer worked his magic through spirit possession. The shaman hedged his bets: in addition to intervening with the spiritual world, he wrote prescriptions for his clients to take to druggists, and he seemed to have some medical knowledge.

Access to the spirit world was much closer to home in 1973. *Candomblé,* whose "spirit mothers and fathers" (*mães* and *pais de santo*—literally, mothers and fathers of saints) are influential religious figures in Salvador itself, was enjoying a new popularity in Arembepe. During the 1960s occasional small-scale *candomblé* ceremonies, consisting of lively rhythms and vigorous dancing leading ideally to the dancer's possession by a spirit, had been organized by a handful of native women who had studied in one of the cult houses during a sojourn in Salvador. Only a few Arembepeiros had attended, and their general goal was not to enlist spiritual support but simply to "enjoy," as on any festive occasion. By 1973 a spirit mother from Salvador had moved to Caraúnas; she was being consulted by Arembepeiros and was helping to organize much better attended ceremonies. One native son had also moved to Caraúnas to promote *candomblé* in his own community after spending several years in Salvador.

Since several villagers had informed me that Arembepe now had real *candomblés,* I was eager to attend a ceremony during my 1973 visit. Just one was held, however, organized by the spirit mother and father who had taken up residence in Caraúnas. That Saturday night in August, I saw several familiar faces among the participants, including one woman who had returned to Arembepe in 1964 after studying *candomblé* in Salvador, and her daughter, who had cooked and cleaned house for members of the 1963 field team. Other participants included Laurentino, the storekeeper whose "devil dog" struck fear in the hearts of some villagers, and his brother, a man who had a reputation for occasionally becoming deranged and running nude through the streets. There were many participants I did not recognize; I learned that they were associates of the organizers and included people from Salvador who had come out for the festivities. The Arembepeiro participants wore colorful costumes, another reflection of the new prosperity. In the old days Arembepeiros could not have afforded to don such elaborate dress for a religious occasion.

Since Marvin Harris had taken the 1962 field team to a renowned *candomblé* house in Salvador, where we had witnessed a proper ceremony, I knew more or less what to expect. However, the Arembepe event, with a much smaller orchestra and fewer dancing "saints' daughters" (*filhas de santo;* assistants of the spirit mother or father) awaiting spirit possession, proved a disappointment. Hour after hour the dancers shuffled lackadaisically around the clearing. When, I wanted to know, would someone be possessed? "Don't you believe that anyone's ever really possessed," warned Alberto. "I don't know when they'll start pretending." The drums beat on insistently, and one woman eventually began moaning quietly, which, someone told me, meant that she had received a saint. This was nothing like the Salvador *candomblé* I had attended, where half a dozen frenzied women had careened across the floor, colliding like amusement park racing cars, and hooting like banshees—leaving no doubt that they had received spirits. By two in the morning I had seen nothing new and decided to go home and get some sleep. The next day, people who had stayed on told me that there had been a few possessions; but my informants said they shared my impression that the event had been unconvincing, or at least unexciting.

From my discussions about *candomblé* with Arembepeiros during my 1973 stay, I formed the impression of a belief system in flux. Villagers neither fully accepted nor fully rejected the beliefs and behavior of *candomblé*. Rumors circulated about which Arembepeiros were clients of the spirit mother in Caraúnas—indicative of the insecurity mentioned previously and of growing mistrust toward fellow villagers. Alberto's middle-aged wife was suffering from a recurring illness, which she and Alberto attributed to magical causes. Soon after my arrival in June she had another attack and moved in with her brother, the spirit father in Caraúnas. Alberto's thirteen-year-old daughter proved susceptible to recurrent malign possession. One evening a frantic Alberto persuaded me to drive her to the pharmacist in Itapoan, since her spirit-father uncle had been unable to fend off what turned out to be her second spirit possession that year. The pharmacist's treatment proved effective—a glucose injection from a syringe huge enough to scare off the most tenacious spirit.

The modes of thought necessary for *candomblé* to succeed during the 1970s could be perceived but were fairly dormant in the Arembepe of the 1960s. The community of my initial encounters had been remarkably ritual-free. All Arembepeiros had been baptized as Roman Catholics, and the resultant ritual kinship (godparenthood and coparenthood), along with individual worship of favorite saints, was the main way in which Catholicism entered community life. Two large-scale celebrations *(festas)* were held annually: Saint John was honored June 24 and Saint Francis, Arembepe's patron saint, on February 20. The latter event, which took place when Arembepeiros were reaping the benefits of their most productive fishing season, was much larger than the former and attracted numerous outsiders. However, religion had little to do with the bacchanalia that typically accompanied the Saint John and Saint Francis celebrations.

By 1973 Arembepeiros' exposure to organized religion had scarcely increased. Although access to churches outside the village was easier, a priest actually visited Arembepe's chapel no more often than in 1965 (twice a year). Despite the fact that Brazil is in theory the world's most populous Roman Catholic nation, with 92 percent of the population claiming that faith, only women and children ever attended chapel in Arembepe; men had nothing to do with formal church participation. On one of the priest's rare visits, I heard him chastise those in attendance for lack of interest in organized religion. Although men claimed to pray to their household and individual saints, and to worship their images in photos and figurines, rituals prior to fishing were absent— even during the season of rainy weather and rough seas.

Although obviously "religious" beliefs and behavior were uncommon in Arembepe during the 1960s, villagers expressed vague belief in such pan-Brazilian spirits as mules without heads, balls of fire, and werewolves. More significantly, however, they shared the common peasant beliefs that individuals in the community could profit at the expense of others (Foster's image of limited good) and that differences in wealth could come as a result of pacts made with the devil. Villagers were particularly fearful and suspicious of the storekeeper who supposedly had caged a private demon.

I believe that much of the *candomblé*-related beliefs and activities of 1973 should be interpreted not as something entirely new but as an extension and generalization of this preexisting belief system, within the context of a community whose socioeconomic structure was changing from graded hierarchy to stratification. Particularly significant was the fact that Arembepeiros had extended their accusations of profiting with supernatural help from storeowners to successful fishermen. I think that increasing supernaturalism was a direct reflection of Arembepe's rapid transformation. Economic changes, alien contacts, and new insecurities favored the growth of religion, as some villagers began to seek supernatural solutions for unfamiliar problems. Increasing belief in *candomblé* was also a cognitive device that villagers were using to interpret what to them, given their previous isolation and poverty, must have been a mysterious fact—that local wealth was growing much faster than ever before. And of course, the community's rapidly increasing cash flow was itself an essential underpinning of the stepped-up ritual activity, which the old Arembepe could not have afforded.

The case of Alberto's wife, Carolina, and their possessed daughter tends to confirm the relationship between increasing wealth, psychological insecurity, and supernaturalism. Carolina's spiritual afflictions had developed soon after she opened a small store, which sold—among other low-value items—soft drinks, lemons, and kerosene, primarily to neighbors and tourists. Carolina's successful small business was one among many that developed in response to the tourist trade and the increasing amounts of cash that flowed through a suburbanizing community. After years of fairly severe poverty, Carolina's new business activities were fast rivaling her husband's earnings as an ordinary fisherman. Their household income had doubled.

Carolina's business seemed to keep on doing well despite her illness. Furthermore, an intensification of Carolina's condition *and* their daughter's attack closely followed *my* return to Arembepe in 1973, which Alberto himself had interpreted supernaturally. Although he had not known that I would be coming back after eight years, Alberto claimed to have had a dream just before my arrival—that I would appear with money that would enable him to finish building his brick house. I doubt that Alberto ever gave up the belief that my return—and my hiring him as one of my field assistants at a good wage—had supernatural causes.

I believe that, unconsciously, Alberto's wife and daughter (spurred on by a closely related spirit father) were punishing themselves psychosomatically for their family's economic success. In the old days Arembepeiros—good captains, for example—had *gradually* acquired reputations for success. However, *rapid* improvement in fortune had been a rarity in traditional Arembepe and was usually explained in supernatural terms. Now, in the 1970s, rapid growth in wealth was a fact of everyday life, a local manifestation of the "economic miracle."

How are miracles explained? Most Arembepeiros were shackled by a value system that mistrusted marked economic improvement and attributed it to devil-pacts. Individuals who had been raised with these traditional beliefs and values found it difficult to cope psychologically with their new success. Some, like Carolina, who came from a more supernaturally oriented family than most, developed psychosomatic illnesses, which they attributed to the same kinds of devilish spirits, working negatively, that they had previously identified as working positively to promote the success of others. In effect they were saying to other villagers, "No, I can't have made a pact with the devil, despite my apparent prosperity. Far from it, since evil spirits are really doing me more physical damage than other people." Leaving the specifics of Carolina's case aside, more and more Arembepeiros *were* being attracted to *candomblé*—almost surely as a means of dealing with stressful aspects of change. We shall see that in 1980 *candomblé* continued to provide a context for expressing contradictions between the old value system—developed in a more egalitarian and stable society—and contemporary forces of rapid economic change.

Facing changes too sudden and complex to decipher, Arembepeiros thus used magical thought to make the new order understandable. Previously they had accused only land-based entrepreneurs of trafficking with the devil. But now ordinary fishermen were extending this traditional explanation for success to their own co-workers—captain-owners who were beginning to act like bosses. And some of the captains were getting nervous. For example, Fernando, previously a successful captain and sailboat owner, had acquired a motorboat and was drawing the new profits that went to its captain-owner. However, Fernando was also deviating noticeably from his former path. He was drinking too much beer and rum, and he was actually attending *candomblé*, thus reinforcing other Arembepeiros' developing explanation for his success. His insecurity had led to a potentially hazardous habit—carrying a revolver, which he assured me he would use against robbers, strangers, and the unanticipated dangers that he imagined to be lurking in the night. (Fernando's case is fully examined in Chapter 11.)

To be sure, it was not just the economy but a variety of changes that had contributed to an atmosphere of unfamiliarity, uncertainty, fear, and insecurity, as Arembepe grew ever more vulnerable to external forces. Nevertheless, I do believe that a number of changes in the relations of production were being expressed in the behavior of Fernando and other fishermen. Captains had to deal not simply with their crew members' hostility but with their own intensifying achievement drives and competitive urges. These psychological manifestations of change showed up in the behavior of Fernando and (in varied expressions) of many other villagers (see Chapter 11). However, a few, such as Tomé, seemed to be managing a comfortable aloofness.

"I know that others resent my success, but I don't care. After all, I've got four successful brothers, five sons, and many sources of income."

Tomé was very secure; but he stood at the top of the local

hierarchy, and character stability and adaptability had been factors in his rise.

Other Changes and the Possible Danger of Overfishing

Although social relations and the psychological adjustment of individuals were suffering in the mid-1970s, Arembepe's economy was thriving. But how long could the boom last? Might not the new technology (combined with industrial pollution from the nearby titanium factory) lead to the rapid depletion of local marine resources?

From informants' accounts and from my own observations over the years, it is clear that fishing productivity in Arembepe has always varied—both seasonally and from year to year. During July 1972, for example, the cooperative's records show that Arembepe's boats caught 125 percent of their average monthly catch, whereas fishing was generally bad in July (and throughout the winter) of 1973. The drop in winter catches between 1972 and 1973 *may* have been due to overfishing. It may also have had something to do with the stream of industrial wastes flowing into the Atlantic only 3 kilometers south of Arembepe's harbor. Bad weather did not seem responsible; fishing boats went out most days in July 1973 but simply didn't catch many fish. However, I suspect that the drop was really just a normal year-to-year fluctuation. If overfishing were to blame it should have shown up in the January–March season; instead, slightly *more* fish had been caught then than in the corresponding months of 1972.

Whatever its cause, the lean 1973 winter fishing season did bring into sharp relief the new diversity and experimentation within Arembepe's fishing industry. New technology was opening niches in addition to those already discussed; and if the old niches were withholding their accustomed rewards, many Arembepeiros were finding substantial profits in the new ones—night fishing and lobster fishing. Previously, a few boats had fished at night, at certain times of the year, using kerosene lamps to catch fish attracted by light. The introduction of bottled gas permitted Arembepeiros to own and operate much more powerful lamps, which they took out in their motorboats to use in night fishing.

By August 1973 the total fishing pattern had changed dramatically. In the 1960s the fleet had set sail in the early morning and returned in the evening—sooner if fishing had been bad, later if good. In the winter of 1973, individual boats left and returned at all hours of the day and night—which again had not been practicable in the absence of local places to store fish until their transport to the suburbs of Salvador.

This economic shift also affected social relations. Previously the boats had left and returned more or less at the same time. After unloading their gear and dividing up their catch, men had shared their evening bath in the lagoon and ambled over to the chapel stoop for talk with fellow fishermen. By 1973, however, boats were leaving and returning individually, and their crew members' activities on land were thrown into disarray. Younger men still got together for the Sunday soccer game; but pollution and the new fishing pattern had forced abandonment of the communal bathing pattern, and the chapel stoop had been relinquished to old men and alcoholics. These were additional ways, then, in which Arembepe's social life was fragmenting.

Like night fishing, lobstering was an innovative adaptation to the lean season in 1973. A dozen Arembepeiros now owned more than 4,000 meters of nylon trammel nets. Trammel nets, which hang vertically in the water and were first introduced to the community in 1965, did not prove much of a boon to traditional fishing, which continued with hook and handline. But about five fishermen (including Tomé and two of his brothers, who together owned more than half the nets) had found them effective in lobster fishing. Previously, a few ordinary fishermen had been particularly skilled at catching lobsters, which had been done on the reef at night—during low tide, when the rocky surface was greatest. The lobster catches of the 1960s were small, and none was exported.

During 1972 and 1973, however, trammel net owners expanded the scale of lobster fishing, so that it contributed significantly to their incomes. Between August and November of 1972, for example, a monthly average of 150 kilograms of lobster were sold to the fishermen's cooperative, at three times the unit cost of fish. These had been the leanest hook-and-line fishing months in 1972, with catches only half the year's monthly average. The same five fishermen resumed lobster fishing in June of 1973, and production increased to over 320 kilograms per month through August. Although the cooperative had held the cost of fish at virtually the November 1972 level, the price it offered for lobster had risen to four times that of fish by June 1973, providing another incentive for an increase in lobster fishing. In June 1973, fishermen's receipts from lobster rose to 80 percent of their total fish sales to the cooperative.

The records of the cooperative show that lobster fishing almost immediately ceased when hook-and-line fishing became productive again. The news that regular fishing was getting better was immediately apparent when the first large catches began to appear on the beach. The news spread quickly, and fishermen headed for the traditional banks and abandoned the rocky areas near home where lobster nets were set.

As I suspected it might be, Arembepe's "lobster boom" proved short-lived. Because lobstering proceeded in a much more restricted territory (the rocky areas near shore), it was much more vulnerable to overproduction than open-sea fishing, whose territory has continually expanded as a result of new technology. The brief popularity of lobstering was attributable to cost-effectiveness—high prices for low labor investment. Trammel nets were easily set and collected—tasks that required two quick trips in a motorboat rather than a hard day in the sun on the open sea.

By 1980, however, nets that had once yielded several kilograms of lobster were catching just 1 or 2 kilograms per setting. Lobster prices had fallen relative to those of fish, and it was hardly worthwhile for Arembepeiros to set their trammel nets. There is little chance of resurgence of lobstering, since catches continue to decline and since Arembepeiros ignore national conservation laws requiring that small lobsters be thrown back. Villagers still eat whatever-sized lobster they are fortunate enough to catch.

In the remaining chapters, we will see that many of the economic and social trends perceptible in 1973 had intensified by 1980. Arembepe's occupational structure grew more diverse; social relations between captain-owners and ordinary fishermen moved further apart, becoming less social and more economic. Fishermen grew more dependent on external supplies, traveled farther, and caught more fish. Population kept on growing, and stratification became more pronounced. Immigrants continued to arrive, and new settlements grew up as a result of lotting. Tourists kept coming, and marine pollution went on. However, Tibrás took measures to stop destruction of the freshwater lagoons, and people washed and bathed there again as in the 1960s. There has been no halt to Arembepe's opening up. Today it is just one turnoff on an asphalted highway that continues north for 20 kilometers and will eventually link up with Bahia's northern neighbor, the state of Sergipe. It is time to tell the story of contemporary Arembepe.

Part Four
Reality

7 Another Sunrise in the Land of Dreams[1]

Pleasantly, my initial encounter with Arembepe in 1980 brought to mind the sleepy, sun-drenched village I had first seen in 1962, and not the sleazy suburb I remembered from 1973. Given the excellent paved road and the quick trip (about fifty minutes) from our seaside hotel in Salvador, I expected to find more cars in the central square on that Wednesday in August. Had I picked a Sunday to return, my first impressions would have been very different. My most trusted informant and former field assistant, Alberto, for example, would have been busy with his thriving bar and store in the lower street. I would have spent the day dodging, and enduring the embraces of, beer-bloated old friends and acquaintances. I would have seen at once exactly the kind of resort that the Arembepe of 1980 had become—a honky-tonk beach town, weekend haven of Salvador's working-class and lower-middle-class population. Among villagers, I would have noticed that excessive weekend drinking, just perceptible in 1973, had intensified as a result of certain changes in the economy.

The fishing pattern, for example, had changed radically. Most of the old open sailboats *(saveiros)* had been sold or abandoned, and the larger ones had been converted into *barcos*, motorized fishing vessels with enclosed cabins. Fishing expeditions now began on Tuesday or Wednesday, when a shipment of ice arrived from the city, and lasted four days, as crews traveled far north of their former fishing grounds, to fish in offshore waters of the villages of Sauipe and Subaúma. Returning on Friday or Saturday, many fishermen spent the weekend drinking alongside the visitors from the city.

On my first 1980 Saturday in Arembepe, the morning was rainy; but it cleared by afternoon, and a stream of automo-

I had difficulty finding a parking place in Street Down There one August Sunday in 1980. (Courtesy Jerald T. Milanich)

biles ran in and out. There were even more cars on Sunday, when we counted 309 automobiles and 3 buses in an area that had only 16 autos and 1 bus the next Monday. In 1973 I had been shocked to see a road sign marked "Arembepe." The 1980 equivalent was my difficulty in finding a Sunday parking place in Arembepe itself.

One Saturday Alberto complained of an especially active Friday night; people had sat on his doorstep until seven in the morning drinking beer and liquor. The weekend Arembepe of 1980 offered still other diversions. Music blasted all day Saturday from a discotheque in the central square, but the heavy dancing began at nine in the evening and lasted until four in the morning. The square and beach even had "Bahianas"—the elaborately costumed women who bedeck corners in Salvador, selling ready-made Bahian food specialties (part of the region's characteristic Afro-Brazilian cuisine). Dora, our former cook and now a barmaid, was one of many women working for wages in bars and restaurants, and for tourists. Her labor netted her a bit less than $10 per weekend.

By no stretch of the imagination could Arembepe be iden-

A Bahiana sells cooked food in Arembepe's central square, while weekend tourists wait for a bus. (Courtesy Jerald T. Milanich)

tified as the predominantly fishing village I had studied in the 1960s. In 1980 just 40 percent of its adult men, and only a third of its total work force made their living from fishing (see Appendixes 2 and 6). Arembepe had become a tourist town. As one informant remarked, there were bars everywhere. A Sunday afternoon stroll down the lower street showed just how complete Arembepe's transformation had been, providing firsthand illustration of the statistics on occupation I subsequently collected. One out of every three occupied houses sold something.

The proliferation of bars had contributed to the breakdown of community solidarity. In the 1960s there had been few bars. *Cachaça* by the glass was available at the two large stores near the central square. Returning fishermen often tossed down one or two shots before taking their evening bath in the lagoon, going home for dinner, and joining the men's group on the chapel stoop. By 1980, men had picked up the habit of drinking in bars close to their home, where they socialized with neighbors and the bartender's family. Rarely did they venture over to the chapel stoop, which was now usually vacant each evening. Neighborhood—and even more narrowly, the subneighborhood group of about a dozen houses whose residents drank at the same bar—had replaced the whole-community evening interaction of yesteryear.

Alberto and Carolina had by now grown accustomed to the business success that they had found psychologically disturbing in 1973. Their oldest daughter, Maria José, a bright and hard-working woman of twenty-five, was living with Ivan, an ambitious migrant from interior Bahia, son of a business-oriented family, who hoped to open his own commercial establishment, preferably a restaurant, in Arembepe. In the meantime, he had moved into Alberto's small house and helped him with his business. Even though Maria José and Ivan had formed a common-law union, he slept on a couch in the living room, while Maria José shared a bedroom with her two younger sisters.

Carolina, Alberto, Maria José, Ivan, and Cosma—Maria José's eighteen-year-old sister, whose 1973 spirit possession has been described in Chapter 6—each sold something different. Alberto sold beer, Arembepe's coldest because of his excellent freezer. Normal wintertime Sunday sales of 100 liters brought him a profit of $25. He and Carolina also sold cigarettes, shots of *cachaça*, fruits, vegetables, spices, herbs, razor blades, aspirin, matches, and sundry items. Cosma was in charge of soft drinks. Maria José sold bread, sweets, and roasted peanuts. Ivan made money from cocktails (he had tended bar before coming to Arembepe); and he and Maria José prepared our meals during our stay. Ivan supplemented his income doing odd jobs, painting, plumbing, and electrical work, mainly for summer people.

The business savvy that Ivan hoped would guarantee his eventual personal success in Arembepe's tourist trade led him to suggest to Alberto that they build a porch at the back of the house, directly overlooking the Atlantic, which sometimes lapped the foundation of the house at high tide. The fishing fleet now anchored picturesquely right behind Alberto's house. Larger boats needed deeper moorings than the old sailboats, which had forced abandonment of the old reef-protected harbor in favor of the slightly rougher area just south, right behind the seaward houses of Street Down There. Ivan and Alberto were correct in assuming that the fresh air and harbor view would appeal to outsiders; each weekend Salvadorians drank beer and ate seafood snacks in Alberto's outdoor bar.

A few houses further down, Aunt Dalia's juice bar also sold beer but specialized in juice and ice cream, and it too offered a porch and view. Aunt Dalia's business success had been built on sales to hippies during the late 1960s and early 1970s. Young outsiders, along with the dozen former hippies who had stayed on, still brought her substantial business in 1980.

The gap in construction that had formerly separated the end of Street Down There from the summer houses farther south was being filled in. One new restaurant, Arembepe's fanciest, with bow-tied waiters, had just opened on the site where Francisca, Arembepe's last slaveowning landlord, had once defended her coconut grove against the pranks of village boys. A former hippie, now considered a permanent resident *(morador)*, ran a restaurant, bar, and rooming house just beyond. He rented (filthy) indoor rooms and several bamboo cabanas just seaward of the restaurant, under the coconut trees. All of these were occupied one Sunday afternoon, and since I saw few bathers in the nearby Atlantic, I assumed that these shacks were Arembepe's version of the "motels of high activity"—places for rapid sexual encounters—located near the beaches on the outskirts of Rio de Janeiro.

It was still the case, I was told, that the number of city people who came to Arembepe on Sundays in August was "nothing" compared to summertime tourism. The woman who ran Claudia's Restaurant reported that her clientele consisted almost entirely of outsiders. Tibrás officials came two or three times per week throughout the year. Although she never knew in advance when they would come, electricity and refrigeration permitted her to store fish and prepare meals when customers arrived. In contrast to the slow winter trade, she reported good business even on weekdays during the summer. In winter, she served twenty-five to thirty Sunday meals, whereas the number doubled in summer. Indicating the extent of Arembepeiros' monetary reliance on outsiders was a series of complaints about reduced business during 1980, attributable to the gasoline shortage. Yes, Arembepe, too, had been caught in the global energy crunch of 1980. Business had been much better in the winter of 1979, people said.

Worlds Apart

As had been the case in 1973, there was still a difference between the weekend visitors and other outsiders who sought leisure in Arembepe. The owners of the substantial and comfortable vacation homes on the town's northern and southern peripheries continued to be wealthy outsiders who belonged to a separate and distant social world. They maintained their aloofness from villagers and from the outsiders who did their tourism in the village proper. At the end of the northern rectangle, just north of houses owned by wealthier Arembepeiros but still south of landlord Jorge's *casa grande*—which marked Arembepe's northern boundary—stood a row of substantial and attractive two-story summer homes, with sea views; many had enclosed garages. When we asked villagers about the possibility of renting one of these houses for our brief stay, their answer was always the same: "They wouldn't rent." Arembepe's highest-ranking municipal official, the former policeman and naval carpenter, who prided himself on his connections to important outsiders and lived nearby, said that he knew little about these wealthy outsiders and could not even tell us their names. They were said to come to Arembepe on weekends, even though we saw little evidence of it in 1980. Villagers assured us that people with such wealth would have no reason to rent.

The same applied to the owners of the houses south of Arembepe, where we had lived in 1973. This area was less isolated than it had been previously, because construction had filled in the gap between these houses and the village proper, and because the summer people now maintained employees who lived in caretakers' quarters and garage rooms. One of the caretakers told us that the new owner of the most opulent house, which had been constructed originally by a high state official, came just once or twice a year but surely wouldn't rent. Our 1973 landlord was himself in Arembepe, recuperating from an operation. Only one house, whose owner, a wealthy woman from Rio, was reported to be traveling in the United States, could be rented through a lawyer in Salvador, for about $700 per month. It was in poor condition, and we decided to seek lodging elsewhere.

Prudencio, who for decades had represented the landlords in Arembepe, had died during our absence. No single individual had replaced him, since some of his roles had disappeared and others had been split up among several people. For example, as a result of lotting, the landlords had divested themselves of many of their coconut trees, removing the need for someone to oversee their harvest and sale. In 1980 the immigrant who ran the newsstand at the entry to Arembepe also took care of several of the summer houses. He knew more about the summer people than any other Arembepeiro, since they usually stopped at his stand when they arrived in the village.

Subdivisions

As lotting progressed, Jorge had opened a real estate office in one of the new western streets that paralleled the northern rectangle. Although he frequently visited Arembepe on weekends, Jorge rarely transacted business there himself, leaving such matters to his younger brother and brother-in-law. One informant told us, insightfully, that with so many social ties to Arembepe, Jorge found it difficult to say no to villagers when they asked for special consideration—for example, an extension of the deadline for a monthly payment. However, his brother-in-law, judged unpleasant by a member of our 1980 field team, acted as the hard-nosed landlord.

Jorge, educated and upwardly mobile scion of the land-owning family that Arembepeiros had known for generations, would forever be considered the village patron, although with Prudencio, his longtime local agent, no longer available as buffer and mentor, Jorge found the patron's role more uncomfortable than ever. After all, he told us, "I'm a professional." His increasingly successful career demanded frequent travel, often abroad. Growing tired of land sales, Jorge complained, "I don't make much money from selling lots. Prices are low and there are all kinds of subdivision ex-

LAGOON

TO CARAÚNAS

STREET DOWN THERE

ALBERTO'S BAR

NEW HARBOR

SQUARE

CHAPEL

BEACH

OLD HARBOR

AREMBEPE IN 1980

penses. For example, the law says that you have to build new roads to provide access to each lot. And that eats up almost all of my profits."

In place of villagers' previous uncertainty about the lotting scheme was general acceptance of continued immigration, sales to outsiders, and overall growth. A few people had complaints. One woman thought that outsiders were being favored in lot sales. Some, she asserted, had bought up two or three lots, leaving little choice for villagers who wished to live near their relatives. "You'd think he might leave land for people from here," she said. Jorge claimed that he wished to

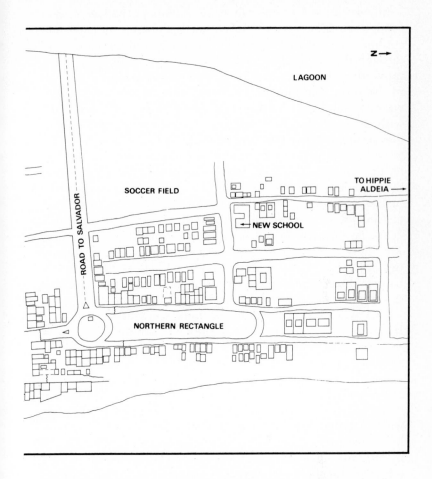

do just that, but his relatives, who were much more involved than he in actual sales, appeared to be less concerned with social ties and more interested in maximizing their immediate economic gains.

In August 1980, lots were selling for 35,000 cruzeiros (about $600) cash, but most buyers were putting down 10,000 cruzeiros and paying 2,000 cruzeiros monthly for two years. The landowners had just announced that the down payment would be raised to 15,000 cruzeiros (about $250), which because of economic changes to be described in Chapter 8, put lot ownership beyond the means of most fishermen.

All of the real estate values in Arembepe had increased faster than inflation. As the national economic miracle had continued, though slowed down a bit, the flow of cash through the community had permitted many villagers to improve their houses. Only 15 percent of the houses surveyed in southern Arembepe in 1980 were wattle and daub, whereas most had been in the 1960s. The rest were brick with tile roofs. In Caraúnas, too, houses were better; most of that settlement's one hundred houses (a doubling since 1973) were brick, and one was sold to Salvadorians during our stay for the equivalent of $600 cash—which was now well beyond the income of an ordinary fisherman. One reason that houses in Caraúnas were now more substantial was the increasing number of salaried workers, including local Tibrás employees, who now numbered forty—approximately 17 percent of Arembepe's adult male work force. Outsiders, too, were buying in Caraúnas, in the new satellite village of Volta do Robalo, and throughout the area being subdivided, viewing any developed land near the beach as a good investment.

Lots were also being sold on both sides of the Coconut Highway near the turnoff to Arembepe. Volta do Robalo, on the northeast corner, already had two rows of houses, about twenty-five completed, another twenty under construction. A successful captain-owner who had just built a substantial house in Volta overlooking the lagoon, and had also bought three adjacent lots for his children, was enjoying his view while it lasted. He envisaged row after row of houses extending down to the high water mark of the lagoon. With lotting in progress on both sides of the highway, and with houses projected for the area between Volta and the lagoon, Alberto remarked that Arembepe would soon be a city. At nightfall, from the highway, viewing coconut palms outlined by hundreds of electric lights, Alberto and I agreed about Arembepe's impending urbanization, and its lingering beauty.

Population Growth

Because of the brevity of my 1980 stay, I did not try to census Arembepe. Talking with the head statistician in the municipal seat, I learned that a sample done in 1977 had estimated 2,500 to 3,000 people in the area from Arembepe to the Jacuipe River, 11 kilometers to the north. The statistician believed that the 1980 census would find Arembepe's population in excess of 2,500, a reasonable assumption, considering the more than 600 houses in Arembepe and its satellites. The actual 1980 census figures turned out to be 617 houses and 1,561 people, which seems a bit low to me. However, Arembepe's population remains difficult to census accurately, because so many of the people who own houses in the village reside there only part of the year. I was able to do my own quick census[2] and survey of 130 houses in southern Arembepe (just 29 less than the *total* number of dwellings in 1964). This included both sides of Street Down There plus the new streets to the west, where houses had been built right up to the high-water mark of the lagoon. Confirming the importance of outside and absentee ownership, 58 percent of the 130 dwellings belonged to non-Arembepeiros. Only 47 percent of the houses were inhabited year-round by anyone, owner or renter. Rentals were prominent in southern Arembepe, as they were throughout the village. In the winter of 1973, when the pattern of tourism and part-time residence was beginning to develop, just 10 percent of the community's houses were rented and only 34 percent had been rented at least once. By 1980, these figures had risen to 30 percent and 50 percent respectively.

Familiar Outsiders

The outsiders who have built, bought, or rented houses in Arembepe proper are not the aloof elites of the northern and southern peripheries. Most of them belong to the lower middle class. Therefore, they are socioeconomically similar both to today's weekend tourists and to the fallen gentry with whom Arembepeiros have dealt for decades. Because of this, there has been no dramatic alteration in the class affiliations of the outsiders with whom Arembepeiros most frequently come into contact. Although encounters with outsiders are more regular and take place for different reasons now, Arembepeiros' behavior with them is not very different from what it was during the 1960s.

Arembepeiros have not begun to kowtow to city folk, as a few observations from Alberto's bar will illustrate. One Sunday a group of strangers walked up from the beach to Alberto's porch and asked if cold beer was available. Alberto's daughter and "son-in-law" ignored them, continuing an animated conversation with a regular customer, Milton, a city man who rented a house across the street for weekend use. When Alberto's daughter eventually offered to take the strangers' orders, they asked for seafood snacks to accompany their beer. However, she told them that the crabs that Alberto usually bought on Sunday from river fishermen had not arrived that week; the tourists then left.

The interactions of Alberto and his family with Milton also illustrate that Arembepeiros maintain their customary, non-obsequious behavior patterns, developed in an egalitarian community, with most outsiders. Alberto called Milton his buddy *(camarada);* their joking certainly suggested a familiar and long-term relationship. Milton told me that he had first visited Arembepe during the 1940s, when he had met Alberto. Once the village opened up, he had rented a house for weekend and summer use, and he always drank (many hours each weekend) at Alberto's bar. Because of Milton's leathered and sunburned skin and his lack of teeth, I was suspicious of his claim to be a member of the middle class, particularly when he urinated off Alberto's porch, announcing to me that he was just "looking at the ocean."

Behind the western side of Street Down There are several new dwellings, most belonging to city people. Many of their owners use them only in summer, and some houses have mammoth gates that are chained and padlocked. Following an urban Brazilian custom intended to deter thieves, some houses are surrounded by high masonry walls with broken glass cemented to the top, giving them, to paraphrase archaeologist Jerald Milanich, a concentration-camp atmosphere. Similar homes had been built due west of all of Arembepe's traditional streets. I had trouble appreciating the tourist appeal of this zone, since none of the summer houses had ocean views, and their placement below the sandy ridge where the old village lies also cut them off from the sea breeze. Some did face the lagoon, which dries up in summer, more now than in the past, since Tibrás uses its water in manufacturing. Villagers said that mosquitoes, which had never been a problem in traditional Arembepe, were a nuisance for residents of the western zone, particularly in the rainy season. Caraúnas had a similar problem.

The Rental Business

Other outsiders, including Milton, the buddy and weekend neighbor of Alberto, had worked out long-term agreements to rent quarters in Arembepe for weekend and summer use. Several houses belonged to Salvadorians, some of whom had built them only as rental investments. Other rental units belonged to villagers. As was true in 1973, many Arembepeiros had sold or were renting their beachfront houses to people from Salvador. Some still followed the pattern of building duplexes; but by 1980 most villagers had decided to stay in the front, generally more comfortable, and to rent the rear portion, reversing the 1973 pattern, as demands to rent increased. Tomé, the spectacularly successful fishing entrepreneur of the 1960s and early 1970s, had left his wife for a hippie (see Chapter 11). They shared a rental house with another family, with only a curtain separating the two households. Tomé cited a housing shortage; he and his partner had been looking for several months for a dwelling, for which they were willing to pay up to $125 per month. But outsiders had cornered the market.

Arembepe's permanent immigrant population (on the basis of the household survey) had swollen from 24 percent in 1964 to 41 percent in 1980. Some were people renting beach quarters while working elsewhere. For example, the back of a house in the northern rectangle was rented to a young man who worked in the booming petrochemical industry near Camaçari, now just a thirty- to forty-minute commute, compared to two to three hours in 1973. Other renters included bus drivers, Tibrás workers, artisans, and still other people attracted by jobs in Arembepe's expanding economy.

Laurentino, the purportedly devil-worshipping storekeeper whose abortive attempt to succeed as boat owner was described in Chapter 4, had sold his store and now made his living from rentals. Operating in Street Down There, he had made money by catering to hippie needs. He rented them rooms; he had also built a rooftop tank to catch rain water and rented shower stalls. His business had prospered, particularly during the pollution crisis of 1973. Although Laurentino's devil worship was believed to continue, it appeared no longer to bother fellow villagers. In 1980 he owned several rental houses. The smallest one, just one room, brought $50 per month. For the larger houses, with two bedrooms and a living room, he charged twice as much.

Several villagers had grown suspicious of still another rental pattern, in which Arembepeiros and outsiders agreed to long-term rental contracts. For example, as a result of a run of bad luck that had forced him to sell one boat and one house, Tomé asked his mother to vacate the home he had built for her so that he might rent it to a man from Salvador. They signed a five-year contract, which, lamented Tomé, who was himself seeking rental quarters in 1980, still had a year to run. One homeowner in northern Arembepe complained to me that "rich outsiders," of whom Arembepe now had too many, were renting villagers' houses and then treating them as their own. Some city folk had even hired lawyers, claiming that they had contracted to *buy* in installments, rather than simply to rent the house. Although no Arembepeiro had yet lost title to a house as a result of such a rental agreement, this eventuality was feared because of the renters' clout in the external legal system.

Boxcar Apartments

Mapping and a household survey of southern Arembepe did uncover new facets of settlement pattern and population growth. In Chapter 6 I reported that in 1973 the poorest villagers, who had formerly been concentrated in flimsy palm-frond and unfinished wattle-and-daub shacks at the northern and southern ends of Arembepe, were moving to Caraúnas. By 1980 there had been a partial reversal of this pattern. Caraúnas itself had become more prosperous. The average brick house (with lot) there was worth $600; virtually all houses had electricity, and some had indoor plumbing. Although only about 5 percent of the real estate in Caraúnas

had so far been bought by city people, more and more outsiders were seeking land there.

As real estate prices rose in Caraúnas and Volta do Robalo,
and as all the lots were sold in these satellites, the poorest
villagers were giving up any hope of affording a home of
their own. They were taking up temporary residence with
relatives, building shacks adjoining the more substantial
houses of their kin. Small shacks had been built behind
many of the houses that faced Street Down There, even on
the narrow Atlantic side of the street. Just a few of these
were rented; most were occupied by relatives, often the married children of the owners of the better house in front. On
the western side of the street, with much more space for
rearward expansion, the developing compound pattern was
particularly obvious. For example, Dora, our former cook, resided down an alley in a crude, two-room unfinished wattle-
and-daub hut with her common-law husband, their own two
children, and her two youngest sons by previous unions. The
shack just west of Dora was the residence of her aunt's former husband. The aunt in question, Dora's mother's sister,
had a shack on the other side of Dora; Dora's oldest son slept
in the aunt's living room. Seaward of the three shacks, and
facing Street Down There, was the brick house constructed
by Dora's aunt and uncle before they separated. This more
substantial structure was now rented by a city person for
weekend and summer use.

Arembepe's increasingly labyrinthine settlement pattern
was most obvious in the southern part of the village. However, the pattern of poorer people living in hovels attached
boxcar style to more prosperous houses opening onto a street
was visible throughout Arembepe, expressing local population growth, a huge demand for rental property, completed
sale of nearby lots, and increasing socioeconomic stratification. The major economic reasons for growing class divisions
in Arembepe are discussed in Chapter 8.

Resident Hippies

The heyday of the hippies in Arembepe had ended by
1980. Informants remembered that the first hippies had ap-

peared during the summer of 1966–1967, but the main hippie years were 1968–1971, particularly 1970 and 1971. I encountered fewer recognizable hippies in 1980 than in 1973; just nine had remained in Arembepe and Caraúnas. In the opinion of many villagers, these people were no longer hippies but had become permanent residents.

Always more numerous than females among Arembepe's hippies, males had found it easier to be accepted as locals. A ten-year resident from interior Bahia whom I remembered from 1973 had persuaded his whole family to move to Arembepe. He operated a restaurant, bar, rooming house, and cabanas in southern Arembepe. His three sisters helped with the business. His parents had retired to a rental house in Street Down There, and his brother worked for Tibrás.

An Argentinian couple, also long-time residents, operated a bar in the northern rectangle. Another Argentinian, a craftsman, had lived in Arembepe for six years. His rental house adjoined Aunt Dalia's juice bar in Street Down There, which had always been the preferred hippie neighborhood. Three Brazilian hippies, two males and a female, occupied separate households in Caraúnas; the woman made clothes, and the men made handicrafts. One of them was reputed to do especially good work; he sold things locally and in Salvador and had been successful enough to buy a lot and build his own house. Three other hippies lived in Street Down There, one in a small shack that he used as shop and weekend bar, toward the southern extremity of the village.

Unique among the hippies was a young man from Salvador who had been in Arembepe for three years. Formerly a craftsman, he had become a jack-of-all-trades and even fished—the only hippie to enter Arembepe's traditional economy. Old Arembepeiros had mixed feelings about him, some accepting him as a serious fisherman and full human being, others disparaging his attempt to fish, considering all hippies to be silly, childlike creatures who could do nothing worthwhile. Illustrating acceptance was the retired captain who told me that the young man's parents had visited Arembepe. Such kinship ties provided villagers with evidence of the hippie's roots and humanity; another hippie's status had also risen when his parents and siblings moved to Arembepe.

Longest-term resident was Sonia, a middle-class native of São Paulo, whose education had included some college. Because of her ongoing affair with Tomé, a once-successful fisherman, Sonia had become Arembepe's most notorious and stigmatized hippie. Their story is told in Chapter 11.

The Hippie Handbook

By 1980 I had overcome much of my previous resentment toward Arembepe's hippie population, so that rather than ignoring their presence, I spent some time investigating their current life style and activities, and trying to understand their place in Arembepe's history. The few hippies who had decided to stay on, and in so doing had opted to become permanent residents, were now just one among many intrusive elements figuring in Arembepe's transformation. The mass media had lost most of their former fascination with the story of Arembepe's hippies; but the hippies' arrival still loomed large in Arembepeiros' own perceptions of change. For villagers, the invasion divided the community's history into eras, before and after. By 1980 many villagers were expressing *saudades* ("homesickness," "nostalgia") for the old days—the prehippie, untransformed Arembepe. They had lost their fascination with the new, and I was happily surprised to discover that they remembered us, members of the anthropological field teams, as part of the increasingly romanticized past.

How, specifically, did Arembepeiros of 1980 view hippies and their historical role? First of all, how does one tell who is a hippie? I found that villagers attributed certain stereotypical traits to hippies, and that even former hippies did exhibit characteristic ways of acting and thinking that set them off from other villagers. In other words, a hippie subculture was still discernible within Arembepe. One Sunday afternoon I sat talking with a sixty-year-old woman on the stoop of her brick home in Street Down There. Through the open window of a house across the street, I saw a blonde young woman who looked very like a *ippa* from Rio I had met in the Aldeia (the hippie settlement to the north, described further in the next section) a few days previously. However, my informant denied that this woman was a hippie. She had no hesitation, however, in using the label for a couple who approached us looking for Sonia, Tomé's stigmatized hippie lover (and my informant's neighbor), a few minutes later. The man, who spoke with an Argentinian accent, was wearing expensive clothes and didn't look like a hippie to me. My companion, however, focused on his beard and his request for information about Sonia in identifying him. Guilt by association! Furthermore, as an expression of her own hostility toward the hippies, particularly toward Sonia, for "taking another woman's husband," my informant knowingly lied in answering the man's question.

For villagers, important traits of hippies were hair and dress. Hippies had long hair; men with beards were hippies. Hippies went around "half-naked": men wore just loincloths; women used brief halters and wore no bras. Males and females bathed together nude in the Caratingi River. (Boys from Arembepe liked to bathe there too, to catch a glimpse of naked *ippas*!)

Speech and diet offered additional subcultural cues. Foreign hippies had accents, but more significantly, hippies spoke more slowly and softly than normal people (reminiscent of "laid-back" Americans). Hippies also differed in diet and consumption patterns. "Bread," I was told, "is the food of hippies." Villagers recounted that during their heyday, Arembepe's hippies had subsisted on bread and soda pop. Villagers also knew that hippies were supposed to smoke marijuana; indeed, there were rumors that certain Arembepe hippies were regular cannabis users. "Walking around stoned" was mentioned as another hippie culture trait.

Villagers seemed more resentful of hippies than in 1973—part of a more general pattern of hostility that had developed since my last visit, as change became less novel and more bothersome. One man who prided himself on his multiple social ties to outsiders chided me for referring to the northern hippie settlement as "the Aldeia."

"Don't use that hippie name," he said. "Caratingi is its proper name; call it that."

Villagers scorned the handful of village youths who were known to associate with hippies. "What a shame," remarked Dora of a twenty-year-old native, "that she has associated herself with that *ruindade* [low life] of the hippies."

Many villagers expressed low opinions of hippie morality.
"Hippies even rob each other," I was told. (On a visit to the
Aldeia, I did encounter an *ippa* from Portugal spending a few
days there who complained of having had $300 in traveler's
checks stolen the night before.) For traditional Arembepeiros, robbery is a highly stigmatized type of antisocial behavior. Both in 1973 and in 1980 I was repeatedly warned of robbers and assailants. The thief is a symbol that has come to
summarize many fears and uncertainties that Arembepeiros
have about the outside world. To classify hippies as robbers
is to place them outside normal social life. As I was frequently assured, Arembepeiros do not rob and have nothing
to fear from each other, "We may be poor, but we're not
thieves." Hippies, however, don't just rob; they steal from
each other. In telling me this, Arembepeiros were like veg-
etarians distinguishing between meat eating and cannibalism.

Another symbol, speech, was also used to establish hippies' lesser humanity. As we know from our own culture, we
feel most at home with people who talk more or less as we
do. However, Arembepeiros used the hippies' speech to diagnose something more subtle—not just a social difference
but an incomplete humanity. Drugged, foreign, or both, people who uttered words without seeming sure of their meaning were seen as parrots *(papagaios)*, creatures capable of
speech but not of understanding.

Until the arrival of the hippies, a German priest and American anthropologists had been the only foreigners that
Arembepeiros had ever known. All of us were initially classified as *papagaios*. During my visits in the 1960s, I always
felt that fieldwork in Arembepe was a linguistic struggle.
Why, I wondered, was my ability to speak and understand
Brazilian Portuguese always good in Rio and São Paulo, but
so bad in Arembepe? Only later did I realize that talking like
an Arembepeiro was as different from conversing in formal
Brazilian Portuguese as the speech of a Liverpudlian worker
is from BBC English. Cut off from foreigners, outsiders, and
even from the national speech patterns that can now be
heard each day on radio and television, traditional Arembepeiros were as much linguistic chauvinists as any similarly
isolated people. To speak was to talk like an Arembepeiro;
anything else smacked of parrot talk.

When Alberto, informed of my return, rushed to Claudia's

Restaurant to welcome me in August 1980, his enthusiastic but tactless greeting was, "Oh, my *papagaio*'s come back." Toward the end of my stay, however, he commented that I used to be a *papagaio*, but now I spoke "more or less right." This new evaluation may have been based on an actual improvement in my speech. More likely, it reflected Alberto's (and Arembepe's) growing familiarity with alien speech patterns.

Consider a final illustration of the stigma attached to alien speech in traditional Arembepe. Incorporated in contemporary village lore is the story of a woman who, in 1964, refused to give us full information when we were attempting to complete our interview schedule with all 159 households. Villagers insist that her daughter, born soon after our departure, never learned to speak like a native Arembepeiro. With speech that was "all mixed up," the girl talked just like the foreigners to whom her mother had been inhospitable. The girl's plight was somehow her mother's punishment. The moral of the story seems to be that in traditional Arembepe, *papagaios*, even though less than human, should still have been treated courteously.

Despite the view of hippies as robbers, *papagaios*, vagabonds, kinless, and in general incompletely human, many villagers simultaneously held a more positive image of the hippie life style. One woman, after lamenting that some village youth were mixing with hippies, went on to say that there were good hippies, too—people who worked making handicrafts, behaved with decorum, spoke respectfully, and minded their own business. In contrast to the unreliable transients, these were mostly the hippies who had become locals. If they were not fully part of the village social system, at least they did not mock its values.

Nature and Culture in the Hippie Aldeia

The hippie Aldeia has grown up near the Caratingi River, a fifteen-minute walk north of Arembepe. One makes the trip along the beach or inland, wading through the lagoon. In summer the lagoon dries up, making it possible to get there by car. Accompanied by Alberto and the entire 1980 field

The southern part of the hippie Aldeia, a beautiful site that has attracted young people from all over the world. (Courtesy Jerald T. Milanich)

team, I visited the Aldeia for the first time on a Friday afternoon. Alberto was surprised to find so few people there. His estimate that the settlement had once contained 200 people corresponded with that of the head municipal statistician in Camaçari.

The Aldeia had three separate sections. The southern area, the settlement's core, had about ten fairly substantial wattle-and-daub huts with palm-frond roofs. Just north of this area was a coconut grove with several flimsy lean-tos made entirely of palm fronds. A bit further north was the river, where there were two pup tents.

Two hippie couples and João, a twenty-one-year-old man who normally lived alone, resided in the southern area. All made their living from handicrafts, but one man also painted. Three of these people had gone into Salvador that day, one for medical attention, and the other two to sell their wares to agents of the city's thriving tourist industry. Two native men—a pair of brothers, one single, the other married—also lived here, along with a native Arembepe woman who washed, sewed, and occasionally cooked for the hippies.

Considered a bit deranged by Arembepeiros and hippies alike, she habitually prayed to ocean and woods, and occasionally made an appearance in Arembepe proper, where she drank too much *cachaça* and sometimes removed her clothing in public. A would-be entrepreneur from Salvador had recently opened a bar where he sold rum. Using a team of animals, he had just brought the Aldeia its first refrigerator, powered by bottled gas. He planned to sell cold beer to tourists on weekends. This would supplement his earnings from the butcher shop he ran in Arembepe on Fridays.

The next part of the Aldeia was a poor person's version of a European youth hostel. No rent was paid for the palm-frond hovels, which barely provided shelter from sun and rain. Lacking owners, the lean-tos were kept up in a desultory fashion by a stream of temporary occupants. This was a transient area, where, we had been told by an Arembepe hippie, we could find American, English, German, Italian, and Danish hippies. It turned out to be the hangout of the "low-life" hippies that villagers had vilified, the place where the Portuguese transient, said to be rich, was robbed of traveler's checks. All the people I talked to here were scantily attired;

A hippie resident of the Aldeia in 1980. (Courtesy Jerald T. Milanich)

marijuana smoke (which Alberto had never smelled and did not recognize) wafted through the walls of one hut.

A bit further north was the Caratingi River, on the banks of which two tents had been set up. One belonged to a young man from Salvador, out for weekend camping. Standing in front of the other was a slight young man in a jump suit. After his rituallike reference to the Jagger-Joplin myth, I learned that this Paulista (person from São Paulo) had come to Arembepe to vacation and to *lose weight*. His daily routine was to walk north to the mouth of the Jacuipe River, a three-hour roundtrip. He reported that his weight had fallen from 90 to 65 kilograms. Two Amazon-sized women, his camping companions, then arrived. Now I understood why he needed to diet, since the pup tent looked hardly big enough for one. One of the women sat down and leafed through a "girlie" magazine that contained photos of women with bare breasts the size of her own. The other went into the tent and began giving orders to the man.

Disregarding the idiosyncrasies of individual personalities, these people, whom Arembepeiros would classify as hippies, are perhaps more appropriately called campers. Participating in an international culture pattern, they travel to the warmer beaches of northern Brazil for the winter, just as young Americans make springtime visits to Florida. Although I had difficulty determining the socioeconomic background of the hippies and young transients, Arembepeiros asserted that it takes money to be a hippie. Villagers believed that many hippies were rich, which made it particularly hard for Arembepeiros to understand why hippies lived the way they did, eschewing the consumer goods that Arembepeiros had done without until recently, and now found tantalizing.

It does take a certain amount of money to adopt the hippie life style. Although he spent most of the year in the Aldeia, twenty-one-year-old João used the cash he made from making and selling mobiles and curtains to travel to other hippie beach settlements—from Belem, at the mouth of the Amazon, to the extreme Brazilian south, a distance of more than 3,000 kilometers. João had last encountered one of his friends—another young man from São Paulo, who was spending a few days in the Aldeia in 1980 as companion to the Portuguese robbery victim—in a beach settlement in southern Bahia. This young Paulista knew something about anthropology and told me that he had taken part in an archaeology dig in Mato Grosso (west-central Brazil)—information suggesting upper-middle-class status.

There was no doubt of the privileged background of the young woman who was temporarily living in João's house. This *ippa* claimed to have been born in Egypt of Jewish parents, to have moved to Brazil when she was five, to have attended French schools in Rio de Janeiro, and to have lived in an Israeli kibbutz as a teen-ager. In addition to the fluent Portuguese and English she spoke with us, she claimed to speak French with her parents and also to know Hebrew and Italian. The reason she spoke so many languages and traveled so much, she told anthropologist Maxine Margolis, is because she was Jewish. To the amusement of Maxine—who is Jewish, speaks several languages, and travels a lot—the *ippa* explained that "all Jews speak many languages and like to travel." (There are fewer Jews in Brazil than in the United States, and our informant felt that we needed to be enlightened about Jewish characteristics.)

The young woman told of how she had given up the professional career she had begun in Rio after receiving her university degree, in order to live a "purer life" away from the city. This was her second visit to Arembepe. Because she believed that world civilization would be destroyed by a nuclear war in three years, her goal was to find a place safe from radiation where she could live on a communal farm. She realized that the Aldeia was unsuitable for farming but planned eventually to settle in the interior, near the city of Goiania, as Doomsday approached.

Along with her rejection of urban life and her search for purity and a communal life style, her dietary preferences helped her to fit into hippie subculture. Like those of João and many other hippies, her meals were usually vegetarian. She and João shopped in urban supermarkets because macrobiotic foods were available there and because prices were cheaper there than in Arembepe. She was concerned about her health, boiling all her water (which she drank in tea) and wearing shoes as a precaution against foot borers (abundant in rural Brazil). Less characteristic of other Arembepe hippies than her vegetarianism was her belief in spiritualist religion, increasingly popular among Brazil's urban elites (see Brown, 1979).

This *ippa*'s interaction with Alberto reveals her ignorance of the local social system and shows that she retained certain prejudices from the urban south. As we were leaving the Aldeia at sundown, I was surprised to discover that the unusual sight 50 meters to the west, which I had initially interpreted as a whitewashed coconut tree stump, was actually a prostrate woman dressed in white. It was Olga, the hippies' washerwoman, praying—apparently to the woods or the setting sun, as we had been told was her practice. When Alberto and I asked João's *ippa* guest what Olga was doing, she offered enlightenment by informing us that it was Friday.

"Friday," said Alberto. "What's so special about Friday?"

"What," replied the *ippa*. "You, a black man from Bahia, don't know that Friday is the day of Oxala?" (Oxala is a deity in *candomblé*.)

"No," huffed Alberto. "I have nothing to do with *candomblé*." (In fact, Alberto's wife has participated in *candomblé*, to which he, however, expresses adamant opposition.)

The *ippa* was stereotyping: because Alberto was a dark-skinned rural Bahian, he must, she thought, be a believer in *candomblé*. She did not realize that *candomblé*'s popularity, though growing, had traditionally been slight in Arembepe. She was also trying to demonstrate to Alberto that she was no spiritual ignoramus, that she was knowledgeable about his presumed religion. In addition to these false assumptions, the *ippa* had also used racial terminology in a way inappropriate to Arembepe. Residents of southern cities see race in terms of black, white, and *mulato*, with far fewer terms and distinctions than in Bahia generally and in traditional Arembepe specifically. Although Alberto's skin is darker than that of most villagers, he is usually classified as a *moreno escuro* ("dark brunet") or simply as *escuro* ("dark"), rather than as *preto* ("black").

Despite these cultural faux pas, João's *ippa* guest contrasted sharply with the transient hippies in the palm-frond shacks, all of whom had facial lesions, suggesting malnutrition. She was a decorous, educated, and apparently healthy transient. Because she and João shared certain goals that had

led them to a hippie life style, she can be seen as a more sophisticated version of João himself. A gentle, articulate, slow-
speaking young man, João did a good job of encapsulating
the ideology of Arembepe's hippies. A runaway from his own
parents in São Paulo, he had accompanied another family to
Arembepe in 1974, when he was just fourteen.

The key elements of hippie thought are apparent in his un-
favorable comparison of present and past Arembepe. João
was one of several hippies who told me that it had been better in Arembepe before the advent of electricity and the
boom in weekend tourism. "Things were more natural, simpler, more peaceful then." When I told him that I had begun
to study Arembepe in 1962, he seemed envious. "Were there
hippies here then?" he asked. When I replied that there
weren't, that I had been in Arembepe before all that, he concluded, with wonder in his drawl, "You were here, then,
when it was really natural."

João went on to lament the loss of the community spirit
that had once thrived in Arembepe and especially in the Aldeia. He recounted the origin myth, the stories of the House
of the Sun on the sand dunes near the river, of visits by Joplin and Roman Polanski, of the year that Mick Jagger had
spent traveling back and forth between England and Arembepe. At one time, João asserted, Arembepe had been the
drug capital of Brazil, with all kinds of drugs sold: cocaine,
marijuana, hashish, heroin, LSD, and other hallucinogens.
Now, however, drugs and rock stars had all but vanished,
and community spirit had failed. (However, archaeologist
Jerry Milanich's inspection of the garbage dump uncovered
evidence of large-scale consumption of cognac and *cachaça*.)
João remembered a few of the hippies that I had met in 1973,
but most were gone without a trace. He had little to do with
the transients who slept in the lean-tos and seemed a bit
wary of their presence. He had fished with the old fishermen
and loved their stories. He preferred the really old captains;
even Tomé, at age forty-seven, was too young for his taste.
The young fishermen knew too little lore.

In Arembepe, as João assessed it, community spirit and
generosity had been replaced by capitalism and self-interest.
Villagers were not as they had been when he arrived. For example, Aunt Dalia's husband, once a good friend and João's

landlord, had changed: "His best friend now is capitalism. He sits in front of his house and counts a roll of 500-cruzeiro [$10] bills."

João complained that although he had tried to do things for Arembepeiros, to be friendly with them, he had finally given up because they didn't appreciate his efforts. More than before, he maintained his distance.

His interaction with Alberto, whom he respectfully addressed as "Seu [Mr.] Alberto," is instructive about the clash of cultural values. When we arrived, João was making a curtain out of seashells and snail shells from the lagoon suspended on nylon fishing line. We had been told by a hippie in southern Arembepe that such a curtain, designed to be hung in a doorway or window, sold for the equivalent of $150. This seemed expensive in view of the meager labor invested. After collecting the shells, João had been working on the curtain no more than six hours and was almost finished. Two completed curtains were hanging nearby, one in a window, another inside his house.

Alberto scrutinized the curtain and asked João if he was going to paint the shells. João replied no, that natural was best. Alberto suggested that it would look better if the shells were red. He then pulled me a bit aside, but still within João's hearing, and remarked that this was the kind of thing (junk, he meant) that tourists buy. "Why don't you buy it," Alberto said to me, "to take back to the United States?"

Alberto also appraised João's living quarters. To my eyes, the house was clean and furnished in attractive, if modest, hippie style. Straw mats made of palm fronds covered the floor, and there were two sleeping hammocks. Alberto found the entire scene absurd. For decoration drawn from nature, João had brought in a dead bush, which lay (rather awkwardly) in his living room. "Is that tree alive?" queried Alberto. He gave me a knowing wink. Who but a crazy hippie would have a dead tree in his living room? João and Alberto also got into an argument about pollution, João citing the (obvious) pollution of the ocean, the yellow foam, which Alberto claimed (incorrectly) had always been there. Alberto played down the danger of Tibrás's sulfuric wastes; João saw Tibrás as part of the assault on paradise.

These interactions between young hippie and old villager

made me think of Claude Lévi-Strauss's (1967) discussions of the opposition between nature and culture, addressed in the myths of many societies. The French structural anthropologist has pointed out that people everywhere are concerned with the contrast between that which is natural and that which, manufactured by humans, is artificial, a cultural product. All their behavior showed that Alberto and João were engaged in a debate about the merits of culture versus nature, about economic development versus preservation of older lifeways. Alberto stood for culture—for lights, electricity, roads, cars, tourism, business—changes that had, he felt, made things better for him. João lamented the loss of the natural, the simple, the primitive. He maintained a romantic vision of a traditional Arembepe that he had never known, whereas Alberto was very sure that his own life style had improved. Some villagers shared Alberto's opinion. Several others, unexpectedly, given their fascination with novelty in 1973, agreed with João. Reasons for dissatisfaction with change will become more apparent in Chapter 8.

A Dimming Symbol

The hippies' era was ending in Arembepe, as it had throughout the world. The vestigial subculture survived in such people as João, the hippie artisans of Arembepe and the Aldeia. Having become permanent residents, they, like many other villagers, catered to the tourist trade, providing handicrafts and running bars. As we worked on the household survey in Street Down There, even Alberto, an observant man who is astute about social differences, was unable to say whether or not some recent arrivals who rented nearby were hippies. The distinction was becoming less salient. Villagers who knew them well asserted that hippies no longer liked to be called by that term; those who had settled in Arembepe preferred to be accepted as ordinary villagers. Furthermore, outsiders now had difficulty identifying hippies in Arembepe, since many kinds of people milled around the village each weekend.

The hippies were only a part, and today are just a small fraction, of the many outsiders who have taken up residence in Arembepe because of its beauty, seaside location, increasing accessibility, and tourist economy. Yet the hippies have a decided symbolic importance, because their arrival separates two eras in Arembepe's history. They provide a reference point that sets traditional Arembepe off from the present. The media accounts published since 1970 have focused on the hippies, according them attention disproportionate to their numbers and importance in village life. Even in 1980 a film crew doing location photography drove straight to one of the hippie bars in southern Arembepe. For urban Brazilians, the image of the hippie still holds more fascination than that of a rural worker or a weekend picnicker in a honky-tonk town. As one municipal official told me, the Aldeia's rock concerts, drug traffic, and nudity created a furor when reported in newspapers and on television. With pollution and hippies to catch the media eye, no wonder traditional Arembepeiros have been ignored.

Yet many other changes, although less sensational, have affected Arembepe. The following chapters explore the more profound alterations, undetected by the media, including a major transformation in the fishing industry that is part of an overall change in the pattern of village economic and social life.

8 If You Don't Fish, You Work for Tibrás

The hallmark of recent Brazilian economic development, according to Sylvia Hewlett (1980), has been the coexistence of great and growing wealth with deepening poverty. Although real income has increased throughout most segments of the Brazilian population, the rich have benefited much more than the poor. The rich include the upper and middle classes, and they constitute 30 percent of the population in the industrial south but only 20 percent in Bahia and throughout the northeast. In 1976, the top 1 percent of the Brazilian population appropriated a larger share of total national income than the bottom 50 percent; and it is estimated that by the end of the 1970s, the incomes of almost one-third of all Brazilians stood below the minimum needed for family subsistence (Hewlett, 1980). In the Arembepe of 1980, local manifestations of growing wealth disparities and increasing relative poverty were visible to the naked eye. Social classes had formed in a once classless community; the poorest were actually getting poorer, and the rich dramatically richer. Nowhere were the changes more obvious than in the fishing industry, where in real terms fishermen were receiving fewer fish per day's labor[1] than they had during the 1960s, while boat owners were drawing ten times their previous profits.

The Arembepe of 1980 was firmly entrenched in a world political economy, partaking through the mass media and direct contact with outsiders in a planet-wide process of cultural amalgamation. Mules and donkeys had become rarer sights than automobiles. Television antennas bedecked even modest homes, conducting transoceanic messages. Soon, we were told, the international telephone system would reach out and touch Arembepe. These developments mirrored what was happening throughout the country: nationally, the percentage of households with television sets had increased from 7 percent to 51 percent between 1964 and 1979 (*The Economist,* 1979), and almost all Brazilian families now had at least one radio. Brazil had become the world's fifth-largest user of communications satellites, used both for phones and for television transmissions. Through "the magic of electricity" Arembepeiros enjoyed the advantages of irons, water pumps, refrigerators, and freezers. Villagers were licking their chops at the inventory of consumer goods offered by "the civilized world." Future archaeologists excavating the Arembepe of 1980 would surely uncover a thousand different products designed and marketed by corporations based 10,000 miles away.

The paved highway had been the most significant factor in ending Arembepe's isolation. Originally planned by an ambitious landlord in order to increase tourism and enhance land values, the road's early completion, which coincided with the international hippie diaspora of 1969–1971, was the achievement of Tibrás, the multinationally owned chemical factory. A flood of ordinary tourists from Bahia joined the hippies and, in fact, contributed much more to rising property and rental values. The end of isolation transformed Arembepe's entire economy, bringing occupational plurality while also changing the nature and role of the fishing industry. Direct sale to tourists in Arembepe itself and easier access to external wholesalers permitted ambitious Arembepeiros to replace outsiders in fish marketing.

Profits were plowed back into more costly fishing technology, including larger and much more expensive boats. As the value of property increased, so did the owners' share of fishing production, exacerbating wealth differentials to the point where traditional leveling mechanisms became ineffective. Social relations within the fishing industry grew decreasingly social, more purely economic, as owners became bosses rather than co-workers. Given their long-established ideology of equality, Arembepeiros resented these changes, and many stopped fishing; but a swell of immigrants helped fill the void.

By encouraging occupational plurality, differential rewards from fishing, and immigration, the new economy produced new social cleavages. As the economy became more complex, so did Arembepe's social structure. Once relatively united through shared poverty and isolation, Arembepeiros were now divided on the basis of social class, occupation, neighborhood, provenience, and religious participation. Furthermore, previously absent forms of social deviance appeared and flourished. This chapter considers the most significant economic changes. Their social consequences are examined in Chapters 9 and 10.

Some of the reasons for Arembepe's increasing occupational diversity have already been mentioned. Tourism, for example, had created new jobs in construction, food preparation, lodging, and sales. Appendix 2 compares primary male employment in 1964, 1973, and 1980—showing, for example, that just 40 percent of Arembepe's employed men fished in 1980, versus 74 percent in 1964. Competing for second place in 1980 were construction (16 percent), business (14 percent), and factory employment (17 percent). Forty Arembepeiros worked for Tibrás. Just a handful were fishermen who had shifted occupations; most were young men, better educated than the past generation, who were working for the first time. With wages ranging from the equivalent of just over $100 to just under $500 per month, their compensation dramatically exceeded the earnings of an ordinary fisherman in 1980. Furthermore, factory work had more fringe benefits and pay was regular—not the fisherman's fluctuating and uncertain income.

However, it was not just increased opportunity on land that was drawing Arembepeiros away from fishing. There had been striking alterations in the fishing industry itself, most notably a change in the relations of production. Reversing the longtime pattern whereby enterprising fishermen had been gaining increasing access to the means of production, which had prevailed from my first visit through 1973, the gap between boat owners and ordinary fishermen had widened enormously. To be sure, the cost of purchasing, outfitting, and provisioning a fishing boat had risen, but the owner's profit had grown disproportionately. In 1965 the captain-owner had drawn 230 percent of the earnings of the ordinary fisherman for a day's fishing; by 1973 his share had increased to 300 percent. By 1980, however, the figure was 800 percent; a captain-owner now received 75 percent of his boat's total catch. Understanding of how this dramatic break with Arembepe's traditional egalitarianism came about requires discussion of major changes in the fishing pattern. We shall see that villagers were simultaneously being enticed away from fishing by better land-based opportunities, and being driven away from it by changes in the pattern of production and marketing.

Larger Boats and Long-Distance Fishing

One obvious contrast with the past was that fleet size had contracted and boat size had increased. Only nineteen boats were fishing in 1980 (versus twenty-six in 1973 and thirty-one in 1965). Two other boats were working for Tibrás, their captains and crews helping to lay pipes that would carry the factory's industrial wastes farther out to sea. Four other vessels were being repaired, while Tomé, the owner of the remaining two, could not afford to have his motors repaired and was fishing as an ordinary fisherman with his sister's husband.

Only one of the old-style open sailboats still fished in 1980, but even it had a small motor. All the rest were classified as *barcos* rather than *saveiros*—the term that for decades had been one of the most common words in daily discourse. Although most of the new boats were much larger than the old ones, with bigger motors and on-board ice chests, the main difference was the enclosed cabin, which theoretically slept three people, actually under very cramped conditions.

Most of the boats in the 1980 fleet had been purchased since 1973. With the cost of just a new motor at more than U.S. $2,500 in August 1980, a fully equipped boat cost a minimum of $5,000. Dinho, Tomé's younger brother, who now owned five boats, had just purchased a large one new for about $10,000—a figure far in excess of anything any Arembepeiro could have afforded during the 1960s. Owning three boats or more, four villagers, including Dinho, were millionaires, in cruzeiros. Even Tomé, with two inactive boats and two houses, owned property worth more than 2 million cruzeiros ($35,000)—testimony to the current value of motorboats and real estate, both critically important as means of production in Arembepe's new economy.

Elements of the experimentation with new fishing strategies that had been obvious between 1965 and 1973 could still be detected in 1980, but the fishing pattern was more set than in 1973. With the end of lobstering, trammel net use had diminished and only a few villagers still owned nets. One of just a handful of old-time fishermen who could still afford to experiment, Dinho had bought a shark net, designed to take advantage of the recent arrival of "red sharks" in the area. Found in other offshore Bahian waters, the sharks, whose meat villagers could purchase for about half the cost of regular fish, reportedly congregated in the area where the Tibrás residues flowed into the Atlantic.

The practice of using gas lamps for nighttime fishing, just started in 1973, continued but had been incorporated into the more general pattern of long-distance fishing or "ice fishing." Initiated by Tomé in 1973, when he purchased Arembepe's first large motorboat with enclosed cabin, the "ice fishing" pattern was one of expeditions to offshore banks located eight to ten hours to the north of Arembepe. Boats left on Tuesday or Wednesday, after loads of ice were delivered by truck from Salvador. During the three or four days they were gone, most fishing took place at night, using bottled gas–fueled lamps. As fish were caught, they were stored in the boat's ice chest, and when the boat returned to Arembepe, they were transferred to the owner's refrigerator, freezer, or ice vault, where they remained until sold locally or to wholesalers from Itapoan—now barely a twenty-minute ride away. Most of the fleet was back in the harbor by Saturday evening, ready for Sunday socializing and a Monday of resting and taking care of obligations on land.

By 1980, crews had plumbed bottoms and marked spots in the waters offshore from the villages of Sauipe and Subaúma. These were also traditional fishing communities, but because neither had the necessary harbor for sailboat or motorboat protection, raft fishing with small crews was the custom. As Arembepe's fishing territory incorporated these northern waters, their fishermen, particularly those from Sauipe, were migrating to Arembepe, where by 1980 they supplied a significant proportion of Arembepe's fishing personnel. Like customary fishing in Arembepe's own waters, most fishing in 1980 was still done over the continental slope, less than fifteen kilometers offshore from northern Bahia, just as with Arembepe itself.

Although most boats did long-distance fishing in 1980, two captain-owners still preferred the traditional daytime fishing pattern. One was Fernando, the captain-owner whose excessive drinking, intense fear of outsiders, rumored *candomblé* participation, and habit of carrying a gun were mentioned in Chapter 6. By 1980 Fernando seemed to have come to terms with the insecurities that had plagued him in 1973 and was content to pursue a relaxed style of fishing, leaving at eight-thirty in the morning and returning around five in the afternoon. Motorization permitted him to reach the traditional banks on the continental slope in just one and a half hours, compared to between four and six hours in the 1960s. But often he fished even closer to shore, where he caught smaller fish that could be used by the ice fishermen as bait for the larger species they sought over the slope. The catches of Fernando and the two ordinary fishermen who accompanied him provided their food and a small amount of cash, but their annual catch was estimated to be no more than half that of the "ice fishing" boats. Alberto called Fernando's fishing style *besteira* ("silly"), even though it was based on a decades-old pattern. The new fishing style was considered (and was) much more productive, more than doubling the average annual catch of a vessel in the 1960s.

Another option was overnight fishing close to Arembepe. For example, one of the boats that had been hired by Tibrás for pipe laying did overnight gaslight fishing when it was not being used by the factory. In times of rough weather, many captains stuck closer to home, fishing overnight rather than making the long trip north. The new pattern had relieved pressure on local banks, perhaps allowing eventual recuperation of fish supplies in the Arembepe area. Note that in 1980 only two crews fished regularly in banks that had once sustained the families of more than 100 fishermen, providing more than 100,000 kilograms of fish annually.

Motorization and the Cooperative

Even more striking than the change in fishing pattern, to one familiar with Arembepe's history of egalitarian social relations, were changes in the allocation of fishing profits and in the relations of production. As noted in Chapter 6, government loans, administered by the local fishermen's cooperative, had facilitated the rapid motorization of Arembepe's fleet, permitting industrious fishermen (captain-owners who already owned boats) to add expensive motors. Also discussed in Chapter 6 was a pattern whereby the most successful fishermen were rapidly paying off their debts, and then withdrawing from the cooperative so as to be able to market their own fish. Tomé had made such a move and was sending his fish to be sold in Itapoan; his next younger brother, Dinho, was about to do the same thing.

In 1973 it had been my impression that the cooperative's days were numbered, since the price it offered for fish was lagging, and since Arembepe's traditional entrepreneurial pattern had always been one of pursuing individual self-interest. Because there had never been much community spirit, cooperatives could not succeed in Arembepe if their goal was presented as community welfare. Success could come only if individuals believed that they were being personally benefited. Thus villagers had been perfectly willing to avail themselves of loans in order to increase their productivity and have access to the cooperative's ice, bait, gasoline, oil, and fishing supplies. However, once more profitable options became available, members felt no compelling loyalty to stick with the cooperative.

The predicted failure of the fishermen's cooperative came soon after my 1973 departure. Seeing that Tomé and Dinho had abandoned their agreed-on support in order to seek individual advantage, all the successful captain-owners eventually withdrew from the cooperative and sought alternative marketing arrangements. Some bitterness was generated by the collapse. For example, Fernando, who remained a member to the last, complained that Salvador-based government employees had robbed the fishermen, but most villagers disputed this story, citing general withdrawal as the reason for failure.[2]

Marketing

Since the mid-1960s Tomé had been Arembepe's most innovative fisherman. The first villager to own his own *saveiro*, to buy an enclosed boat, to do "ice fishing," and to use a seafloor map to locate new fishing zones, Tomé also started a new marketing pattern. Unfortunately, for reasons spelled out in Chapter 11, it was not Tomé but his brother Dinho— an equally enterprising if opportunistic follower—who reaped the benefits. Beginning in late 1973, rather than selling either to the cooperative or to local land-based entrepreneurs, Dinho arranged to have his catches transported to Itapoan, where a fish store offered a more profitable deal. Like Tomé, whose game plan he was following, Dinho reinvested his profits in a second fishing vessel, this one a large *barco*, like Tomé's.

But unlike Tomé, Dinho used this new source of income as a means of retiring from fishing, which he had always done reluctantly, both in Rio de Janeiro and in Arembepe. In contrast to Tomé, who spent four days a week fishing many miles north of Arembepe, Dinho could now devote full time to fish marketing. Dinho joined two other nonfishing entrepreneurs who by this time had also bought boats with enclosed cabins and hired captains to pilot them to the new, distant fishing banks.

However, in contrast to one of these land-based businessmen, who still farmed and marketed coconuts, and to the other, who ran a store and restaurant, rented small houses and rooms, and also farmed, Dinho devoted his full attention to fish production and marketing. By 1980 he had become Arembepe's most successful fish marketer and its richest inhabitant. Owner of five boats, Dinho had paid the equivalent of $10,000 for the largest and most recently purchased one. The first floor of his opulent two-story house (the second story was the village's newest status symbol) was his fish store, with Arembepe's only ice vault, plus freezers and refrigerators (other fish merchants had just the last two appliances). In addition to owning five boats, Dinho bought fish from other boats. He arranged for the transport to Itapoan of fish that were not sold locally.

Other Arembepeiros maintained a similar relationship

with a second Itapoan fish store. No longer was Arembepe visited by agents from Salvador, since marketing opportunities were ample in nearby Itapoan and in Arembepe itself. Representatives of two other Itapoan retailers also came on Fridays and Saturdays, when the fleet returned, hoping to arrange to purchase some fish for their establishments. Another agent drove in from the county seat. A recent immigrant who had built a house in Volta do Robalo rented his pickup truck to Dinho and other local merchants to transport surplus fish to Itapoan when the fish stores sent no agents. The same man also made money using his truck to take Arembepeiros to Camaçari, where many now picked up monthly pensions.

Across the street from Dinho's house, in the shack just above the harbor where the cooperative had formerly been housed, was another fish store, this one jointly run by a captain-owner and two nonfishing owners. The shack contained three large freezers, where the catches of five boats could be stored. Like Dinho's fish store, this one had several scales, checked regularly for accuracy by municipal offi-

As part of the new marketing system, trucks transport fish to Itapoan. Other fish is sold in the local fish store, shown here to the extreme left. Also note the 1980 fleet in the new harbor. (Courtesy Jerald T. Milanich)

cials—another illustration of the increasing penetration of village life by the nation-state, a prominent aspect of changing Arembepe that is examined more closely in Chapter 9. Fish were still unloaded in the old harbor, prior to the boat's anchoring in the new, deeper harbor, which lies farther south. But in contrast to the past, when fish had been deposited on the beach and divided up among fishermen and owner, they were now carried directly to one of the fish stores, where they were laid out on the cement floor. Another difference from the past; half (by weight) of each fisherman's catch was now turned over to the owner. Gone, along with the joint line system of pooling the small fish, was the fiction of "the boat's fifth." In 1980 the owner's share was more accurately called "the boat's half."

A Double Profit

As Alberto explained, the owner now made a double profit. "First, he gets half of each ordinary fisherman's catch. The captain gets to keep his entire personal catch—twice, therefore, the ordinary crew member's share. But even here the owner profits, since the captain, like the ordinary fishermen, has to sell his fish to the owner for 70 cruzeiros [$1.17 at 60 cruzeiros per dollar]. The owner always sells the fish for much more than he pays the fishermen. Sometimes he finds local buyers for the fish, at 120 cruzeiros per kilogram; sometimes he has to sell some to one of the Itapoan fish stores for just 100 cruzeiros." Assuming half local sales and half exports, the owner's average resale profit (at 110 cruzeiros per kilogram) was 40 cruzeiros.

Illustrating this differential allocation of the rewards of fishing is division of the catch of a boat that returned one Saturday in August 1980 after four days of fishing near Sauipe with a five-man crew. The owner also acted as captain. Weighed in his fish store, the total catch was almost exactly 200 kilograms. Each fisherman saw his catch, now always identified with his "mark," weighed separately. The weighing was done in the fish store by a salaried employee who also recorded the weight in a notebook. Each fisherman would eventually be reimbursed for half his catch, at 70 cruzeiros per kilogram, after loans had been subtracted. (Fishermen often asked boat owners for advances against the week's work, money for their wives to buy food during their absence.) Assume, to illustrate simply, that all five fishermen, including the captain-owner, had each caught 40 kilograms. Each ordinary crew member would receive only 1,400 cruzeiros (less than $25) for nearly 100 hours of grueling work on the open sea. The captain-owner would add the 80 kilograms turned over by his crew to his own 40 kilograms. Sold for an average price of 110 cruzeiros per kilogram, these 120 kilograms would bring the captain-owner 13,200 cruzeiros. Add to this 3,200 cruzeiros—the owner's profit between paying fishermen 70 cruzeiros and selling their fish for 110 cruzeiros—and the captain-owner's receipts amounted to 16,400 cruzeiros. Once owner's expenses (4,000–6,000 cruzeiros per trip for diesel, bait, ice, food, and drinking water) were deducted, the profit was 11,000–12,000 cruzeiros, or about $200, eight times the earnings of the ordinary fisherman. That means $10,400 versus $1,300 annually.

On the basis of various measures of Arembepe's fishing productivity,[3] actual annual earnings were only about 85 percent of these figures ($9,000 and $1,100 respectively). Depreciation of the boat and the owner's much greater risk (none of the boats was insured) have not been taken into account; nor has the fishermen's "subsistence share": crew members were allowed to keep between 3 and 5 kilograms of the fish they caught before beginning to share equally with the owner. Still, Dinho and other owners of two or more boats were making incomes far in excess of those of ordinary fishermen. And it is no wonder that Dinho could afford to pay $10,000, one year's profits from one boat, to buy another boat in July 1980.

By 1980 the hope of making enough money to purchase his own boat—a realistic aspiration for an enterprising fisherman in the 1960s—had become an impossible dream. A *barco* cost between five and ten times the ordinary fisherman's annual income. Just to repair a boat in July 1980 cost one nonfishing owner over $300—more than an ordinary fisherman made in three months.

Intelligent and successful entrepreneurs had always existed within Arembepe's population. A particular group of men, however, just happened to make their fortunes at the right time, when the amount of wealth entering Arembepe was greater than ever before, when entrepreneurial efforts could be parlayed into permanent assets. In the once-egalitarian community, as the volume of wealth had grown and as the traditional leveling mechanisms had become less and less effective, separate socioeconomic strata had appeared, and people were very much aware of their existence. And because of property and class, the Protestant ethic could no longer ensure a fisherman's success.

The Genesis of Stratification: Capital and Land Time

The roster of successful Arembepeiros did not change much between 1965 and 1980. Tomé had been replaced by his brother Dinho, and some new fortunes were being made in tourist-oriented businesses. Still, the surest predictor of success in 1980 was success in 1973, and even as far back as 1965. Most of Arembepe's 1980 boat owners had owned vessels for more than a decade. The conversion of a ranked hierarchy into a stratified hierarchy happened like this: People who had worked hard and innovated intelligently during the 1960s had acquired productive property. They were therefore good risks for loans during the early 1970s and were able to motorize their boats. Motorboats cost much more than sailboats, and reflecting greater purchase price and operating costs, owners demanded a larger share of fishing profits to compensate for their greater investment. The differential between boat cost and fisherman's earnings never stopped growing.

As capital (initial wealth) had been a factor in continued success, the new fishing pattern accentuated the value of a new input—time—to devote to a plethora of new land-based concerns. Undoubtedly Dinho's decision to retire from fishing in order to work full-time on the land side of the fishing business was critical in his success, for several reasons. First, the new pattern demanded that all fishermen, including the captain-owner, spend three to four days at sea. This left just one workday, Monday, to attend to essential land-based concerns of the fishing business. And one day was not enough.

By 1980, Arembepe's fishing industry had relinquished the

autonomy that wind power, locally manufactured supplies, seasonal adjustments in fishing strategy, low consumer demands, and production for immediate consumption had formerly permitted. Like a thousand other formerly isolated communities, Arembepe's life style was converging with our own, as villagers gave up more and more of their self-sufficiency. The whole fishing operation now depended on external supplies. For example, each fishing expedition required thirty sacks of ice, at a total cost of $35. Crews had to await ice trucks from Salvador, which often arrived behind schedule, forcing delays in fishing. Much of the bait used in 1980 was shrimp from faraway São Paulo. Since villagers no longer relied on casting for schools of tiny bait fish in the harbor, most of the local casting experts and netmakers had let their skills lapse, and no youngsters had replaced them.

Refrigeration is essential to the preservation of fish and bait. Vulnerability to power failures and to breakdown of refrigerators and freezers illustrates another aspect of Arembepeiros' current dependence. Motors need to be oiled and fueled. A malfunctioning motor could cause a tragedy. Two local men did simple repairs, but both held other jobs and were frequently not available. Often, mechanics had to be sought in the city and persuaded to come to Arembepe.

Shopping around for a new boat or a new motor might also require several trips to Salvador. Borrowing money from banks or through government programs was also a time-consuming process. If one wished to market his own fish, he had to supervise weighing, keep records, occasionally arrange transport to Itapoan, and maintain relations with the fish stores there. A hundred other minor matters occupied a boat owner in 1980. Tomé complained that as owner and marketer for two boats and captain of one, he had never gotten enough rest.

The new pattern of uninterrupted long-distance fishing plus dependence on external inputs therefore posed almost impossible demands on the captain-owner. Realizing this, Dinho retired from fishing to devote his full attention to landside matters, and make a fortune in the process. Of the other three multiple boat owners, none fished. One had fished briefly in 1973, but quit when his wife's inheritance permitted him to buy two more boats. The other two had never been fishermen.

A few men, however, had found ways of combining the duties of captain with the owner's varied responsibilities. For example, two captain-owners did only daytime fishing. And one captain-owner who did long-distance fishing employed someone to weigh and sell his fish, keep records, and do the simpler jobs on land. When this owner had unavoidable business on land, he cut fishing to three days or fished for even shorter periods in nearby waters. Most captains could not change their fishing habits so easily, since their crew members depended on four days at sea and the better catches available in the northern waters. But this one had close kin connections with two crew members, his son and brother-in-law. He occasionally trusted them to take the boat out alone, or he told them and his third crewman, a nonrelative, to try to find another boat to fish in that week. This use of kinship was a successful strategy for retaining the roles of captain and owner of a single boat, and two others employed it.[4]

Thus as demands on land increased, time placed limits on the once-common dual role of captain-owner. Nor, in strictly economic terms, were the owner's efforts as captain particularly cost-effective. Assuming the same 200-kilogram catch previously used for calculation, the owner received just $47 less for employing a captain, cutting gross profits by 17 percent, and net profits by 25 percent per trip. However, the value of the dual role of captain-owner had never been simply economic but social as well. As was discussed in Chapter 4, owners who were also captains, who shared daily fellowship, inconvenience, fatigue, and dangers with ordinary fishermen, had traditionally commanded greater crew allegiance than nonfishing owners.

New Crews: Strangers and Debtors

The matter was not nearly so simple in 1980. For example, the special expertise of the captain was less valuable, since crews fished in strange waters and since almost all the fishing was now done over the continental slope, where there was little landmarking of the sort that was once believed to separate captains from ordinary crew members. Furthermore, the differential rewards of owner and crew had become much too obvious to mask behind the captain's "ordinary-fellow" behavior. Unless crew members were kin, resentment was inevitable. How could strain be absent when everyone was well aware that fishing owners received ten times the ordinary fisherman's share for the same day's work, and when even captains made twice as much?

Another change in the relations of production in fishing between the 1960s and 1980 was that ordinary fishermen no longer had set places in crews. Since the degree of loyalty of crew member to captain and owner had diminished, there was more shifting around. However, the extent of shifting reflected fishing strategy, with greatest crew fluctuation on short-term expeditions. For example, one fisherman arranged to fish overnight in another craft when his regular boat was hired out to Tibrás. I saw several crews assembled on the spot for daytime or overnight fishing.

In contrast, long-distance fishing had more stable crews. Both owners and fishermen counted on a four-day work week. These owners had to make larger investments in perishable ice, bait, and food, and therefore needed to ensure that fishing would take place. One way of maintaining crew loyalty was to make cash advances against the week's catch. Indebtedness had become a new technique used by owners to retain their crews, providing still another example of the ongoing and pervasive shift from social to economic relations of production. That is, in 1980 many men fished for someone not because he was a relative, friend, or *compadre*, but because they owed him money.

In the context of these changes, fishermen were fascinated by televised reports of a fishermen's strike in southern France, going on during my 1980 visit. Arembepeiros had grievances, too, fishermen told me. For example, the price of fish had not risen rapidly enough. Although sympathetic to the French actions, Arembepeiros could not understand how those fishermen could afford to stop working. "They must have some kind of insurance," surmised one villager, "in Arembepe there is no such thing."

Another grievance was living conditions during long-distance fishing. Arembepeiros who for years had done daytime fishing in sailboats found the new style unpleasant. "Grown men have to try to sleep in crowded quarters alongside a noisy motor. And the cabin holds only three men, so that the other one or two have to sit outside. And sometimes it's cold, especially when there's a wind." Fishermen also faced the danger of sudden storms in distant waters. Although owners did not directly share this threat, they did fear the loss of their investments.

At the end of August 1980, coinciding with the unusually high and low tides that accompany a full moon, Arembepe experienced an unseasonable storm, one of the worst I had ever seen there. Most of the boats had returned by the evening of August 29, but a few were still out. The churning waves brought Tibrás residues close to shore; the sea was yellow and strong, making entrance to the harbor very dangerous. "On a day like this," one fisherman said, "the cold at sea slaps you in the face."

"There are people out there," remarked Alberto, "thinking that they are going to die if their motor fails."

Alberto's nephew stood for hours on Alberto's porch, trying to sight his boat, which he had allowed an inexperienced captain to take out for the first time. The young man had just borrowed money from a bank in Salvador to finance a new motor. He had barely begun to make payments and now, lacking insurance, just like all Arembepeiros, he faced loss of his means of livelihood.

Alberto's nephew, whose boat soon arrived without mishap, was luckier than another owner, who got the news that two of his craft, not daring to risk returning to Arembepe, had anchored in Praia do Forte, 25 kilometers to the north. The owner's son drove him up in their automobile. The boats were undamaged when they arrived, but the owner made the mistake of tying them to one another in the harbor. That night the storm threw them together, causing damage that would lead to the loss of several days of fishing time. The two crews thought the owner silly to have tied the vessels together and had warned him against it, but he had never been a fisherman and made a mistake. His crew had feared to press their point, since he was a rich owner, and they were just ordinary fishermen.

From Fellowship to Exploitation

Thus within Arembepe's fishing industry the shift from social to purely economic relations, detectable in 1973, had proceeded rapidly. From beginning to end, fishing had become a business in which an owner—usually a nonfishing owner—expropriated more than half the labor product of the ordinary fisherman. No longer independent producers, ordinary fishermen had become employees. They resented captains and owners, and lacked trust in each other. In contrast to 1973, when a few crews had still used the joint line system, every fisherman now marked his catch individually. Each crew member had his distinctive mark, incising one side of the tail, both sides, the head, or the area below the throat once or twice. It was rumored that some fishermen stole from others by adding a second cut to the neck, or making an extra slash in the tail, if that was their mark. Concern with the individual share persisted on the land, as fish were weighed separately.

Division and weighing of the catch had moved inside, from public space (the beach) to private space (the shacks and fish stores owned by land-based entrepreneurs). With boats coming and going at different times, the daily public ritual of the 1960s had ended. No longer did the village assemble to greet the boats as they returned in the late afternoon and watch the fishermen pool their catches, deciding how much would be sold, how much kept for their families, and how much given away to destitute onlookers. The village poor still begged; but now they were often cursed for their behavior or ignored altogether, and they rarely received pieces of fish.

The 1980 pattern of social relations in fishing may not continue indefinitely. Given other opportunities to make a living, most Arembepeiros will not continue working for fellow villagers under conditions that contrast so sharply with tradition. In fact, the 1980 pattern was dependent on immigration and could not have developed in its absence. Furthermore, villagers' perception of the industry's reliance on fishermen from outside was even more obvious than the actual dependence. I was told again and again that most of Arembepe's 1980 fishermen were immigrants, people from the northern coastal village of Sauipe in particular. As noted, Sauipe lacks a good harbor and its only fishing vessels have been small rafts. As Arembepe's fishing expanded to include the continental slope offshore from Sauipe, the northerners began to move to Arembepe in order to catch more fish and make more money than before, riding Arembepeiros' boats to their own fishing grounds. More isolated from a city than Arembepe, Sauipe's traditional fishing economy had been less cash-oriented. Sauipeiros were willing to work for less than Arembepeiros, because their 1980 cash incomes still exceeded what they could make back home.

Stepped-up immigration and job seeking also reflect rapid national population growth. The population of Brazil, the Western Hemisphere's second most populous country, has an annual growth rate of almost 3 percent. It tripled between 1940 and 1977 and was about 130 million in 1980. Arembepe's own population had doubled between 1964 and 1980. Because of immigration and the new relations of production, the percentage of natives among Arembepe's fishermen had fallen from 79 percent in 1973 to 63 percent in 1980. The proportion of fishermen from Sauipe in 1980 (20 percent) was about equal to the percentage of all immigrants in 1973. Sauipe's representation among 1980 captains was even greater: 26 percent, versus 57 percent native Arembepeiros and 17 percent other immigrants. This reflects Arembepeiros' own reluctance to work as underpaid at-sea agents of the nonfishing owners they had grown up with. There was another reason to hire Sauipeiros as captains: they were familiar with the waters where Arembepe's boats now did most of their fishing. It was too early to tell whether these Sauipe immigrants would reside permanently in Arembepe or were simply working temporarily for cash, as Arembepeiros themselves had once done in Salvador, Ilheus, Rio de Janeiro, and other ports.

Where Are the Arembepeiros?

However, current relations of production in fishing can continue only as long as immigrants keep on arriving and accepting relatively low wages. One thing has not changed: boat owners cannot make profits from fishing unless they have a supply of fishermen, and Arembepeiros *are*, as any villager would agree, deserting fishing for other sources of income. The number of native Arembepe fishermen in 1980 (fifty-seven) had fallen to less than half the 1964 figure.[5]

Many villagers asserted that the trend was for fishermen to go to work for Tibrás, but statistics did not bear them out. Data on the 1980 occupations of the 105[6] fishermen who lived in Arembepe in 1973 are tabulated in Appendix 4. Only 8 of these had shifted to Tibrás jobs by 1980.[7]

To be sure, one aspect of Arembepe's overall economic transformation was that more native sons, although not more ex-fishermen, were doing factory work (17 percent in 1980 versus 11 percent in 1973 and 2 percent in 1964). Of the forty Arembepeiros employed by Tibrás in 1980, 80 percent were natives—a sharp contrast with fishing, where only 63 percent were native. Most of Arembepe's Tibrás workers were men younger than thirty, some of whom, of course, might have fished in the traditional economy. Many, however, would probably have entered professions other than fishing, either in Arembepe or outside. Today's Tibrás worker is less likely than today's fisherman to have a family background of fishing. Only 49 percent of the 1980 Tibrás workers had fathers who were or had been fishermen, whereas 80 percent of 1980 fishermen had fathers who were or had been fishermen.

The Basis of the New Order

The dramatic shift from social to economic relations within fishing can now be seen in a larger context that includes Arembepe's overall economic transformation, increased immigration, and growing heterogeneity. Gone with the wind was the socially cohesive kin-based crew of the 1960s. Only four 1980 crews had close kin ties, compared to over twenty in the 1960s. As native Arembepeiros worked in factories, construction, businesses, and tourism, covillagers who would in the past routinely have labored alongside one another in a fishing boat were now working separately in varied locales. Crews were relying more and more on recent immigrants, whose social links to Arembepe were weak. Nor did immigrants have much time to forge such links, since they spent four days each week at sea. In this context the immigrants remained strangers, emerging from their usual isolation only to take part in weekend drinking. The outsiders, in turn, resented other villagers, particularly the nonfishing natives who exploited their labor. An atmosphere of distrust pervaded social relations in crew and village alike.

Related to these changes, the Fishermen's Society had declined in importance. There were fewer meetings, and the candidates for president in 1980 were both nonfishermen. Boats no longer gave as units, but each fisherman was supposed to give 200 cruzeiros [less than $5] for the annual *festa* of Saint Francis in February. Villagers lamented that the festival had become an affair mainly for tourists. "The festa used to be the fishermen's thing. But now it's for outsiders. You can't imagine the people who come here in February for São Francisco. The cars park along the highway all the way to Volta do Robalo. If you get here on the eve of the festa you're trapped until it's over. The cars are so thick no one can get out." Storekeepers and other business people now played a larger role in the society and in organizing the festival. And of course they reaped far larger profits.

By 1980, along with boat owners' cupidity, the increased

Owner of multiple boats, the man with the purse inspects and helps unload the catch from a four-day fishing trip. (Courtesy Jerald T. Milanich)

costs of an industrial technology had bloated the owner's share of fishing profits from less than 25 percent to 75 percent of the catch. More productive fishing had also contributed to larger profits. The annual catch of the average boat had risen from 3,500 kilograms in 1965, to 5,500 kilograms in 1973, and 9,000 kilograms in 1980—amassed through long-distance fishing. In 1965, the cost of a fully equipped sailboat had equaled the retail sales proceeds from just 400 kilograms of fish. The motorized leviathan of the 1980s was worth 5,400 kilograms of fish. The most glaring contrast, however, was between the 1980 owner's share of the annual catch and the ordinary fisherman's: 6,750 kilograms for the owner and 500 kilograms for the fisherman, versus figures of 850 and 600, respectively, in 1965.

Arembepe's history between 1973 and 1980 had played out on a small scale a generalized and concurrent Brazilian development. By and large, those who were lucky enough to have been prosperous when the "economic miracle" began were its prime long-term beneficiaries. In Arembepe, as throughout the vast nation, the poorest, after just a few years of increasing real incomes, found themselves in many respects worse off than in 1968. Thus by 1980 Arembepe's ordinary fishermen were actually getting to sell fewer fish than in 1965,[8] whereas the owner's share had increased eightfold. No wonder Arembepeiros were leaving fishing to outsiders. And no wonder people who used to deny wealth differences now carried purses and called each other millionaires.

And things might get even worse—not just for Arembepe's poor but for its *nouveaux riches* as well—if chemical pollution continues threatening northern Bahian fish supplies. Fishermen asserted that Arembepe's old spots now had fewer fish than they used to and complained that the harvest of the horse-eyed bonito, which usually accounted for just over half of Arembepe's annual catch, had been below normal in 1980. Yet they contended that the more distant banks produced larger catches than Arembepe's traditional territory had; and an increase in annual fleet production from 108,000 kilograms in 1965 to 130,000 (average of SUDEPE figures for 1977–1979) bore them out. Fishermen did not agree about why the northern waters were more productive. Tomé thought that overfishing was becoming a problem all over and said that northern territory yields had been much better when he had started fishing near Sauipe around 1972.

Some fishermen blamed Tibrás for the decline in fishing productivity near Arembepe. In a heated argument with a skilled painter who worked for Tibrás, one captain-owner contended that Tibrás was destroying fishing in Arembepe. He had seen dead fish, and he knew that pollution had driven fish from their old homes. The Tibrás employee retorted by citing an observation made by other fishermen: that horse mackerels now congregated near the end of the Tibrás pipes, where they apparently feasted on the wastes. "Isn't mackerel fishing better than ever before?" he asked. Others told of the yellow (sulfur-covered) turtles and of the red sharks that seemed also to enjoy their seafood with sulfuric spicing.

However, the experts I talked to in Salvador had no doubt that Tibrás's pumping of sulfuric acid 2.5 kilometers out at sea, just 3 kilometers south of Arembepe, was affecting Atlantic waters to the north and to the south. The yellow foam that was so obvious in Arembepe's ocean could be detected several kilometers up the coast and may have been affecting yields as far away as Sauipe. One marine biologist attributed a series of recent sea gull deaths to Tibrás pollution and thought that effects of pollution would soon begin to show up in fish. Arembepeiros complained only about declining yields; they had not noticed physical deformities in the fish they caught.

The problem of ocean pollution seemed less immediate than the lagoon scandal of 1973, because the ocean is much vaster and destruction takes longer to show up. Still, many of Arembepe's tourists will eventually conclude that bathing there is insalubrious, and evidence for contamination of fish, and ultimately of the people who eat them, can be predicted. In the meantime Tibrás pollution has been a likely factor in the change in fishing pattern, even as the factory has also altered Arembepe's economy by providing good jobs for many of its better-educated young men. Much more than in 1973, when its attitude seemed to be "let the community be damned," the Tibrás of 1980 had worked hard to improve its image and was doing its best to maintain a generally positive reputation among villagers.

Factory Work at Tibrás

Providing relatively well-paying jobs for young men who had finished junior high school, the titanium dioxide factory, Tibrás, which stands 5 kilometers from Arembepe, employed forty Arembepeiros in 1980, 80 percent of them native sons. Next to fishing, factory work just exceeded business and construction as the second most common occupation of male villagers. Most of the Arembepeiros who worked for Tibrás held unskilled positions—doing kitchen work, gardening, sweeping, and cleaning. The factory's public relations chief told me that the business gave preference to locals (people from between Itapoan and the Jacuipe River) for such menial employment, while most of the skilled workers were bused in daily from Salvador. Of the 1,032 people working for Tibrás in 1980, about 20 percent (195) came from the local area.

The company official asserted that since 1974 he had been working with a German priest stationed in Abrantes, the district seat, which is almost as close to Tibrás as is Arembepe. The aim was to provide better educations for local children so that they might eventually fill higher-paying jobs. The Tibrás chief complained about the cost of transporting over 800 workers from the city, mentioning that eighteen busloads were brought in daily for the shift that began at 8:00 A.M. and ended at 4:00 P.M. One company plan for cutting gasoline and bus maintenance costs was to build, near Abrantes, a town with 400 well-constructed two- and three-bedroom houses. Workers' purchase of these dwellings would be financed by Tibrás, with monthly installments payable over fifteen years, the amount to be determined by salary level. The aim was to get skilled employees who lived in Salvador to move closer to the factory.

As previously noted, Tibrás began operation in 1970. South America's only titanium dioxide factory, its 1979 output was 22,000 metric tons. 1980 output was projected at 50,000 tons, 60 percent of national consumption, rising to 70,000 tons in 1984 or 1985. An increase in the work force to 1,300 was anticipated by 1985, creating an additional twenty-five to thirty jobs for Arembepeiros, assuming that skill levels remained the same or improved slightly.

The reputation of Tibrás had improved substantially since

1973, mainly because of the many services it provided for neighboring communities. As noted, the factory had worked with the recently installed peripatetic Roman Catholic priest to improve the school in Abrantes, base of his parish. Although educational opportunities had improved significantly in Arembepe itself, where there were now competently staffed elementary and junior high schools supported by state and municipal funds, certain subjects, physics, for example, were taught only in Abrantes. Twice weekly, Tibrás bused over 100 children from the Arembepe-Jacuipe region to study physics in Abrantes.

Tibrás provided several other services. Although Arembepe now had its own medical post, where a physician from Salvador spent two days a week, villagers preferred the medical care available at Tibrás. Two physicians worked at the factory each weekday morning, and one in the afternoon. Registered nurses covered the lighter shifts, from 4:00 P.M. to midnight and from midnight to 8:00 A.M. The Tibrás medical staff treated not just factory employees but any local resident. In theory the Tibrás doctors and nurses were consulted only under emergency conditions, but in fact people went there with routine maladies. In extreme emergencies, factory vans had carried physicians into nearby villages, and an ambulance was available to take people to hospitals in Salvador.

Phone service had not reached Arembepe by 1980 but was projected for the near future. In the meantime a token-operated phone stood at the corner of the highway and the turnoff to Tibrás; and when it was not working, phone calls to the city and even long-distance calls could be made (free of charge) in the factory. Still sensitive to the water-pollution issue, Tibrás maintained a faucet outside its gates where anyone could get purified water certified as drinkable by the state health department. The public relations officer I talked with explained that the lagoon problem had been solved by treating factory wastes and redirecting them out to sea. Pipes now extended 2.5 kilometers out to sea and had reached a depth of 30 meters. He downplayed the current marine pollution problem but told me of the company's plan to end the pollution potential "once and for all," by using tankers to carry wastes some 12–15 kilometers out to sea. The tankers would be loaded from a floating platform to be placed seaward of the factory. My informant did not mention the likely end to any remaining tourist appeal of the seaside subdivision just north of the projected loading area.

Publicity about its community services was a major component in the Tibrás campaign to improve its image. Factory tours were also available, and I found the public relations official I interviewed extremely cooperative. The factory itself was a world apart, its security maintained by armed guards. To enter, one had to leave a passport or identity card, and Arembepeiros warned me to wear long pants; shorts, the usual male dress in Arembepe, were not permitted. Once inside, I was impressed by the physical plant. Gardens made the inner courtyards attractive; workers could do their banking at a branch of the Banco Econômico here. I passed a lunchroom where a waiter in white shirt and bow tie was laying out slices of melon, fried fish, and abundant quantities of rice. Decorative plates, vases, and clean tablecloths contributed to the pleasant atmosphere. Next door was an activity room, where workers could play pool; some men were playing checkers at a table outside. No sulfur wastes or job hazards were allowed to intrude on this comfortable ambience; they belonged to another part of the plant. I was passing the area where workers could relax.

Arembepeiro Jaime, an old friend of the anthropological teams of the 1960s, a boy of eight when I first met him in 1964, was now a married man and a semi-skilled (grade 3) Tibrás worker. Jaime's mother had died when he was just two, and his father had remarried, leaving Jaime and his brother to be raised by an ancient great-aunt. Anthropologist Carl Withers, who led the Columbia University Brazil field team in 1963, had found Jaime charming and bright. Knowing that Jaime's chances of being educated were poor without outside support, Carl had sent money for many years to pay for Jaime's education in Salvador.

My 1980 trip gave me a chance to observe in Jaime's life style some of the results of Carl's support. Jaime had studied beyond junior high school and had obtained a grade 3 Tibrás position, for which he received more than $300 per month, which included double pay for overtime. Jaime had worked for Tibrás for five years. He had married in 1979 (legally and in a religious ceremony) and was father of a month-old boy.

Because of his good education, Jaime had never been a grade 1 worker. This category, in which most Arembepeiros were employed, included the unskilled custodial tasks mentioned previously. Still, even the grade 1 salary ($115–$150 per month) was twice the minimum wage. Grade 2, in which Jaime had begun, now paid $215 monthly. The highest positions (grade 4) paid a monthly salary of almost $500 to the most skilled factory workers. Some workers also received special pay for particularly hazardous work, and wage indexing provided between one and three inflation raises annually.

Jaime seemed neither pleased nor displeased with the nature of his work. Like Arembepe's forty other Tibrás workers, Jaime was bused to work each day in vans sent from the factory. He usually worked the daytime shift but sometimes chose to make double pay from night work. The benefits of Tibrás employment showed up in his life style. The good company lunches were obvious in his girth. His new brick house in Caraúnas (now a more respectable neighborhood than in 1973) had a refrigerator, black-and-white television, gas stove, and bathroom. His plumbing system awaited running water; his well would be finished soon. When I visited his house, his well-dressed wife was ironing with an electric iron on a real board—novelties never seen in Arembepe in the past, when women had ironed on tabletops, using charcoal-stuffed irons.

Jaime had become an investor and a consumer. He had bought some land and was looking for a car; he asked me costs of particular models. He knew that a used Volkswagen beetle could be had for about $1,500. He had bought his refrigerator for the equivalent of $250, and his television for half that. To be sure, Jaime earned less than owners of the most productive boats, but his work was less risky than fishing, and his salary was regular, with protection against inflation and such fringe benefits as good retirement, widow and child benefits, and disability insurance. Nor was Jaime's income reduced by tax. "No one in Arembepe pays income tax," he asserted. "No one makes enough money." (He was wrong about that but correct that no villager paid.) Although income tax was deducted from Jaime's wages, as with all Tibrás workers, he could file for reimbursement in Salvador, since his salary remained below the taxable level. Thinking that anyone could get their tax payments back in this way, he saw taxation as just a functionless bother.

Like other Arembepeiros, Jaime was much more knowledgeable about the external world than previously. He asked me about strikers in Poland and about the 1980 presidential elections in the United States. He had followed news of strikers in São Paulo but reported no union activity or strikable grievances at Tibrás, or in the Salvador area. Like a few other Arembepeiros, Jaime had moved into the upper working class. His life style contrasted sharply with that of most fishermen. Arembepeiros clearly saw Tibrás, as they had regarded the national oil company in the 1960s, as a step up.

This became apparent one Sunday afternoon when two villagers, a captain-owner and a skilled Tibrás employee, tried to engage me as a referee in a dispute about the relative value of Tibrás versus fishing as a profession.

"I'm proud to have a better job than my father," asserted Pedro, the Tibrás worker. "I wanted to be better-educated than my father, just as he wanted to have a better education than his father. Don't you want your children to do better than you?"

Valter, a captain-owner, provided the counterpoint: "You may be doing well at Tibrás, but it's bad for Arembepe. The fish are leaving, and they are dying."

Pedro argued that fishing would eventually end in Arembepe, that the new economy was better. His own grandfather, he said, had been a fisherman, but he would have been proud of Pedro for advancing himself. "Fishing is unskilled work; anyone can catch a fish."

Valter defended his own work. "Here's my card showing that I'm a professional fisherman. Do you have such a card?" he asked Pedro.

His will to defend the fishing profession heightened by several bottles of beer, Valter insisted on the value of his work. "I'll take you out in my boat tomorrow. Let's see if you catch anything. Let's shake on it."

They never shook, and Pedro, alas, seemed unconvinced, though he ended the discussion peacefully, contending that he had nothing against fishing—some of his best friends . . .

Thus Tibrás had influenced behavior, life styles, values, and opinions the Arembepe of 1980 in numerous ways. Villagers—and not simply those who were employed by the factory—relied on Tibrás for services and for jobs. Arembepeiros sold prepared foods to the workers who arrived each morning from Salvador; they got the business of Tibrás workers and officials in their bars and restaurants; and some hired out their boats and labor to lay pipes for Tibrás on the ocean floor.

Although Tibrás had restored the lagoon and been forgiven for the scandal, tourism and fishing, two major components of Arembepe's economy, remained vulnerable to the pollution hazard. So did the health of Arembepeiros and other Bahians—from rural inhabitants of tiny coastal settlements to clients of the most elegant seafood restaurants in Salvador, which were buying some of the fish caught offshore from Arembepe and neighboring communities.

In the long run, Arembepe's fate will be determined by Tibrás activities, and the future remains a mystery. In 1980, however, the nearby factory had filled the gap left when the national oil company stopped hiring Arembepeiros because they lacked secondary educations. Much more accessible, Tibrás worked to improve the education of locals so as to stock a cost-effective pool of labor close at hand. But listening to Jaime talk of television and Volkswagens, I wondered what Carl Withers, now dead, would think if he could see what his investment in Jaime's education had wrought—a contented, well-fed factory worker with an all-American appetite for consumer goods. Jaime's story is probably one of the happier chapters in the assault on paradise, but it does provide one more illustration of Arembepe's dependence on external forces and of the quickening erosion of cultural differences. Taxes, government forms, pensions, national wage indexing—all are aspects of the increasingly obvious presence of the state in the lives of Arembepeiros. The impact of contemporary Brazilian nationhood, particularly on Arembepe's public health and family life, is the subject of Chapter 9.

9 The Web of Government

One of the most noticeable contrasts between the 1960s and 1980 was Arembepeiros' increasing familiarity with external services and institutions. This reflected the nationwide improvements in transportation and communication, and increased government efforts to enhance health, education, and welfare. Because of their own and their municipality's easy access to nearby Salvador, Arembepeiros enjoyed early exposure to the new and expanded national programs of the 1970s. The role of government in villagers' lives had become far more prominent. National benefits were funneled through municipal seats; bus service now linked Arembepe and Camaçari, and a local man also sold villagers rides there in his pickup truck. One reason why more than a dozen Arembepeiros went regularly to the municipal seat was to collect monthly pension payments. Although glad to have these federally sponsored benefits, which just one villager had drawn in the 1960s, people complained about having to stand in line in Camaçari to receive their stipends, the amount of which varied from month to month, averaging about $40 for a retired fisherman.

Welfare and Education

The age at which eligibility began had just been reduced from sixty-five to sixty years. The availability of government pensions was one of the main reasons why many Arembepeiros (14 out of 105) retired from fishing between 1973 and 1980. During the 1960s, about 10 percent of Arembepe's fishermen had been over seventy, and 31 percent over sixty years old. Adjustment to the new fishing pattern would have been especially difficult for older men; the availability of pensions made it possible for them to opt for a more leisured life style.

Women also drew government stipends, some as fishermen's widows, others in their own right as retired businesswomen. More would do so in the future. For example, Alberto's wife, Carolina, and their two grown daughters, who worked in their parents' store, each made monthly payments equivalent to about $10 for their eventual social security and retirement benefits. Most of Arembepe's growing population of business people were doing the same thing. The even more ample benefits available through factory employment have already been mentioned.

Arembepeiros made the trip to Camaçari for several other reasons. The town had grown enormously since my last visit there during the 1960s. New employment opportunities had fueled this growth. A booming petrochemical industry had been established on the outskirts of the municipal seat—like Tibrás, a local manifestation of Brazilian national development goals. Small amounts of oil had been discovered in Camaçari and adjacent municipalities, but much more impor-

One example of Arembepe's penetration by the nation-state is the registration of boats. (Courtesy Jerald T. Milanich)

tant were factories that transformed petroleum into such products as polyurethane. Even a few Arembepeiros commuted (an hour's round trip) to work in petrochemicals near Camaçari. The town now included several one-way streets, two supermarkets, a "commercial center," several pharmacies, physicians' offices, laboratories, and other medical services. I reintroduced myself to the head of statistical services for the municipality, who told me about plans for the national census, scheduled to begin in September 1980. Would he send me the results for Arembepe, I asked. "Certainly," he replied. "Or better yet, take down my number and give me a call next year. I'll give you the information on the phone." Given my recollection of the sleepy county seat of the 1960s, I had difficulty imagining myself sitting down in my Ann Arbor office and making a long-distance call to Camaçari, Brazil.[1]

In the municipal seat I also saw a dozen lawyers' offices, testimony to increasing litigation, which extended even to Arembepeiros. Our former cook Dora, for example, traveled to Camaçari with me to see the attorney who had agreed to represent her in a suit she had brought against a former neighbor. The case originated in Dora's decision to tear down her old wattle-and-daub hut in northern Arembepe, in order to build a brick house on the lot she rented from the landowning family. Before construction could begin, the man who owned the brick house in front of her built a fence around her lot, claiming it as part of his property. Trying to avoid a feud between her relatives and his (both belonged to large, long-established Arembepe families), Dora took the case to court—an ambitious move but probably a lost cause because of her lack of experience with legal procedures.

Many Arembepeiros now paid licensing fees to the municipality for their stores, bars, and restaurants—another contrast to the 1960s, when only the owners of the two largest stores had paid such fees. Municipal officials inspected weights and measures. Mail was delivered regularly in Arembepe, and its streets now had formal names, proclaimed in street signs, and house numbers. The names were those of the landlords who had owned particular areas of the village. Even residents of Street Down There were abandoning this traditional designation for a new, landlord-derived name.

The numbers, which had been there in 1973, facilitating my village census, had originally been painted on each house during a malaria-eradication campaign by the state health department. Additional numbers had been added subsequently, as in Caraúnas and Volta do Robalo.

Villagers themselves were now identified in the more detailed and impersonal terms of the nation-state. Full names were used in legal documents, and Arembepeiros were increasingly familiar with the last names of fellow villagers. Most adults now had identity papers. Alberto's entire family, including his twelve-year-old daughter, carried them whenever they left Arembepe; Alberto told me that people could be jailed if they were stopped by police and could not produce identification. The military and police presence in Bahia seemed, however, less obvious and ominous than on my 1973 visit, when on each visit to the city I had been depressed by ubiquitous teams of uniformed, rifle-wielding agents of the nation's hard-line military government. Even Arembepe was invaded briefly in 1973 by the military police, seeking drug dealers (and probably political undesirables) among the hippies.

Another new pattern concerned Arembepeiros' participation in the armed forces. On completion of junior high school, many village boys now presented themselves to the army, air force, or navy for the military service that, in theory, is required of all healthy young men in Brazil. Along with education beyond primary school, a stint in the armed forces provided experience and documents that helped young men find jobs with Tibrás and other externally managed organizations. Jaime, the Tibrás worker introduced in Chapter 8, had joined the military after completing some high school; both experiences had helped him obtain employment at Tibrás as a semi-skilled worker.

State and municipality had combined to bring better educational opportunities to Arembepe. This reflected implementation of the Basic Education Reform Law of 1971, which mandated eight years of primary and intermediate education (in primary and junior high school). The new national law also established a compulsory core curriculum of general studies, including practical courses to determine vocational aptitudes (industrial, commercial, agricultural, and domestic) in grades five through eight. Preparation for employment was one of the main goals of national educational reform. Arembepe's new junior high school and two elementary schools were staffed by five competent teachers—two local people and three outsiders. Two were state employees, two municipal; and the principal, an Arembepe native who had been educated at a teachers college in Salvador, was paid partly by the state and partly by the municipality. The 1980 classroom differed radically from the educational setting of the 1960s, when children had wandered in and out of an always crowded one-room school, sporadically supervised and barely taught by a local woman who herself had received just a third-grade education.

Education was a much more serious, and costly, matter in 1980. Children were now required to wear uniforms, pay fees, and purchase books and supplies. They paid attention in the classroom and were taught by people who had adequate training for their jobs. Still, education beyond junior high school eluded most villagers. Just one native was a college graduate, having passed the extremely difficult "vestibular" exam, on which the rate of success in Bahia was barely 10 percent.

Public Health

Along with education and welfare, the health services available to Arembepeiros had improved but remained inadequate. In addition to the Tibrás medical staff discussed in Chapter 8, other health benefits were financed by various levels of government. A medical post in Arembepe had been established in 1978 and was supported by Fundo Rural, the agency in charge of administering social services to fishermen. The two practical nurses who staffed the post full-time were municipal employees. Fundo Rural paid the salary of the physician from Salvador who spent two days each week in Arembepe and three in Abrantes, the district seat. Preferring the Tibrás medical staff, many Arembepeiros complained about this doctor, saying that he did little to relieve their health problems and just wrote prescriptions. For treatment of emergencies, villagers had to travel to Tibrás or a

Salvador hospital. Arembepe still lacked a pharmacy, although a limited selection of free medicines was kept at the medical post, while aspirins and other simple remedies could now be bought in most local stores. Many prescriptions still required a bus ride to Itapoan, where there were several pharmacies. The physician came to Arembepe on Tuesdays and Thursdays and usually worked a six- to seven-hour day, scheduling sixteen appointments in the morning and an equal number in the afternoon. As at Tibrás, no fees were collected for consultations.

In both Arembepe and Abrantes urine, blood, and stool specimens were collected and sent for analysis to laboratories in Camaçari. On the basis of the lab tests, the doctor wrote prescriptions, frequently for worms, still viewed as Arembepe's main health problem. The head nurse at the post told Maxine Margolis that virtually all Arembepe children had intestinal parasites, which she believed came from their playing in the lagoon, making reinfection likely. The nurse also mentioned dysentery, measles, and schistosomiasis as health problems. As Tibrás pollution of the lagoon ended, the snails had returned, and with them more frequent diagnoses of schistosomiasis. The nurse asserted that schistosomiasis was a much more severe problem now than during the 1960s.

Many changes in knowledge and customs had benefited public health in Arembepe, but problems remained. A lingering effect of the pollution scandal was greater caution about lagoon water. Many villagers got their drinking water from deep wells that had been excavated throughout the village; these had electric pumps. Others preferred the water from wells in Volta do Robalo—farther from sea and lagoon—or obtained drinking water from the faucet in front of Tibrás. If very few villagers would now risk a drink of lagoon water, many had returned to their traditional bathing spots. Several others, however, still avoided the lagoon; they had built showers in their homes and used well water for bathing and for washing dishes. Alberto, for example, took care of a summer person's house across the street and drew water from its well for bathing, dishwashing, and even his toilet. Arembepeiros whose homes, like Alberto's, directly bordered the ocean had to rely on others for well water, since their own dwellings stood on an inland extension of the sandstone reef, and it was too rocky to excavate wells underneath. These villagers hoped that the municipality would eventually drill for a public fountain in the central square.

Problems with public sanitation remained. Although four men were employed by the municipality to sweep the streets and keep the village clean, much of the burden of garbage disposal rested on traditional agents—animals and tides. Buzzards still ate fish innards and other organic remains on the beach. Horses, donkeys, chickens, and ducks scavenged garbage dumps throughout the village; but the livestock population had decreased noticeably since the 1960s, as access to animal products in supermarkets became easier. Villagers still set domestic refuse below the Atlantic high-water mark in the evening, to be taken out by the tide. Toilets heavily outnumbered septic tanks; Alberto's simply poured down to the beach, and sanitation was left to the high tide that lapped the foundations of his house twice a month.

Villagers without toilets still used bushes on the fringes of the lagoon to relieve themselves, but housing developments had cleared many of these once-favored areas. The Atlantic reef was another favorite spot. One day Jerry Milanich watched a small boy defecate on the reef near Alberto's house, then wipe his rear end on rocks nearby. A few minutes later a man arrived with a basin and began washing dishes with sea water in the same place. These are some of the public health practices that helped maintain the high incidence of parasitic infestation, dysentery, and resultant malnutrition among Arembepeiros.

On the other hand, there had been progress in combating certain diseases. The government had sponsored a campaign to control malaria by antimosquito spraying. And as we arrived in August 1980, parents throughout Brazil were being exhorted to bring their children for their second dose of oral antipolio vaccine. In this successful campaign, medical personnel were sent into rural areas to offer the preventive treatment. German measles control had been less successful because many children had not received the vaccine. Some physicians discouraged males from being vaccinated, since, they pointed out, the danger of rubella is mainly to pregnant women. The disease will continue to be a problem, of course, as long as vaccination is not universal.

Arembepe still lacked facilities and equipment for full pre-
natal care and medically supervised childbirth, but childbirth was much less of an adventure than it had been during
the 1960s. Most deliveries then were entrusted to two native
midwives, who had acquired their skills locally, as appren-
tices. Betty Kottak was present at a childbirth in 1964. This
was to prove a more difficult delivery than most, since the
mother was in labor for several hours. As she endured con-
tractions, the room filled with smoke from the midwife's
pipe. Thinking that birth was imminent, the midwife splashed
her hands with a bottle of alcohol, only to relight her pipe
after it turned out to be a false alarm. There would be no second dousing when the baby finally did emerge.

Current conditions are much more sanitary, if also more
impersonal. By 1980 pelvic examinations were being done in
Abrantes, but women were sent there only if a pregnancy appeared risky. Most women had never had a gynecological ex-
amination and strongly feared pelvic inspection. Just one of
Arembepe's traditional midwives continued her practice; the
other had retired in 1975. Most women now went to the maternity center along the Salvador highway, less than twenty
minutes away, to have their babies. Villagers' only complaint
was that the maternity center did routine episiotomies, for
which Arembepeiros saw no reason.

By 1980 Arembepeiros routinely journeyed outside for
many other health-related services. They visited the nearest
dentist, in Itapoan, to have teeth pulled. However, no one received preventive dental care, nor were teeth ever filled.
Even poorer Arembepeiros now bought vitamin syrup for
their children, helping to correct the severe malnutrition that
had been marked during the 1960s, when Alberto and Carolina had lost ten of their thirteen children to illnesses made
more severe by an inadequate diet. Use of antibiotics that
would have saved many lives during the 1960s had also increased. Avoidance of drinking lagoon water produced other
health benefits: most mothers now breast-fed their babies,
and I detected less use of bottles and powdered milk than
previously. I was struck by the number of villagers with eyeglasses, prescribed and ordered in Salvador.

New government programs and the expansion of others
also made it possible for many Arembepeiros to obtain specialized care in Salvador hospitals. A few had been treated

for mental problems in city institutions. However, hospitalization benefits available to fishermen through Fundo Rural were much less complete than those provided by INPS (Instituto Nacional de Previdência Social), the national social welfare fund, into which many of Arembepe's business people were paying. Special medical benefits available through factory jobs were even better. Indigents and unemployed people were eligible for free hospitalization.

The case of an infant born with a club foot illustrates inequities between the benefits available to fishermen and other rural producers. Examining the baby two weeks after its birth in 1974, a physician recommended consultation with specialists at a children's hospital in Salvador. Once there, the parents (a fisherman and his wife) were told that the boy needed an operation but that the particular hospital did not accept payment by Fundo Rural. They were sent to an adult hospital that did take fishermen's benefits, but the child was kept there for two months without being operated on. During this time the baby, still less than a year old, was visited by his parents, who had to take the bus in from Arembepe, and by his godmother, who lived in Salvador. The parents tired of waiting for the operation and removed their son from the hospital. They eventually found a physician who certified (falsely) that the father was an agricultural worker so that the operation might be done in a children's hospital that accepted the benefit program for cultivators. The operation, which required just two days' hospitalization, was declared a success, and the child was fitted with orthopedic boots, which were supposed to be replaced each six months.

All these matters necessitated numerous trips to Salvador, which taxed the time and energy of the parents and their relatives. In 1980 they were told that a second operation would be necessary, and the mother lamented that she had not been able to replace the boots at the required time because of another pregnancy, her sixteenth, at the age of forty-two, six years after the birth of her last child, the one just discussed. Of course, one might argue that Arembepeiros because of their proximity to Salvador were relatively fortunate, despite the obstacles, to have access even to these benefits. Use of hospitals by rural Brazilians in more remote parts of the country remained much less practicable.

Enhanced medical awareness was another aspect of Arembepeiros' increasing familiarity with the outside world. One woman told me that her father had recently died of a heart attack and her mother of pulmonary edema. Villagers would not have used these terms during the 1960s, nor did many know the cause of death of relatives. Alberto's father, a man of about seventy, had dropped dead on the beach as he was loading his fishing gear one morning in 1965; villagers had suspected a heart attack; but there was no postmortem, since the nearest physician was in Salvador, then three hours away. The absence of a death certificate later prevented Alberto's mother, who had been legally married to his father, from receiving the fisherman's widow's pension to which she was entitled.

In addition to new diagnoses, there were new causes of death. Traffic accidents and weekend brawls had become public safety problems in Arembepe, as throughout the "civilized" world. For example, the woman who had cleaned house for me in 1962 was one of two villagers who had been run over by road-construction trucks near Arembepe. Automobile traffic had affected child-rearing practices. Previously, small children had been assigned the task of caring for their even smaller siblings, since Arembepe in the 1960s contained few dangers. One day in 1980, however, I heard a fisherman yell at a hippie couple that they should do a better job of looking after their toddler, who was wandering in the street at the point where the Salvador highway entered Arembepe. With the advent of strangers and their machines, the job of supervising children has become more difficult.

There had been little change in birth-control methods since the 1960s. Four village women had undergone tubal ligation, one of them a woman with twelve living children out of twenty live births, including four sets of twins. One thirty-year-old woman with five living children had asked for a tubal ligation (which could be done at the maternity center) following the birth of her fifth child. A physician there tried to dissuade her, however, arguing that she was still young and might one day regret not having a larger family.

Arembepe's medical-post doctor used to prescribe birth-control pills but, like many other physicians, had stopped doing so after a national media campaign publicizing health hazards associated with the pill. He warned one woman that the pill might be bad for her varicose veins. At forty-two, after sixteen pregnancies, with a new daughter who was a year younger than her youngest grandchild, this woman hoped she would soon go through menopause, which she saw as the only means of birth control realistically available to her. Another woman mentioned that she had heard of a male contraceptive pill but doubted if men in Arembepe would agree to take it. Nor did the mass media encourage population limitation: "Stop taking the pill," crooned a male vocalist singing the nation's number one song, "I want my child to be born."

Faced with restricted access to the more humane means of limiting population, a few villagers took extreme measures. When, soon after my 1980 arrival, I asked about an old acquaintance, a woman who would have been in her late thirties, I was told that she had died. A destitute woman married to a notorious alcoholic, she had drunk a remedy designed to abort the fetus she discovered she was carrying. The abortion was successful, but the prospective mother became violently ill and never recovered; she died after a few months. The old woman who told me this sad tale ended it with a proverb: "One kills a child in order to eat" (that is, to feed oneself and one's family). But, my informant concluded, "The woman who aborts her own child may herself die."

Despite such unfortunate cases, the trend in Arembepe was toward better health and reduced infant and child mortality. Immigration had also contributed to Arembepe's rapid population growth, a doubling in less than two decades. Increasing government impact and immigration had also transformed certain relationships based on kinship and marriage.

Marriage and the State

Significant modifications in marital arrangements took place in Arembepe between the 1960s and 1980. The main reasons for these changes in social organization lay in Arembepe's increasing participation in external systems, including the social-welfare programs of a nation-state. Compared to the 1960s, when almost half (47.3 percent) of the marital unions in the village had been formally sanctioned (by state or church, usually both), there were strikingly fewer (34.8 percent) legally sanctioned unions in 1980 (see Appendix 5). Several informants commented on the decline in formal marriages—all the more striking in view of much easier access to agents of both state and church, including a justice of the peace and a Roman Catholic priest in the district seat, now just minutes away. Asserting that marriages had become rare events for Arembepeiros, one woman could recall only three local people who had married during the past two or three years. Ivan, the *noivo* ("fiancé") of Alberto's eldest daughter, said that he had no plans to make their union official. He had little use for formal marriage, calling it "something for old people." "Nowadays," he said, "young people are *amaziado* [they have a common-law arrangement]." I asked Arembepe's highest-paid municipal employee, who is also the village's most active male Catholic, about my perception that there were fewer formal marriages in 1980 than previously. After reflection, he agreed, saying that some young people now lived together for a few years and then married, whereas others didn't bother to get married at all.

The reduced frequency of formal marriage was attributable to several factors. Most significantly, government regulations concerning the allocation of pensions had discouraged many people from marrying, since a married couple could not draw two pensions simultaneously. Alberto, for example, would be eligible for Fundo Rural benefits as a retired fisherman. Carolina, his common-law wife, made monthly payments to INPS, from which she expected retirement benefits at age sixty. Alberto was uncertain about whether both he and Carolina could receive their pensions if they married legally (which they had no plans to do). They might still be eligible, he thought, since different government programs were involved. However, other villagers expressed certainty that a legal widow could not receive her own INPS benefits and inherit her husband's Fundo Rural benefits as well. Nor did informants think that spouses could both draw benefits from INPS.

Villagers obviously did not control national welfare laws. Nor were they certain about all the legal ramifications of formal marriage. Because of this, government regulations (at least, as Arembepeiros interpreted them) reinforced a traditional pattern. Common-law unions had never been unusual in Arembepe; although such living arrangements had lacked the prestige of formal marriage, they had never been particularly stigmatized. Now, however, the common-law arrangement guaranteed that both partners could receive retirement benefits, and this consideration was more important than previously because of growing female participation in the changing economy. Many women, not content with the prospect of merely receiving benefits as widows, wished to draw pensions in their own right as owners and operators of stores, restaurants, and bars. The most enterprising single women therefore avoided formal marriage, since it might mean forfeiture of future benefits.

Along with pensions, Arembepeiros also considered inheritance rights in making decisions about marriage. Brazilian law grants legal spouses equal survival rights. In traditional Arembepe wives usually outlived their husbands and men were the principal producers; this meant that young women of the 1960s wished to marry formally. They tried to preserve their virginity as a commodity to be traded against eventual inheritance rights, as was discussed in Chapter 3. This consideration was less compelling in 1980, in view of improved business opportunities that permitted women to prosper in their own right.

Arembepeiros have always been well aware of which spouse owns property. Women were especially adamant in remembering that women, rather than their mates, were the owners of particular items. Dora, for example, pointed out that the boats that most village men considered to belong to her brother actually belonged to his (legal) wife. He had purchased them with his wife's inheritance from her father. Dora complained about her sister-in-law, calling her a domineering woman who constantly issued orders to her husband. After the wife received her substantial inheritance, Dora's brother gave up the common-law union he had maintained "on the side" for several years, although he did employ one of his illegitimate sons as a fisherman. In marriage as outside, in Arembepe as elsewhere, differential wealth entails differential power.

A legal marriage was necessary only to guarantee the inheritance rights of *spouses*. If children of a common-law union were registered in the name of both parents, they could inherit from either, and the other parent usually had access to their inheritance. Because of this, there was no incentive for Alberto and Carolina to marry legally, he told me, since their only significant property was their two houses, one in his name and one in hers. Since all three daughters had been registered in both names, they would jointly inherit the property of whichever parent died first. And if Carolina died first, Alberto would still have access to her house in Volta do Robalo through the children.

In 1980 some villagers were even questioning the special inheritance benefits accompanying formal marriage. They had heard that a stable common-law union of at least two years' duration might also confer inheritance rights on the partners. If true, this would theoretically remove the main economic incentive to marry legally. However, few Arembepeiros had the knowledge, connections, or money to litigate for such rights. Because Arembepeiros lacked legal experience and political clout, even legitimate rights based on formal marriage were sometimes denied. For example, Alberto's mother had been attempting to obtain her fisherman's widow's pension for several years. Although she had marriage papers, government officials refused to approve benefits because no death certificate had been filled out when her husband died—years before Arembepeiros had convenient access to physicians, coroners, and state officials.

A final cause of the decline in formal marriages may lie in villagers' observation of hippie life styles. Even during the 1960s Arembepeiros' decisions about marriage had been partially modeled on outsiders' behavior. Wealthier Arembepeiros, who were more likely to marry legally than poorer villagers,[2] were not just ensuring mutual inheritance rights but also emulating the norms of middle-class and upper-class Brazilians. Subsequently, however, villagers had regular contact with hippies, whom they considered "rich," and who actually were often young people with middle-class backgrounds. Because these outsiders placed little value on legal marriage and permanent relationships, many Arembepeiros had modified their own opinions about external norms concerning marriage and sex.

An anthropology textbook axiom is that marriage is a mechanism for creating alliances—social ties beyond the particular spouses. In traditional Arembepe only formal marriage created obligations between spouses and their families. In 1980 as previously, a common-law spouse was not one's "husband" or "wife," but one's "man" or "woman." Recognition of "in-law" relationships came only with formal marriage. To avoid marriage was to avoid the plethora of extended social obligations (particularly to the wife's family) that accompanied the legal bond. More people were avoiding marriage, and hence social alliances, in 1980 than in the past.

Nevertheless, there were compensatory social conventions that helped to support stable common-law arrangements. For example, customs about naming children could be used symbolically to strengthen a marital union. Parts of each parent's name could be incorporated in their children's. For instance, the children of Atahydes and Odete, who had a long-term common-law relationship, included Ozete, Valdete, and Crispina. The name of Crispina, a twin, did not combine her parents' names. Twins stood apart from the ordinary system, taking such mythology-derived traditional twins' names as Cosma and Damiana (Cosme, Damião for males) or Crispim, Crispina, and Crispiana. In this way twins (who rarely survived as a pair) were symbolically separated from other children.

The ritual kinship (compadresco) system offered another way of shoring up common-law arrangements. Fernando's daughter, aged twenty-one, was not formally married to the father of her two children. The couple had eloped but contended that they planned eventually to make the arrangement legally binding. Asked if he was pleased with the relationship, Fernando asserted that he couldn't help being pleased, since his daughter's mate was his godson, as was their first baby. Even if the union lacked legal sanction, Fernando was nevertheless godfather both of his daughter's partner and of his own grandson, and compadre of his daughter and her partner. Here we see that the compadresco system permitted close social ties between a woman's family and her partner and children in the absence of a legal bond. Similarly, when I asked Dora if she considered her niece's common-law mate, whom she spoke of frequently and warmly, to be her nephew, she responded negatively. He was her *compadre*—because Dora had asked her favorite niece and her husband to stand as godparents of her own youngest son. Thus *compadresco* relationships could, and often did, take precedence over in-law relationships in common-law unions.

Throughout the world, marriages create alliances in which many people other than the immediate partners wish, and work, to maintain the union. If parenting partnerships in Arembepe increasingly become informal individual arrangements, rather than social concerns, more frequent separation and household instability seem likely. Even though ritual kinship can provide compensatory social links, the decline in formal marriage and thus in the alliances it engenders may contribute to the increasing atomism and social fragmentation noted in previous chapters. There were already some signs of this in 1980. For example, affinal links between fishing crew members had decreased along with kin ties. More research will be needed to determine the implications of the decline in formal marriage. However, yet another change—a reversal of the sex ratio, so that males now outnumber females—may help balance pressures toward marital instability.

The Sex Ratio and Female Status

This surplus of males reflects a final factor—immigration—that produced significant changes in marriage and household composition in Arembepe between the 1960s and 1980. In 1964 the village's population was 49 percent male and 51 percent female,[3] and 17 percent of the village's 159 households were headed by women. By 1980, in the sampled area of southern Arembepe, there were 164 males (52.4 percent) and 149 females (47.6 percent). Of the 61 inhabited households in the survey area, only 4 lacked a co-resident adult male, and only 6 (9.8 percent) were headed by females. These figures confirm a pattern that became obvious to me after a few days of talking with old acquaintances. Virtually all the women who had lacked permanent, co-resident partners in the mid-1960s had acquired them by 1980. Dora, for example, had been living with an immigrant fisherman from Sauipe for several years. Another of our former employees had established a stormy but stable common-law relationship with a bricklayer.

Arembepe's expanding and diversifying economy, while attracting men to the community, had also brought breadwinners to many village women. Although few of these were formal unions, the social status of the women involved had improved markedly. Most had previously been considered village prostitutes (*raparigas*), scorned by other villagers, especially women, because they lived off other women's husbands (in secondary, unstable unions with polygynous males). With "husbands" of their own, no longer posing a threat to other families, such women as Dora (see Chapter 11) were no longer regarded as *raparigas;* they had become ordinary village women. Polygyny, too, had declined as a result of male immigration. Women's greater economic prominence, coupled with the surplus of adult males that immigration had provided, may help maintain marital and household stability despite opposing pressures.

10 Social Differentiation and the Origin of Deviance

Because of the new surplus of males, the label *rapariga* ("village prostitute") had lost most of its salience as a social category. However, this ran counter to a general trend in Arembepe toward more social divisions and greater social complexity. Several variables had created new divisions within this once fairly homogeneous and egalitarian community. For example, the native sons and daughters who had taken up residence in Caraúnas and Volta do Robalo were no longer considered to be Arembepeiros. Occupational diversity also meant different activities and associations for villagers. And many kinds of outsiders played regular roles in community life.

The process of social change in Arembepe provides clues about the means whereby any egalitarian or simply ranked society is transformed into a stratified social order. Not just in Arembepe but more generally during such a process of sociocultural evolution, attributes that once were associated with particular *individuals* eventually come to be considered markers of different social *groups*. For example, during the 1960s a handful of villagers had had psychological problems. However, they were considered classificatory oddities; people didn't know what to make of them, how to explain their behavior. So they simply ignored them. In other words, during the 1960s, the *role* of the "mentally ill person" was undeveloped. However, the mentally ill had become a salient social category with characteristic generalized behavior by 1980. In the realm of religious expertise, too, the idiosyncratic perceptions and special talents of individuals had found no social reinforcement in traditional Arembepe. By 1980 they had. For example, no one cared in 1965 that one woman claimed to be able to discern in dark corners faces that others missed and to receive spirit possessors. A niche for her, and others with similar talents, had opened up—in *candomblé*—by 1980. Another individual trait that had been transformed into a social category by 1980 is linked closely to the development of socioeconomic stratification out of a hierarchy of graduated wealth contrasts. Although there were relatively wealthy Arembepeiros in the mid-1960s, villagers had always insisted that no one in the community was really rich. By 1980, however, "rich people" had also become a salient social label.

The Rise of the Bourgeoisie

Arembepeiros had adopted the term *burguês* ("bourgeois") to describe wealthy people, including some fellow villagers. Alberto said that a *burguês* is a person who makes more than 50,000 cruzeiros (about $850) per month; he assigned some boat owners and, somewhat jokingly, one Tibrás employee to this category. Although many people, including Alberto himself, appeared to be more comfortable with success than they had been in 1973, others were wary of the rapidly broadening wealth differentials. One man complained, "There are so many rich people here now that it scares you."

Two of the most characteristic statements of traditional Arembepe—"We are all relatives here" and "We are all equal here"—were no longer heard. Immigrants, tourists, summer people, and hippies were certainly not relatives of native-born Arembepeiros; and men like Dinho and a few others who carried purses and owned cars and large boats were clearly not the equals of an ordinary fisherman. The huge contrast in earnings between the fishing boat owner and the crew member—since that relationship was at the heart of Arembepe's traditional economy—was particularly impressive to villagers, and it led some of them to exaggerate owners' profits and the existing wealth contrasts. Alberto, usually accurate in numerical estimates, told me that rich boat owners such as Dinho could gross 100,000 to 200,000 cruzeiros ($1700–$3400) *daily* from their fishing interests. I told Alberto that these figures were impossibly high; and after we had figured out the actual profits (see Chapter 8), he saw his error. His uncharacteristic mistake is indicative, however, of villagers' heightened perception of wealth differences within their community.

Still, since there had been too little time for such wealth differentials to be transmitted across the generations, familiar themes continued in villagers' explanations for success. Arembepeiros still cited luck as a major determinant of economic ascent and decline, particularly in fishing. Through a series of minor incidents, one's fishing luck could erode. For example, as Alberto observed, "Someone loads up his boat with ice, leaves port, and the motor malfunctions. He loses all the ice and that day's, or week's, fishing, too. This happened to Tomé, who then started fishing in his other boat, only to have the same thing occur a few weeks later." While Tomé's luck was declining, that of his younger brother Dinho was rising, said Alberto.

Villagers were right: luck (chance, more accurately) along with entrepreneurial activity did still contribute to differential success. Certainly, as we shall see in Chapter 11, Tomé had been mistaken to overextend himself financially and to rely too much on external resources. However, he was just as definitely *unlucky* to lose the use of both his boats at the same time. Furthermore, Dinho and the other wealthy nonfishing owners would never have been able to get quite as rich had there not happened to be fishermen from Sauipe ready to replace native Arembepeiros who had qualms about having nonfishing covillagers as their bosses and, besides, could find more lucrative work on land. Even the business success of Alberto and Carolina rested as much on luck as on their hard work, foresight, and innovation. They were among the first Arembepeiros to electrify their homes, permitting them to buy a reliable refrigerator and freezer and to sell cold beer. However, they had controlled neither the arrival of electricity nor the harbor shift that enhanced their view and made their bar especially attractive to outsiders.

An Irrational Fear of Robbers

Use of such terms as *burguês* and *ricos* ("rich people") suggests that consciousness of class differences within

Arembepe was beginning to develop, but locals still defended their community's integrity. Many projected their hostility toward the rich against outsiders. One Friday afternoon as several boats returned, I saw a small man nervously clutching a purse near the fish weighing stations. Alberto identified him as a prospective fish buyer from Itapoan. "A gunman's going to come and take that purse away from him," suggested Alberto, but the assailant would surely *not* be an Arembepeiro. The man who had told me that rich people scared him also focused his comments on outsiders. Only one local boy was recognized as having gone astray, becoming first a marijuana-smoking hippie and then a vagabond who robbed people. However, he had left the community and had thereby become an outsider, too. Thus although the life-style differences they saw each day made Arembepeiros envious of one another, villagers projected onto outsiders their unconscious wish to level wealth contrasts. Strangers, not natives, would be the poor who robbed from the rich.

Both in 1973 and in 1980 I found villagers' fear of robbers enormously out of proportion to reality, particularly since, remarkably, no Arembepeiro had ever been robbed or assaulted by a gunman. The only armed robbery that had taken place in Arembepe involved outsiders. An engaged couple, emerging from Aunt Dalia's juice bar one Sunday, had been accosted by a young man with a revolver who had demanded their car keys and driven off, leaving them stranded. The only other incident during the past several years had been even milder: Sunday visitors in the beach-home area south of Arembepe had found their car trunk prized open and their money and documents taken. Arembepe in 1980 still lacked effective law enforcement. The local "policeman" was feebler than ever. Outside police officers appeared from time to time—for example in June 1980, as part of a widespread search for a man who had raped, robbed, and murdered in a suburb of Salvador. He was later apprehended near Itapoan.

Even though, on the basis of actual happenings in Arembepe, I was a hundred times more likely to be possessed by a spirit than to be robbed, my old friends still reiterated the warning "Don't give rides to *anyone*." Beware, they said, of men who dress up as women and hitch rides with the intent to rob. Alberto always insisted that I park my car in front of his house or near that of an acquaintance so that someone could watch it. "In the old days," reported Aunt Dalia, "no one used to lock their doors. Now, everyone does, even to walk across the street." Knowing that I had lived in Africa (Madagascar), Alberto asked me if *candomblé* and robbers existed there. I explained that people I knew in Madagascar feared witches. He found their fears reasonable and promptly declared such witches to be perpetrators of black magic.

I believe one reason for Arembepeiros' exaggerated fear of robbers is that this preoccupation with external threats provided an outlet for their own envious wishes toward covillagers. Part of Foster's image of limited good (see Chapter 3) is that wealth differences are allowed if they demonstrably come from outside the community. This had definitely been the case in Arembepe. Virtually all the new wealth generated since 1970 had come from outside—whether from tourists, hippies, summer people, factory employment, or the cheap labor of immigrant fishermen. This may be the main reason why, even in a community with a history of egalitarianism and leveling mechanisms, the envy associated with emerging class consciousness was still projected onto outsiders. Villagers' exaggerated fear of robbers may also have expressed resentment against outsiders for the radical alterations in community life.

But there was an additional reason for Arembepeiros' fears. My 1980 visit to Rio de Janeiro, conversations with numerous urban Brazilians, perusal of newspapers, and television newscasts all convinced me that Brazilians in general were much more concerned with crime than previously. Military hard-liners blamed a purported surge in criminal activity on government liberalization. However, it was unclear whether it was actually crime, or simply media attention to it, that had increased. Whatever the reason, the 1980 Brazilian concern with crime, which Arembepeiros could share because of their exposure to the mass media, did remind me of the preoccupation with "law and order" in my own country during the Nixon years. And as had been the case in the United States, the effect of disproportionate interest in crime was to direct national attention toward offenses against individuals and away from social problems. This outlook, of course, was eminently compatible with Arembepe's traditional world view.

Alcoholism and Mental Illness

Despite their fear of outsiders, Arembepeiros remained fairly tolerant of the unusual behavior of covillagers. As noted, no definite social sanction had yet been applied to the wealthiest boat owners, and community disapproval of *raparigas* had abated as most of the women who once bore this label established unions with immigrants. However, there was more alcoholism than ever. Arembepeiros had always recognized that certain individuals drank too much, and they used the term *bebado* ("drunk") to describe those whose alcoholism kept them from holding steady jobs. By 1980, membership in the category had swollen, and the new weekend drinking pattern was promoting new cases of alcohol addiction even among regular fishermen. But this new alcoholism

Illustrating the weekend drinking pattern that intensified between 1973 and 1980, tourists consume several bottles of beer in a shack overlooking Arembepe's old harbor. (Courtesy Jerald T. Milanich)

was expressed in the weekend binge, rather than in daily drunkenness.

In 1980 the constant drunks seemed to be everywhere. Lacking regular employment, they wandered through the village seeking odd jobs and doles that would allow them to buy another drink. I found it almost impossible to avoid them when I walked in Arembepe, even on weekdays. Arembepeiros were just starting to see "the alcoholic" as a prominent social category with characteristic (role) behavior, rather than viewing excessive drinking as simply an idiosyncratic problem for a few individuals. Theories about the nature of and reasons for alcoholism were therefore just developing. Only a few villagers I queried about the matter considered alcoholism an illness; most seemed to view it as a character defect that individuals could remedy if they wished. Alberto reported that a few people began buying *cachaça* at his house as early as five in the morning and were drunk by ten o'clock. One such customer was an unemployed loner who, said Alberto, was waiting to die. Alberto considered the life style of this old man and of others who drank excessively on a daily basis to be reprehensible. But there was still no stigma attached to heavy weekend drinking; and the people who did it, including some regular captain-owners, fishermen, and business people, were not labeled alcoholics (though many would have been in the United States).

Anthropologist Mac Marshall (1979) found that on the Pacific island of Truk, where he did an ethnographic study of drinking, alcoholics were powerless people. The same was true in Arembepe. However, whereas on Truk the powerless were young people, their Arembepe equivalents were women and older men. Most were single or separated; none was financially secure. Generally, Arembepe's *bebados* were passive bums; few seemed angry or belligerent. Typically they attempted to ingratiate themselves, becoming maudlin as they begged for money.

Arembepeiros believed that character defects, including alcoholism, could run in families. For example, Dora attributed separate angry assaults (apparently not alcohol-related) by two brothers on other villagers to the defective character of their mother's (immigrant) family. Future research will be necessary to determine just how much alcoholism in Arembepe does run in families, and why. However, there were several sets of alcoholic brothers and at least one mother-daughter pair of heavy drinkers. Incipient or actual alcoholism was also related to participation in *candomblé*, a point that is discussed in the final section of this chapter.

Like violence and alcoholism, mental illness also seemed to run in families. Villagers regarded two middle-aged brothers as mentally ill; one received a disability stipend from his former factory employment. He checked himself in and out of a mental health facility in Salvador, as needed. His older brother, who had never been institutionalized, was a recluse who paced constantly indoors and talked to himself. Villagers also attributed the uneven behavior of their sister and the psychological problems of one of her sons to the family proclivity for mental illness. Two of Alberto's nephews, his brother's children, had become functionally incapacitated following their mother's premature death. One was institutionalized in Salvador; the problems of the other were identified as alcoholism rather than insanity.

Mental problems were often connected with a mother's death or with childbirth. The wife of a very successful captain-owner "went crazy" after the birth of her first child during the 1960s; she recuperated and was considered perfectly normal in 1980. As noted, the problems of Alberto's nephews developed soon after their mother's death. The most dramatic case, however, was that of Julia, a hippie-like young villager with a penchant for nudity. We encountered Julia the very first day we returned to Arembepe in 1980. As we ate lunch in Claudia's Restaurant, we were startled to see an almost naked woman saunter up to the window. At first I suspected that this young woman, whose head was shaved and body painted orange, might be an international *ippa* (female hippie) who had been misinformed that a photography team from *National Geographic* was in town. However, it did not take me long to learn that she was a local girl who had become mentally disturbed in adolescence, following her mother's death.

Julia had been institutionalized in Salvador several times, including once during our stay, but she always managed to escape or talk her way out during periods of rationality, and return to Arembepe by bus. She was considered particularly adept at convincing mental health specialists that she was sane. Back in Arembepe she would revert to deviance. Julia had burned her father's identity papers and had entered some homes and destroyed possessions. However, her most characteristic expression of deviance was nudity, which flouted Arembepe's double standard for male and female dress. Although villagers considered an unclothed female much more offensive than a naked male, they had grown used to Julia's behavior. No one appeared to notice her each day as she drifted through the main part of town, clothed in a skimpy towel, or less.

Julia was said to have been normal until adolescence; but after her mother's death in 1975 she began to remove her clothes in public—at first occasionally, then, following the birth of her baby, frequently. Villagers recounted that a totally unclothed Julia used to carry the baby around Arembepe. The deviance of other villagers was also expressed in nudity. The hippie Aldeia's washerwoman, nature worshipper, and *candomblé* participant, mentioned in Chapter 7, had gotten drunk and removed her clothes in Arembepe. A middle-aged man had also run amuck nude through the village.

Research in many cultures has demonstrated that feelings of inadequacy and guilt are engendered by birth and death, and there is no reason to doubt that this was also true in Arembepe. Indeed, we shall see that imagery drawn from kinship and reproduction was important in *candomblé,* to which many insecure and potentially deviant individuals had gravitated. The burden of guilt fell heavily on twins. Twin births were common in Arembepe, but few twins survived as a set. I believe that surviving twins were particularly likely to experience psychological problems, expressing their irrational feelings of responsibility for their twin's death. For example, Alberto's daughter whose spirit possession was described in Chapter 6 had a history of mild mental disturbance. She found some solace in *candomblé,* where there are prominent sets of spirit twins. Her uncle, also a surviving twin, was Arembepe's highest-ranking *candomblé* member. Still another twin was an authentic lunatic, becoming crazed *(meio maluco)* when the moon was full. At such times he fought with people and threatened to kill them. At other times, however, he was normal and held a regular position in a fishing crew.

From Individual Idiosyncrasy to Group Label

Most studies of conformity and deviance—which authorities usually regard as opposite sides of the same coin—have been done in social systems more stable than that of Arembepe. There has been little research on the *origin* of social deviance. Arembepe therefore sheds new light on this matter. Developments there suggest that as new groups, including potentially deviant ones, emerge within a formerly undifferentiated social system, attributes once seen merely as idiosyncratic personality traits of individuals serve as models for the construction of the new (deviant) social categories. Thereafter, individual behavior of a certain sort is used to assign many people to a particular social category. Once individuals have been so assigned, and as they accept their new "label" or social identity, their behavior becomes more restricted and more stereotypical of their category. They acquire a "role personality," to use a term borrowed from "labeling theory" (see Lemert, 1951; Becker, 1963; Farrell and Swigert, 1975). (For one illustration of this process, see Dora's case in Chapter 11.)

Anthropologists interested in social evolution have tended to base their theories of culture change on such major, generations-long alterations as are revealed by the archaeological record or chronicled in historical documents. However, there is also value in studying sociocultural microevolution—the change process that Arembepe was experiencing. Some of the more intimate and gradual modifications in individuals' experiences, attitudes, and behavior that accumulate over the years, so that they are finally perceptible as major structural changes, can be observed in a living context in places such as Arembepe, where the forces of change are acting rapidly and dramatically. It is likely, for example, that the modeling of social categories out of individual idiosyncrasies—such as is illustrated by this discussion of the rise of social deviance—is an important generalized characteristic of social microevolution, and that it is one of the most powerful mechanisms whereby social complexity is increased.

Accordingly, by 1980 the behavior of unusual individuals in Arembepe was no longer regarded as simply idiosyncratic but as diagnostic of membership in newly recognized social groups: the rich, alcoholics, the mentally ill, *candomblé* participants, and so on. However, this process of social differentiation was ongoing, as yet incomplete. The new categories were still neither fully nor consistently stereotyped or stigmatized, so that their members were not yet recognized as full-fledged social deviants. Arembepeiros were still in the process of building stereotypes (fully developed in modern urban settings) to go along with the new labels.

Missing in Arembepeiros' evaluations of other villagers in 1980 were the criticism, anger, and outrage that in other places accompany a clear image of deviance as rule violation, as going beyond acceptable social behavior. Just two social categories were noticeably devalued, but neither described a native Arembepeiro. Partially stigmatized were the hippies and other "parrots" who spoke incompletely or inappropriately. True outrage, however, was reserved for just one label, the robber, always an outsider. Images of hippies and robbers helped Arembepeiros distinguish their own social system from the outside world, since no such labels set one group off from another among native-born Arembepeiros.

Another reason why full-fledged social deviance had not yet developed in Arembepe as part of the process of social differentiation is that deviance requires conformity, in which Arembepe has always been relatively deficient. Arembepe had never fully fitted anthropologist Robert Redfield's (1948, 1960) stereotype of the "folk society" or "little community." Like Redfield's folk society, traditional Arembepe *had* been small, relatively isolated, homogeneous, and nonliterate. But in contrast, Arembepe had never developed a strong sense of social cohesion. To identify and stigmatize deviant behavior and individuals, strong community solidarity and concordance are needed. People must be aware of their society's rules and expectations concerning appropriate behavior. They must share a generalized set of understandings about what is right, proper, and allowable. However, Arembepe never did have, and still lacked in 1980, the uniformity, the cohesion, and the shared standards necessary to stigmatize internal deviance. Arembepe had always been an individualistic community with divergent views and explanations of behavior. Furthermore, after 1970 the village experienced unusually rapid change, and Arembepeiros came into contact with varied models of behavior associated with many external groups.

As had been true during the 1960s, when the range of personality variation meant that one could distinguish almost as many *types of individuals* as there were actual people in Arembepe, there was still no "typical Arembepeiro." Who could say what category was normal or typical in 1980: businessman/businesswoman, boat owner, fisherman, captain, immigrant, factory worker, construction worker, hippie, weekender, summer person, alcoholic, twin, mentally ill, *candomblé* participant, landowner, anthropologist? Deviance, labeling, conformity, and the setting of group boundaries are discussed further in the context of Tomé's and Dora's cases in Chapter 11.

Race Relations and Sex Roles

One noteworthy feature of Arembepe's traditional social structure, race relations, seemed mostly to have escaped the process of social differentiation. There was still no evidence for discrimination among Arembepeiros on the basis of color or recency of slave ancestry. For example, Dinho, Arembepe's richest native, had very dark skin. Working for him as a fish carrier and washer was one of the lightest men in town, brother of a prominent storekeeper. Two other very light men also worked as menials for much darker boat owners. An extremely light teacher, who would be classified as white in the United States, maintained a common-law liaison with a very dark merchant, to whose baby she had just given birth. Although multiple terms were still employed in Arembepe in 1980, it was my impression that fewer racial labels were being used than during the 1960s. Awaiting testing through future research is the hypothesis that Arembepe's racial terminology may be changing because of contact with outsiders who make fewer, but more consistent, racial distinctions.

Compared to race relations, village sex roles were in more obvious flux in 1980. Emulating external styles and reflecting greater independence, women's dress was more informal and revealing than during the 1960s, when Betty Wagley Kottak had been embarrassed to wear even a one-piece bathing suit to take a dip in the Atlantic. By 1980 bikinis and halter tops had become common attire of young women. One afternoon I saw Alberto's twenty-five-year-old daughter washing dishes outside in her bathing suit while a neighbor of similar age danced to disco music on the verandah, wearing a skimpy halter and shorts.

Women's work, like men's, had become less communal. Formerly, once the men had left for fishing, the women would gather the pots and pans from the previous night's dinner and go down to the lagoon to wash them. In the afternoons, before the fishermen returned, the women would use the lagoon to do their laundry and bathe. By 1980, however, women with access to well water did much of their washing at home—removing for them, as for men, an excellent opportunity to socialize with others of their sex.

Males still controlled public space, as my observations of behavior around the fish stores one afternoon reveal. As several boats were unloaded, I wandered in and out of the two principal fish weighing stations located just south of the chapel. This whole area had always been male territory. Men used to sit on the chapel stoop in the evening; the only women who would approach them were aged crones and little girls sent to seek their fathers. In 1980, the broken strings of kites littered the electric wires here; only boys played in this area, the behavior of juveniles foreshadowing the sex-linked privileges of adulthood. In the shacks, men engaged in pseudo-homosexual play and called each other *viado* ("queer"). Said Alberto to a little boy wandering by with no pants, pointing to the child's genitals: "If I see you walk by my house like that I'll castrate you." Male territory. Only certain females could enter.

One was Dinho's wife, who sat in front of their fish store, a well-to-do modern woman wearing glasses and an attrac-

Adeli, a successful businesswoman, in her restaurant-boarding house. (Courtesy Jerald T. Milanich)

tive dress; she seemed to have left Arembepe's traditional sex roles, limiting female access to outside social space, far behind. Another was Amy, daughter of Claudia, proprietor of Arembepe's most successful restaurant. Along with the restaurant, she had inherited her mother's right to move through male social space. Amy strode into the fish store and soon received a choice fish. On the counter where the fish store employee cut up and sold fish sat his five-year-old step-daughter. Slightly older girls arrived to fetch fish, but they were shy and soon left. An old alcoholic woman stood in the crowd of would-be buyers; she was pestering the fish store employee for a dole, but he grew tired of her raucous entreaties and called her a *rapariga*.

The most spectacular female entrance was that of Julia, the psychotic nudist, who had returned that day from Salvador, where she had again talked her way out of a psychiatric facility and taken a bus home. Scantily dressed as usual, she began dancing (to no apparent music) just outside the fish store. Gradually she removed the towel wrapped around her upper body; she lit a cigarette and continued dancing. I was distracted by the arrival of a van marked "Civil Police," which pulled up in plain sight of Julia. As three officers stepped out, I had visions of Julia being returned to Salvador. But this intrusion of the state on Arembepe's internal affairs was not to be. Like two dozen other men, the police officers had simply come to buy fish. They totally ignored Julia, who, apparently deciding not to test her luck, wandered off. But the news spread rapidly of Julia's return and her near encounter with the law. Other villagers, including Julia's aunt, said that they had been as apprehensive as I.

These women—Dinho's wife, Amy, Julia, and the alcoholic beggar—illustrate the limits of Arembepe's sex roles, the persistence of public space as a predominantly male domain that only certain females could enter. The females who shared male access to outside social space included businesswomen, small girls, alcoholics, and the mentally ill. In the old days, *raparigas* had also occasionally encroached on this male territory.

The Birth of Religion

Although specific categories of deviance had not yet fully formed, potentially deviant individuals had one thing in common: they were more likely than other Arembepeiros to take part in *candomblé*. *Candomblé* participants included alcoholics, twins, former *raparigas,* audacious women, Arembepe's only known native male homosexual, and troubled immigrants such as Fernando, who had an extraordinary fear of outsiders (see Chapter 11).

The increasing popularity of *candomblé* in Arembepe since the 1960s was yet another aspect of the village's opening up to the outside world. Whereas several regular *candomblé* participants resided in Arembepe in 1980, none had lived there during the 1960s. At that time, however, two natives had been learning about *candomblé* in Salvador. One, Crispim, had returned to Arembepe by 1973 and was regarded as its main *candomblé* figure in 1980. Crispim was a full-fledged *pai de santo* ("saint's father") whose reputation extended beyond Arembepe. The *filhas de santo* ("saint's daughters") who assisted him came from neighboring villages as well as from Arembepe. There was even a tourist from Rio de Janeiro studying *candomblé* with Crispim—for a fee of about $165—hoping that he would help her receive spirits. The other native who had been active in *candomblé* in Salvador in the 1960s was Maria, who returned to Arembepe in 1964 but was unable to show her skills as a recipient of spirits until the arrival of a saint's father (Crispim) around 1973. By 1980 Maria, mouthpiece for twenty-one spirits, was regarded as merely the most talented of Crispim's dozen saint's daughters.

Crispim had some competition as the community's spiritual leader. An equally competent *mãe de santo* ("saint's mother") also began holding *candomblés* in Caraúnas in the mid-1970s, but she was a native of Salvador and was still building a local social network. Crispim, of course, could draw on lifetime associations as a native Arembepeiro. Two other saint's mothers visited irregularly. One had a *candomblé* house in Caraúnas, active only part of the year. The other woman practiced *candomblé* only in Salvador and in Arembepe was simply a summer person. One Tibrás employee, a nonnative, was viewed as dependent on a young male *candomblé* expert, who shared his home in southern Arembepe. This would-be spirit father was biding his time in Arembepe prior to moving to Jacuipe (the hamlet at the mouth of the Jacuipe River, about 10 kilometers to the north), where he planned to study further with a spirit father who practiced there. As part of his training, he planned to shut himself in a room and prepare special foods, dictated by his instructor, for his saints. Thereafter he hoped to emerge as a full-fledged spirit father with the right to his own house of *candomblé*, which might be in Arembepe.

I was surprised to learn the extent to which *candomblé* was yet another expression of Arembepe's involvement with external systems. *Candomblézeiros*, it turned out, were not autonomous individuals but part of a larger organization. In order to call oneself a spirit father or mother and to open a house of *candomblé*, Crispim and the others had to be licensed, with an official card provided by a central *candomblé* organization in Salvador. Licensing followed instruction from a member. Maria and the other saint's daughters lacked these cards and could practice only through attachment to saint's fathers and mothers.

Religion's new prominence in Arembepe reflects both local and regional changes. Arembepe's previous isolation had shut it off from agents of all organized religions. Even the Pentecostals, who had made converts in nearby Abrantes, the district seat, had avoided Arembepe, where there was only one Protestant. The Roman Catholic priest who had taken up residence in Abrantes in 1974 visited Arembepe regularly, holding weekly Monday-night masses and a daytime mass one Sunday each month. At about the same time, a group of nuns had moved into Caraúnas, to live in a house constructed for them by villagers led by the former policeman, who had become Arembepe's highest municipal official. This man ·had replaced Prudencio, the deceased landowner's agent, as the main articulator of Arembepe's relations with church and state, and he felt strongly attached to the church as godfather of "more than a thousand" children.

The nuns, he said, had been good for Arembepe; they had helped a dozen old people obtain pensions. Villagers had come to view the sisters as an ordinary part of community life. (Particular nuns were replaced by others every few years.) No one thought it strange that the nuns often attended *candomblé,* to enjoy the festive atmosphere. Arembepeiros regard Catholicism and *candomblé,* although both local manifestations of larger religious organizations, as different systems rather than as competing religions. The church seemed to have absorbed the general urban opinion that *candomblé* was part of traditional Bahian culture—like the regional cuisine, good for tourism and no threat to organized religion per se. Indeed, the syncretism of Roman Catholic, African, and Native American behavior and beliefs in *candomblé* is well-known.

A higher level of ceremonial activity rested not just on better access to external religious systems but on Arembepe's new economy. Previously villagers had lacked sufficient disposable cash to lodge prospective spirit fathers or pay for instruction in how to get possessed. Increased cash flow through Arembepe, attributable to new employment opportunities, made it possible for villagers to take advantage of curing systems of many sorts: spiritual curers, medical doctors, pharmacies, hospitals, and government health and retirement programs.

With more disposable cash, the Arembepe of 1980 could support both Catholicism and Afro-Brazilian cult activity (candomblé). *Shown here is Arembepe's decades-old chapel and the currently non-operational Hotel de Arembepe.* (Courtesy Jerald T. Milanich)

As in other societies, ceremonial activity intensified during the season of prosperity, the summer, which always has been Arembepe's festive period. Villagers complained that the annual February *festa* for their patron saint, Saint Francis, had become an affair for tourists and that it was maintained mainly by local business people rather than by the fishermen, who in the past had formed a procession of boats and made offerings to supernatural entities associated with the sea. However, villagers could now enjoy the large-scale *candomblés* of December and January. During these months, but very rarely in others, the spirit father and mother in Caraúnas were possessed by the goddess Oxun, a principal spirit, representing a higher hierarchical level in the *candomblé* pantheon than the lesser spirits (*cabôclos* or Indians) who came regularly.

To be sure, Arembepe's *candomblés*, which did not last longer than three days even during the summer, could not rival those of Salvador, where they might last a month. Furthermore, Crispim himself was a piddling *pai de santo* compared to the masters in the city. His house, made of unfinished wattle and daub, did not look very prosperous. His "saint's room" was considered worthy enough, but women complained that he should be more generous with his assistants. He and Maria had argued about her complaint that he called on her only when he needed her services and never did anything in return. Like the big man in a tribal society (see Harris, 1974), a *candomblé* leader was clearly expected to share with other members of his spiritual community, especially in a traditionally egalitarian setting such as Arembepe, where potent leveling mechanisms could operate against arrogance and stinginess. Maria lambasted Crispim to his face for his lack of generosity.

One woman who had also assisted Crispim during the 1970s, even though she had yet to receive a spirit, had curtailed her participation because he never gave her anything. "He never gave me a saint," she complained. "His saints never gave me anything, and the saints that he got for other people never gave me anything." She was especially bitter after a saint at one of his ceremonies called on her to "kill the animal." The person who is invited to kill the sacrificial chicken or lamb at a ceremony usually receives some of the money or goods provided by the ceremonial sponsors. (Fresh blood is necessary to feed the devil [*diabo* or bad *cabôclo*] before enlisting the aid of good spirits.) This woman, however, had received nothing.

Candomblés were often organized as part of a curing process that might also prescribe a few days' fasting. The spirit father or mother provided the person for whom the *candomblé* was being "beaten" (music and dancing accompany any *candomblé*) with a list of items to be supplied, including food and money. The spiritual leader was supposed to use some of the cash to buy ceremonial paraphernalia, and to share the rest with his or her saint's daughters.

Arembepeiros regarded *candomblé* as complementary rather than opposed to other curing techniques; many people turned to *candomblé* only after unsuccessful attempts at cures by physicians. Similarly, religious people, especially women, hedged their bets by attending mass, taking part in *candomblé,* and holding prayer meetings (*rezas*) for Catholic saints. The *reza*, a small-scale prayer session attended by female neighbors and kin, had been Arembepe's most common religious event during the 1960s.

Villagers told me that some fathers and mothers of spirits prescribed cures on their own. Others, like Crispim, relied on their spirits to diagnose and treat. Although both spirit parents in Caraúnas received several spirits, each had a regular *cabôclo* used for curing. Leaders (or spirits) diagnosed by tossing and studying shells. Patients were not supposed to name their affliction. If the *candomblézeiro*, in the client's opinion, correctly identified the malady by reading the shell pattern, the patient would follow the advice of the spiritual leader or spirit. As noted, this usually involved fasting and sponsorship of a *candomblé*. Patients then elicited specific information about curing procedures by filling spirits' requests for beer, wine, *cachaça*, or chicken or lamb blood. Spirits frequently requested money for small cures as well as for major curing ceremonies. "The spirits are like children," said one woman; "they expect their demands to be satisfied no matter what the circumstances."

Curing was just one reason for a *candomblé;* others were special occasions, such as the leader's birthday. Many sponsors might contribute to the large-scale summer *candomblés* mentioned previously. Villagers believed that *candomblé* could be used for both good and evil. Alberto asserted that people used *candomblé* to become rich. He said that Laurentino, the arrogant storekeeper described in Chapter 4, had abandoned *candomblé* but still used the devil dog he had relied on all his life. *Candomblé* could summon evil spirits *(diabos)* to cause sickness and death. Our former cook Dora had heard of soul loss: when victims' souls were extracted or imprisoned by a *candomblézeiro*, they could weaken and eventually die. Release and survival could come only through *candomblé*.

Alberto's statements to me about *candomblé* were extremely negative, even though he admitted that he sometimes attended "just to enjoy." Ashamed even of his mate's infrequent participation, he called *candomblé* "a bad thing that leads to ruin." "People *say* they get possessed," he asserted suspiciously.

Dora, an occasional participant, was more positive. She, Maria, and others provided information about cosmology.

The only male role in Arembepe's *candomblé* in 1980 was that of spirit father (but many spirits were male). There were no sons, just daughters, of saints, although Crispim had once had a male assistant. *Candomblé* thus continued Arembepe's traditional male avoidance of religion. Its cosmology also reflected Arembepe's male chauvinism; women were routinely possessed by male and female spirits, but Crispim received just one female being, the goddess Oxun. When male spirits possessed females, the women's voices deepened. The same spirit might flit from person to person, and the same human might receive several saints in one session. Possession followed hours of drumbeating, dancing, and drinking—often to the point of exhaustion. Sometimes possession was quick; at other times it took hours.

"A wind comes and enchants the *filha de santo,* causing her to enter a trance and to become receptive to the spirit world."

"Everyone has a spirit within, a guardian angel," explained Dora, "but some people also have the ability to receive spirits. Unfortunately, I don't."

Possession rested on a talent that some people were born with, others acquired, and many never got. Recognizing their talent, some people decided to enter *candomblé.* Maria, for example, reported that as a girl she had always been spiritually adept. In the shadows of domestic corners she had made out of the faces of spirits that other people had missed. Although she recognized her supernatural abilities, she let them lie dormant until her daughter entered adolescence. Thereafter, Maria turned to *candomblé* in earnest, and by 1980 had received twenty-one saints.

One of the most interesting features of *candomblé* cosmology is its reproductive and kinship imagery. As in Roman Catholicism, *candomblé* agents employed a kinship model to enclose their spiritual community. The leaders—fathers and mothers of saints—symbolically gave birth to saints by permitting themselves to be possessed. The fathers and mothers also had children in the flesh—the daughters of saints, who assisted them and were themselves possessed by inferior spirits, who were like the leaders' grandchildren.

Maria's case makes the link between reproduction and spirit possession particularly clear. Although she had always recognized her own supernatural abilities, she did not join *candomblé* until her only daughter was twelve years old, when Maria began to have pains. She sought relief in Salvador's *candomblé* community and has been active in *candomblé* ever since. Maria despaired of having another child; unlike most Arembepeiros, she was never even pregnant more than once. Her participation has produced twenty-one symbolic children, the *cabôclos* that regularly possessed her. (Remember that spirits, with their childish, whimsical demands, were likened specifically to children.)

Maria's own daughter's career as saint's daughter began when one of her sons fell sick, and she sought a cure in *candomblé*. While at the ceremony, she had a vision that her son would improve and that she would receive a saint. Both events came to pass. Unlike her mother, Maria's daughter received just one saint but had many actual children. One village woman who was active in *candomblé* routinely became possessed during childbirth, again linking this religious system to reproduction. This was also an effective way of dealing with the pain, letting a spirit have the baby.

Villagers' comments suggested that a slight stigma was attached to *candomblé*, even by participants. (However, they may have thought that I disapproved of this new dimension of Arembepe's religious life.) Alberto clearly detested *candomblé* and avoided telling me that his wife and daughter had received saints. Because of the people who most often took part, *candomblé* in Arembepe in 1980 might be characterized as "a training ground for deviance."

Some examples. Laurentino, an unusual Arembepeiro, who now relied only on his devil dog, had once taken part in *candomblé*, as still did his brother, the nude amuck-runner mentioned previously. Maria's ability to see imaginary faces might have been taken as evidence for psychosis in our society, but in hers it showed she had a talent that could blossom in religious activity. Both Maria and her daughter were incipient alcoholics; both had once been classifed as *raparigas*, and their usual female companions had similar habits and reputations. Unusually assertive and audacious, neither mother nor daughter fulfilled Arembepeiros' expectations about feminine behavior. They drank, told dirty jokes, and got possessed. When Maria, a large woman, saw me again in

1980, she yelled a greeting from a block away, rushed up, and practically lifted me (180 pounds) with a bear hug: "Oh, Conrado, you've come back to take me to America!"

It should be emphasized that women, who have always been less powerful than men in Arembepe, were also much more active in *candomblé*. As noted, twins, people with a history of mental problems, and Arembepe's only known homosexual were also *candomblé* regulars in 1980. I investigated whether other potential deviants—the rich and recent immigrants—were also especially active in *candomblé*, but found just the opposite. There was no evidence to confirm my hunch that villagers might still be suspecting that economic success was linked to use of *candomblé* magic, as they had in 1973. I could find no one who believed that boat owners were *candomblé* participants, or even believers. Nor did I find evidence for greater participation by the immigrants from northern fishing communities—low-paid workers who could be expected to be envious of native Arembepeiros. I had speculated that they might be trying to discover means of magical redress in *candomblé*, but they weren't. Instead, they were spending most of their time on long fishing trips and weekend drinking bouts. *Candomblé* therefore remained mainly a domain for a few unusual men and many unusual women.

Nevertheless, although Arembepe's more powerless and unusual residents predominated among participants, the stigma attached to the community's newest ritual activity was slight indeed. In old Arembepe there had been diffuse knowledge of, and faith in, aspects of the *candomblé* belief system, but the actual rituals and ceremonies had been absent. By 1980, if even the Roman Catholic nuns could attend and enjoy *candomblé*, villagers reasoned that there could be little real harm in it. So, with a local economy that could now support religious activity, Arembepeiros were adopting external rituals to accompany and enlarge preexisting beliefs. And the growth of religion thus became yet another manifestation of sociocultural change, of Arembepe's increasing complexity.

11 A Community of Outsiders

What academics call "social change" is a process lived by real human beings. Of the many Arembepeiros who have befriended me and shared their knowledge, I have chosen four who, over the period between 1962 and 1980, have been affected by the forces of change discussed in previous chapters. By considering in detail how the lives of a few actual people have been altered, I hope to give concrete human meaning to this story of rapid change, as I bring it to an end. All four are people that I know well. I met Dora, Fernando, and Tomé in 1962. Dora cooked for members of the 1962 field team: Betty Wagley, David Epstein, field leader Marvin Harris, and myself. Fernando, captain and part-owner of a sailboat, was the common-law husband of Dora's only full sister. Tomé had recently returned from Rio de Janeiro, where he had spent seven years in commercial fishing. Soon after our arrival, this enterprising captain-owner invited us to a birthday party in his well-furnished brick house in Arembepe's northern rectangle. There we drank vermouth and listened to music on a small battery-operated phonograph, a rarity then in Arembepe.

We saw little more of Tomé during the first stay; but I went out fishing with him in 1965, and we had long conversations in 1973 and in 1980. Dora washed clothes for us in 1964, 1965, and 1980 and was our cook again in 1973. Fernando always enjoyed talking with us but visited us most frequently in 1973, when we lived farthest from his house. He seemed to fancy himself our protector during our residence in the isolated area of summer houses to the south; beginning a period of problem drinking that lasted until 1976, Fernando also enjoyed our ample stock of beer and Bacardi rum.

I don't remember having met Alberto in 1962, but he was

Atahydes, a fisherman, in 1964—one of the many Arembepeiros who have befriended me and shared their knowledge. (Conrad P. Kottak)

to become my most trusted informant, best friend, and in 1973 and 1980, my field assistant. I learned about Alberto from Niles Eldredge, a member of the 1963 field team, who had found him an excellent informant and suggested that I look him up. Fostering my acquaintance with Alberto and our working relationship as anthropologist and informant was our employment of his younger sister as cook in 1964. The woman from whom we rented a house that year insisted that we hire this local woman, whom she trusted. Following a pattern that he had established with Niles, Alberto visited us virtually every night to converse and instruct me about Arembepe, particularly the fishing industry.

None of these four people—Alberto, Dora, Fernando, and Tomé—can be considered a typical Arembepeiro, since, as noted in Chapter 10, there is no such thing. One obvious characteristic, present in many other villagers but especially developed in them, is an attraction toward outsiders—witness their friendships with us. Although no single story can encapsulate the "typical Arembepeiro's" experience with change, the four twenty-year histories discussed here nevertheless offer concrete illustrations of the impact of many forces on village life. Alberto's story, for example, samples the shift away from fishing toward the tourist industry and a more diversified economy. So does Fernando's, but with an added component of the new economy—the Tibrás employment of one of his sons. Fernando's case also illustrates, though in extreme form, Arembepeiros' hostility toward external forces. Dora's life between 1962 and 1980 demonstrates the impact of male immigration on domestic arrangements, the declining significance of the *rapariga* ("village prostitute") label, and the continuing poverty of ordinary fishermen and their families. Perhaps most interesting, the case of Tomé, an unusually ambitious man, demonstrates the importance of innovation and its rewards and pitfalls, the force of leveling mechanisms, and the continuing impediments to class mobility in northeast Brazilian society.

These contrasting stories also demonstrate the wide range of personality variation even in a relatively egalitarian community such as traditional Arembepe. The anthropologist must pay attention to such personality contrasts, since they affect choice of informants and personal relations in the field, and thus influence both the direction and the results of ethnographic research. By considering these four cases, we may also see that in Arembepe as elsewhere, any individual's fate is jointly determined by several factors, including "pure chance," idiosyncratic experiences and thought patterns, personal and family planning and decision making, cultural expectations, and socioeconomic limitations—both local and regional.

The Teacher

Born in 1923, Alberto is the oldest of the four villagers considered here. A native-born Arembepeiro, Alberto enjoyed the role of informant about his home community, particularly teaching Niles Eldredge and me about the fishing industry. Alberto began his fishing career relatively late in life, at the age of twenty-four, after spending a half-year in Salvador, where he was employed successively as store clerk and domestic. Prior to his sojourn in the city, Alberto had never held regular employment; he had done odd jobs in Arembepe. However, once Alberto discovered his dislike of urban

life, he decided to return to Arembepe and become a
fisherman.

He began fishing in the same crew as his father, an ordinary fisherman, but soon joined his godfather-uncle, who
owned a half-share in a boat and was its captain. This man
taught Alberto most of what he knew about fishing. Thereafter, he fished in more than a half-dozen boats, sometimes
with kinsmen, sometimes not. By 1973 he was fishing irregularly, devoting more and more attention to the store that
Carolina, his common-law wife of about thirty years, had
started a few years previously. Tired of fishing, Alberto was
delighted to work as my field assistant between June and August of 1973, for a regular wage.

Alberto's story between 1965 and 1980 was one of consistently improving but unspectacular fortune, and his success,
in accordance with Arembepe tradition, had been based on
innovation and luck. In 1980 Alberto asserted that his life
had improved: "Hasn't yours?" he asked me. He attributed
his success to electricity and especially to his refrigerator.
Alberto and Carolina's household had been Arembepe's
third to install electricity, which permitted them to buy a refrigerator and eventually a freezer. Electric refrigerators, explained Alberto, are much more reliable than the old kerosene models that a few storekeepers had previously owned.

Note the element of luck here: old-time business people
had already made substantial investments in kerosene refrigerators before electricity arrived. They held on to the old
models and did not invest immediately in electric appli-
ances. This opened a niche for an enterprising business
move by Alberto and Carolina: they sold the small farm plot
in which they had previously invested profits from their store
and used the cash to buy an electric refrigerator. Adding a
freezer a year later, they acquired the reputation for having
some of the coldest drinks in Arembepe, a valuable resource
given the increased consumption of alcoholic beverages, especially beer, by villagers and outsiders alike.

Electricity reached Arembepe in 1977. Alberto and Carolina began by buying two cases of beer (each containing
twelve 1-liter bottles) for resale. By the winter of 1980, they
were selling 100 liters per weekend, producing a profit of
about $25, a figure that almost quadrupled in summer. Also

contributing to their success was the paved highway, which permitted not just weekend and summer people but beer and soft-drink trucks to include Arembepe in their regular delivery schedules.

The success of Alberto and Carolina therefore rested on a combination of luck and business skills—enterprise, foresight, opportunism, and hard work. Arembepeiros did not bring electricity or the road to the village, nor did Alberto and Carolina have anything to do with the shift to larger boats that demanded a deeper harbor, necessitating the move of moorings to the south, which gave Alberto's house its valuable view. But in the face of luck, they innovated opportunistically—converting a distant farm plot into a refrigerator, an at-home generator of additional income. Furthermore, Alberto and Ivan, his daughter's partner, convinced Carolina that they should expand their house seaward and construct a balcony where weekend tourists could drink their beer. Again, a strategic innovation led to success. Alberto's household continued to plow its profits back into the business, adding the freezer, a stereo system that permitted dancing in the balcony bar, and a second refrigerator when the first one broke down.

Continued profits permitted Alberto and Carolina to buy a lot in Volta do Robalo and build a house on it, which they were renting in 1980. This house was registered in Carolina's name, whereas their Arembepe residence belonged to Alberto. Alberto and Carolina had also been wise not to sell their house in seaside Arembepe to outsiders, as many villagers had done. Along with the view, they retained a favorable location for selling beer; the only nearby source of competition in cold beer sales was Aunt Dalia's bar, which specialized in juice, ice cream, and sales to hippies. Alberto and Carolina could take advantage of sales to locals as well as to weekenders who owned or rented houses in Street Down There and in the new neighborhood to the west. For those willing to wade through the lagoon in winter, even Caraúnas was nearer to this part of Arembepe than to the central and northern parts, and the best swimming areas were also closest to southern Arembepe. The location of his bar (and his reputation among outsiders for success and reliability) had also brought Alberto the job of caring for a house across the street, owned by a summer person from Salvador. This added about $35 per month to his income, while the summer person's well and electric pump gave his family ready access to clean water for washing dishes and bathing.

For sales of vegetables and sundries, Carolina and Alberto had competition. One out of every three inhabited houses in this part of Arembepe sold something. Although the reselling of limes, onions, tomatoes, herbs, and other produce from the agricultural estates located to the west of Arembepe had originally been Carolina's idea, Alberto blamed her for being insufficiently aggressive in meeting competition. He complained that Carolina had ignored his suggestions to buy more fruits and vegetables for resale. To illustrate his spouse's shortsightedness, Alberto recounted that a man from Salvador had arrived, rented street-front quarters across the street and a few doors to the north, and begun to sell cheaper fruits, vegetables, and sundries. Their produce sales had fallen off as a result. Alberto knew about the practice of first underselling to try to drive competitors out of business and then raising prices, but he thought that his own seaview and drink sales would shield them from such a tactic. Still, he complained, if Carolina had built up a larger sales volume years ago, they would have been able to match the newcomer's prices and keep their advantage.

Alberto's story illustrates successful adaptation by individuals and a household to Arembepe's transformation from isolated fishing village to economically diverse suburban resort community. Alberto and Carolina's economic advance showed up in their life style. A small house that in 1964 had been mostly wattle and daub was now completely brick. Only one room had been plastered and painted when I first met Alberto, and his house had a dirt floor. Years of gradual improvement added up to decidedly more comfortable quarters in 1980. A third bedroom and a toilet had been added, along with the seaward addition; all inside rooms were plastered and recently painted; the floor was cement; the house was spic and span. In addition to refrigerator, freezer, and stereo, they owned an electric iron, a gas stove, and a black and white television—posing a sharp contrast with 1964, when

Carolina had cooked on a simple wood-burning grill and ironed with charcoal, and the family could not afford even the cheapest transistor radio.

Along with their new life style, Alberto's family seemed much more comfortable with their success than in 1973. Carolina took part in *candomblé* less frequently than before, and their middle daughter, though now a grown woman and a regular *candomblé* participant, no longer suffered from possession by unwanted spirits. The health of the entire family had improved. Once a constant complainer about her ailments, Carolina seemed cheerier in 1980. Alberto attributed his persistent slight afternoon cough to years of pack-a-day cigarette smoking, which he had given up in 1977. He maintained his slim and fit-looking physique despite his fifty-seven years and his retirement from the daily manual labor of fishing. However, his hearing was failing noticeably, and his eyesight, which had troubled him in 1973, continued to be a problem. An opthalmologist we consulted in Salvador in 1973 diagnosed Alberto's problem as caused by the optic nerve, attributing visual deterioration to years of glare at sea.

Psychologically, Alberto exuded a new confidence. When presenting me to an immigrant neighbor and friend he remarked, "You remember my boss *[patrão]*, don't you?" Alberto was openly acknowledging and addressing years of gossip about our relationship. Villagers had always suspected that I paid Alberto for being a regular informant, which I never did, except with occasional presents and departure gifts, until I hired him as a field assistant in 1973 and 1980. Alberto had grown accustomed and entitled to his own moderate success; he felt less threatened by covillagers' envy than previously. Furthermore, all Arembepeiros were now more familiar with economic success and conspicuous consumption, and these life style changes were often the result of contacts with outsiders.

One afternoon in 1980 as Alberto and I were inspecting boats that had been beached for repairs near the fish stores, he pointed to a large vessel that belonged to a man from Salvador and joked with me, in plain hearing of a neighbor, "You're going to buy that boat for me, aren't you?" What a contrast with the 1960s, when he had often complained to me that other villagers were making him uncomfortable by accusing him of taking money to reveal their secrets. In 1964 and 1965 I had often wondered why Alberto sometimes did not appear for our nightly chat; I later learned that he was avoiding me after particularly disturbing gossip attacks. Even in 1973 Alberto had avoided head-on confrontations with village gossip about our relationship. By 1980, however, his self-confidence had grown immensely.

Of the four people discussed in this chapter, Alberto might be considered the most typical in certain ways. In contrast to Dora, once stigmatized as a *rapariga*, and to Fernando and Tomé, captain-owners, Alberto belonged to no deviant or statistically restricted social category. For about thirty years he had been an ordinary fisherman. Like many others, he had reduced his fishing and then abandoned it in response to new opportunities. His parents and grandparents were old residents of the Arembepe area, having been born either in Arembepe itself or in one of the agricultural estates just a few kilometers to the west. His grandparents had been among Arembepe's original settlers, and Alberto remembered a great-grandmother who had told him stories of her life as a slave. Like the other three, Alberto would be considered a black in the United States, but his skin is darkest of the four. My records show that he used various racial terms for himself: *moreno escuro* ("dark brunet"), *escuro* ("dark"), and even *preto* ("black") on occasion. He seemed to be using the last, once heard only rarely in Arembepe, more frequently in 1980. This may have been a sign that Arembepe's classification system was being simplified. However, it may also have been yet another reflection of Alberto's new self-confidence. He was now freely using a term that was once uncommon locally, probably because it carried over into Arembepe derogatory Brazilian stereotypes about people with very dark skin.

Despite his more typical economic role and native birth, Alberto's individuality stood out in obvious ways. During his youth he had suffered an accident that left him with a minor but easily detectable physical disability. Another aspect of Alberto's personality soon became even more apparent to me—his interest in teaching. During the 1960s he often mentioned his friendship with the learned German priest who had married one of Arembepe's landowners. He took me to the man's apartment in Salvador, and I saw that Alberto was indeed friendly with the elderly man and his two sons, both university graduates. Only in 1980 did I learn of Alberto's "middle-class" buddy, described in Chapter 7—another outsider who had been visiting Arembepe and had known Alberto since the 1940s. This man's wife had been a schoolteacher. Although Alberto was barely literate, having obtained only the limited elementary schooling available in Arembepe during his boyhood, he valued education. He and Carolina had burdened themselves with the expense of educating their oldest daughter in Itapoan, and their youngest daughter was taking advantage of the improved schools in Arembepe. Alberto had often told me that one member of the landowning family had become a high-school teacher; and he spoke with pride of the college education of another landlord.

Alberto knew that I planned to become a university professor; he appreciated the fact that I found Arembepe worth studying, and he very much wanted to instruct me. Both Niles Eldredge and I found that he liked particularly to teach about the fishing industry. He labored with both of us on maps of the ocean floor, detailing the zones where different species could be found, making sure we had the correct names of the zones and pointing them out when we went on fishing expeditions. In 1973 he went over the ocean floor map in my doctoral dissertation, chiding me for mistakes and penciling in corrections.

Perhaps other anthropologists have forgotten after long absences, as I did between 1973 and 1980, the specific talents and personality attributes of a particular informant that originally led the anthropologist to value him or her especially. In 1980 I found myself rediscovering the full range of Alberto's special qualities. A key marker of a good informant was Alberto's habit of admitting when he did not know the answer to a particular query. Other informants would simply give me a wrong answer; Alberto would go out that evening or the next day and discreetly check out the point. Despite (or perhaps because of) his failing vision and hearing, Alberto had always paid close attention to what he saw and heard. Through observation of what went on around him, he amassed an unusually broad knowledge of village life, and he had a good memory. I was also struck by the accuracy of his estimates and figures, particularly since other people who theoretically should have known particular facts better than he were much less accurate. Accuracy, memory, knowledge, attentiveness, and willingness to admit lack of knowledge are qualities that make a good informant, and Alberto had these in abundance.

A final point: Alberto considered his village's story well worth telling, and he wanted to make sure that I got it right. Unlike others, who insisted on directing my questions about their society back at me ("Are there camels in the United States?"), Alberto pondered even my most naive questions and usually made a sincere attempt to answer them.

In retrospect, I now realize that my association with Alberto was no accident, no chance throwing together of compatible souls. Through Niles Eldredge, I had discovered Alberto; but on the other hand, through Niles, Alberto had also found me. In a community of outsiders, Alberto was the native-born participant observer, the teacher searching for a student, probably as determined to teach as Niles and I were to learn. This book therefore reflects joint accomplishment of a common goal, Alberto's and mine—to bring Arembepe's story to the outside world.

The Village Prostitute: What Happens to the Deviant Once Deviance Disappears

I met Dora, who was born in Arembepe in 1937, two years before I met Alberto. Betty Wagley Kottak knows her even better than I, and I have drawn on Betty's knowledge and a published article (I. Kottak, 1977) for a good deal of the material in this discussion. Dora, our employee during each visit to Arembepe, is an exuberant, sentimental woman with a strong sense of family—a domain where, unfortunately, she had until recently enjoyed little success. In contrast to Alberto, an excellent informant, Dora has never been a particularly good one. Often she grew impatient with our questions and cut them off, telling us she didn't know things it was obvious she did. One trait she seemed to share with Alberto was a dislike of gossip; she didn't usually like to enlighten us about the soap-operatic details of other people's lives. Neither did Alberto; but he nevertheless always tried hard to answer factual questions. However, Dora did love to visit people; when we planned short trips outside Arembepe she often asked to come along. In 1980 she still remembered a trip that she and her then four-year-old son, whose congenital heart condition killed him at age thirteen, had made with us to Camaçari in 1962. There the boy, Dora's first-born, had met his father for the first time. Earlier, Dora had lived for a few months in Camaçari with the boy's father, whom she had met while working as a domestic servant in a Salvador suburb. She had abandoned him following abuse and rivalry with another woman.

Although she was normally a reluctant and frustrating informant, Dora did often help us by "facilitating"—telling people that we wished to talk with them, arranging meetings, accompanying us, and introducing us to strangers. For example, when Betty told her in 1980 that she was interested in talking to the nuns and to the *candomblé* people in Caraúnas, Dora wanted to go right over. To visit was her joy; our hosts could answer the questions.

During our 1980 visit, Dora reported several times "I've had a feeling lately that my Americans would be coming." Whereas Alberto needed us to satisfy his desire to teach, Dora had continuing material needs. She had lost the only house she had ever owned. She wanted a new one, a home of her own, for her growing family, and she was determined that we were going to help her get it. From our first through almost our last conversation in 1980, she insisted on this, until she got part of what she wanted. Persistence was another of her personality attributes, which is why she always managed to arrange meetings with hard-to-contact people.

From the mid-1960s until the early 1970s, when Dora began living with her current common-law spouse—an immigrant who worked as an ordinary fisherman—she had been one of a dozen Arembepeiros classified as *rapariga*, village prostitute, a uniquely stigmatized category that lost most of its significance as the majority of the women so labeled found marital partners among the flood of men who migrated to Arembepe during the 1970s. To a greater extent than the few alcoholics who were socially stigmatized as "drunks" *(bebados)*, Arembepe's *raparigas* were the objects of the community's scorn. Other villagers attributed the plight of these women to mistakes on their part, rather than to the economic and demographic factors that made a "husbandless" category inevitable. That is, the village economy offered women few ways of making a living for themselves, and the marriage-aged population contained a surplus of females. The stigma of being a "manless" woman therefore reflected Arembepe's overall poverty, competition for resources, and the traditional belief that obligations associated with legal marriage and the nuclear family took precedence.

Most of these conditions changed during the 1970s, when women's job prospects improved, many males migrated to Arembepe, and legal marriage became less frequent. In this context the deviant status of *rapariga* all but disappeared, although the term was sometimes heard as an insult. The following discussion, of how Dora got to be a *rapariga* and of what happened to her as the deviant category lost its salience, is based on an article by Isabel (Betty) Kottak, which applied "symbolic interactionist" or "labeling" theory to Dora's case, and on our field notes from all five visits. I. Kottak (1977) analyzes Dora's deviance in terms of Edwin Lemert's (1951) eightfold progression—from primary deviation (first departure from a norm) through ultimate acceptance of deviant status and role.

Dora's primary deviation, getting pregnant, occurred when she was twenty. Note that Dora's deviation was not sexual intercourse, which many young women experienced prior to elopement or marriage, but pregnancy. The obvious anatomical change removed her from the virgin (*moça*) category and made it incumbent on her to find a mate. Accordingly, she joined her lover in Camaçari. But their common-law union broke up after eight months, and she returned to Arembepe with her infant son. In ironic contrast to villagers' subsequent evaluation of Dora as a *rapariga* seeking to live off other women's husbands, Dora had actually made a concerted attempt to improve her own economic and social position. She had journeyed into an unknown world outside Arembepe, where she had arranged employment as a domestic. Like many other Arembepe women, she had had an affair with an unmarried man—lighter in skin color and wealthier than most men back home. Again she had hoped for socioeconomic advance. Luck, however, which had contributed to the rise and fall of so many Arembepeiros, was a factor in Dora's subsequent plight: an inexperienced young woman away from home, she chose the wrong man.

Dora returned to Arembepe and moved into the wattle-and-daub house of her grandmother, where her childless brother and his wife also lived. Even though these people helped Dora care for her son, her chances of attracting a man had been reduced by childbirth. Young men preferred younger women than Dora and generally avoided acquiring stepchildren. The partners that Dora was able to find were "losers." The father of her second son, who lived only two years, was an alcoholic. Following this brief affair, Dora took up with the father of her oldest surviving son, aged eighteen in 1980. This was an unsuccessful fisherman, and again the union did not last.

Thereafter, Dora suffered further penalties and social rejection, which are common aspects of a deviant career. Her material needs increased as her children grew older. Dora's brother's wife began to bear children, and the support of Dora and her children became more burdensome for her brother. Dora realized that she and her children were depriving her brother (a nonowning captain) of resources he needed to invest in a boat of his own. To increase her independence she took various steps: she sought work from the few outsiders, like us, who filtered into Arembepe during the mid-1960s. She became more aggressive in meeting men and trying to obtain their support. She began to associate less with her brother's family and more with women like herself, unmarried females who lived alone. She flouted canons of proper female behavior by visiting the beach as the boats returned in the evenings, by staying out late on festive occasions, and by dressing garishly. In short, she began to act like a *rapariga*.

As a final step, in 1965, she began her first affair with a married man, a successful captain-owner, whose two sons she eventually bore. Other villagers began to regard her as someone who was depriving a legal wife and family of their legitimate rights. After our departure in 1965, Dora, in order to make her ongoing affair (as secondary wife in an informal polygynous union) easier and to relieve tension in her brother's household, left home. With her consort's help, she constructed a new wattle-and-daub house (the first home of her own) in northern Arembepe. This hut was blatantly located near her consort's primary home, in a neighborhood where Dora had never lived before. Dora was regularly abused by her lover's relatives and in-laws, all of whom lived nearby. When she fought with her lover's wife, her own relatives did not intercede on her behalf. The stigma applied to Dora had become generalized and community-wide; the label of *rapariga* was applied to her more frequently. "Decent women" told their children not to play with hers.

During the late 1960s, Dora's relationship with her consort began to deteriorate. As he contributed less and less to feed Dora and her children, she began "entertaining" men for money and food on a nightly basis. This had become easier, as Arembepe's access to outsiders gradually improved. Such behavior had not been possible while Dora still lived in her brother's household. By this time, most of Dora's associations were with other members of the *rapariga* category (including Maria and her daughter, the *candomblé* participants discussed in Chapter 10). Dora gradually became a leader of the *rapariga* group, smoothing over arguments between other members, employing her "facilitating" skills to help them find jobs. (The economic opportunities available to such women were also increasing as the 1960s ended.) With Dora's support and encouragement, the *raparigas* would occasionally invade male territory, visiting the beach, where they would laugh, joke, and poke fun at fishermen and outside fish buyers. Dora had become more aggressive and was regularly visible in domains not ordinarily open to village women. She moved at will through public space, entering stores and bars and freely interacting with outsiders, including tourists and anthropologists.

By 1973 it was apparent that Dora's role as *rapariga* and the deviant behavior associated with it had intensified, as had her labeling by covillagers. Dora's *rapariga* status blocked her access to many usual female areas of social participation: normal home life, an adequate diet, the possibility of advancing in socioeconomic status through a husband, the likelihood of good health, legitimacy, and inheritance rights for her children. This closure caused Dora much anguish,

268   REALITY

particularly through the deaths of several of her children. On the other hand, as is generally true of membership in deviant social categories, Dora's role as a member of this subculture opened compensatory areas of social participation normally closed to ordinary women. For example, along with other *raparigas*, Dora was particularly active in *candomblé* during the mid-1970s.

Members of any social system are concerned about deviant people only if and when there are well-established deviant roles, and that of *rapariga* was disappearing from Arembepe in 1980. Dora's social status had risen because her common-law union with an immigrant fisherman had lasted about seven years. However, her life style had not improved dramatically. Like other ordinary fishermen in the Arembepe of 1980, Dora's husband received low wages. His employer was a wealthy storeowner and local entrepreneur, from whom Dora took weekly cash advances, to be repaid, they hoped, out of the next catch. Dora regarded her partner as a good man; she ignored his excessive weekend drinking and stressed that he was a kind father both to their own two young children (including Dora's only daughter) and to her three sons from previous unions.

Through her husband's earnings, Dora had hoped to convert her wattle-and-daub, straw-roofed hut in northern Arembepe into a brick house; but a former neighbor had seized her land, fencing it off and calling it his own when she tore down the hut in order to start building the new dwelling. Dora was dubious about winning the court case she had initiated against him. In the meantime she had temporarily lived with another brother, with whose wife she frequently argued. Her 1980 residence was a hut loaned by her aunt.

The lives of Dora and her sons had been spent in tiny hovels with mud-wall parasites, bare earthen floors, and leaky, insect-infested palm-frond roofs. By 1980 Dora was desperate for a home of her own, to bring her family together, to have all her children around her. She felt especially sorry for her oldest son, aged eighteen, who slept next-door in her aunt's living room. About to finish junior high school, after which he planned to enter the army, obtain work papers, and eventually find a steady job, Dora's son had no classes until afternoon. Dora lamented, "Sometimes he likes to sleep late in the morning because he doesn't have anything to do. My aunt calls him lazy when he does. I wish he didn't have to take that. I want a house of my own so that my son can sleep late if he wants to. I wish my man and my sons had steady jobs. Nowadays fishermen aren't earning enough to pay the bills.

"People in town treat me funny sometimes. They look at me in a strange way. I think it's because I don't have a house of my own. But my boys are all handsome and strong and I have hope for the future."

Dora looked to her sons, particularly the three oldest ones, aged fourteen, fifteen, and eighteen, to bring an end to her continuing poverty. Their future incomes would help her construct a house on the lot she arranged to buy at the end of August 1980. With the down payment in hand, she believed that she could afford monthly payments on the balance. For a few months before our arrival, Dora had been working in a bar recently opened in the village square by her *comadre* (godmother of her second son). She thought that tips and weekend wages would enable her to pay off her mortgage. She pinned her hopes on kinship—on her sons' eventual success and on that of her *comadre*, whose ritual kinship with Dora had lasted for twenty years, despite the premature death of the son whose baptism created the relationship.

Recalling past taunts and exclusion, Dora said that she trusted few others. She liked the brother with whom she had first lived and his mate and children, her full sister, a half-sister, and some of her nieces and nephews. Aside from these people, she claimed to be "close to no one in Arembepe." Now she locked her door each time she left her hut. "You can't trust people not to fool around with your stuff," she explained.

Though Dora was no longer classified as a *rapariga*, her former status had left its mark. She believed that "people look at me funny," though she couldn't explain exactly why. She felt cut off from most other villagers. Still, in 1980, twenty-three years after the primary deviation of her first pregnancy, Dora, through her sons, could glimpse an end to years of extreme poverty, miserable living conditions, and social isolation. It was the wish, now a more realistic hope, to escape all this that was symbolized in Dora's desperation to bring all her children together in a home of her own. Her ascent, however, was still uncertain, and if it did come, it would surely be no more rapid than her fall.

The Stranger

I first met Fernando, born in 1933 in the interior of Bahia, in 1962. His mate, Ivone, was Dora's only full sister (they had two brothers). Fernando was then twenty-nine; he had come to Arembepe in his early teens and had been living with Ivone for six years. After a year of courting, which had begun at the Saint John celebration one June, they decided to elope. One evening Ivone went to her house and packed a few of her things to take to the house that Fernando had been building for his future family. She moved the rest of her possessions after a few weeks. Their first child, a daughter, came a year later. By 1980 they had ten children, and during the almost quarter-century of their union Ivone had miscarried six times. Fernando, an illiterate man who never received any formal education, remembered that the total number of his progeny was ten; but he had to count names on his fingers to tell me how many girls and boys.

When he was eight years old Fernando had run away from a fairy-tale home, replete with wicked stepmother, in the interior. Following Fernando's mother's death, his father had taken another wife. Fernando decided to leave home when he saw his stepmother place his younger brother's hand in the fire as punishment for taking something. The runaway skirted Salvador and was taken in by a man in Itapoan, who after eight days beat him, spurring further flight, to Abrantes, Arembepe's district seat.

In recalling his childhood, Fernando stressed incidents of physical abuse. A man in Abrantes had kept him for four years and used to beat him for lying. In 1942, at the age of twelve, Fernando moved to Arembepe, where he worked successively as mule driver for two businessmen; they offered him room and board in their houses in the central square. He liked the first, another outsider, better than the

second—Prudencio, the landowner's agent. Fernando recalled another beating—from Prudencio's wife.

Fernando began fishing in 1951 when he was eighteen. As
an immigrant, he had no kin ties to captains or crews and
started fishing with a man from Jauá, whose boat was temporarily working out of Arembepe. In 1960 Fernando became captain and half-owner (with a local businesswoman) of
a sailboat. In the mid-1960s he joined the other captains who
were dissolving their relationships with nonfishing owners
in favor of full ownership. "I don't want to have to fish and
divide my profit between myself and someone who sits on
shore doing nothing while I do all the work. And I'm not the
only one who feels this way."

During the mid-1960s, Fernando was a reasonably vigorous and successful captain-owner. He followed a behavioral
model provided by people like Tomé, but Fernando was
never as daring, innovative, or enterprising, and this showed
up in his good but unspectacular catches. As was required by
the model, Fernando maintained a stable crew, using ritual
kinship to compensate for his lack of kin ties and legal marriage links with other villagers. Enjoying the good health of
a man in his thirties, Fernando fished regularly, varying his
fishing strategy with the seasons but never straying far from
fishing patterns set by others and by tradition.

This pattern of following rather than leading persisted into
the 1970s, when Fernando was one of the last captain-owners to withdraw from the fishermen's cooperative, which had
provided him with the loan necessary to motorize his boat.
And in 1980 he was one of just two people still following the
old pattern of daytime fishing in Arembepe's traditional
banks, while others were doing distant nighttime "ice fishing." In the mid-1960s I shared what seemed to be other
Arembepeiros' general impression of Fernando as an ordinary, respected, noncontroversial, good man. My perception
changed during my 1973 visit.

Of all the Arembepeiros I spent time with that year, Fernando seemed most fearful and hostile toward change. Social
scientists have commented that outsiders often exhibit the
strongest antipathy toward external forces and people. Fernando provides an excellent example. So uneasy was he

about his nighttime visits to the summer house we were renting south of Arembepe that he began carrying a revolver for protection. To my knowledge, no one in Arembepe had possessed such a weapon during the mid-1960s, and gun ownership was still rare in 1973. More than my other friends, he reiterated that thieves and armed robbers would surely attempt to storm the domicile of "Americans, who, they think, must be rich." These would be outsiders, of course. "You have nothing to fear from Arembepeiros." His fear was strong and contagious, and his warnings soon unnerved me; I suspected every set of headlights that crept into my isolated neighborhood after sundown. "Get a gun," he said; "otherwise you'll be killed." It was Fernando who during our absence one evening devised the idea of throwing firecrackers from our windows to convince would-be thieves that our house was armed. Fernando was also more vocal than other Arembepeiros in denouncing other outsiders, the hippies, for licentiousness.

Another manifestation of Fernando's unease was excessive alcohol consumption, in sharp opposition to his previous habits. During the 1960s Fernando had hardly ever drunk *cachaça*, but in 1973 he requested not just beer but ample glasses of Bacardi rum when he visited us. (Alberto's drinking habits provide a contrast. During the 1960s he always took at least one shot of *cachaça* each evening, to "warm up" after the day's fishing. But he remained a controlled and moderate drinker in 1980. I have never seen him drunk.) Fernando, however, had gone from one extreme to the other.

1973 was a time when Arembepeiros felt insecure about many changes—Tibrás pollution, hippie stragglers, weekend hordes of boisterous outsiders, a booming economy, and a dramatically increased cash flow. Alberto's family expressed its unease through his wife's psychosomatic illnesses and his daughter's uncontrolled spirit possession. Both of them sought relief in *candomblé*, as eventually did Fernando, who often mentioned to me that ordinary fishermen had been accusing certain captains of using black magic. He hinted to me that other captains, including Tomé (who never did), were participating in *candomblé*, and that this partially explained the dramatic increase in the wealth of certain individuals. Fernando stood out among Arembepeiros in giving a magical explanation for a down-to-earth but unfamiliar process—rapid commercialization and the economic boom.

When I left Arembepe in August 1973 I predicted that Fernando would increasingly seek solace in alcohol and in *candomblé* participation. (I based the prediction about *candomblé* on Fernando's belief that it contributed to economic success. I suspected that Fernando, attempting to get richer himself and to guarantee his protection against others, would seek the most available magical solution.) My prediction was correct, but fortunately only in part. Villagers reported that Fernando did drink too much between 1973 and 1976. Although Arembepeiros realized that Fernando was drinking excessively, they never labeled him an alcoholic—a term reserved for someone who worked sporadically, hung out around bars, and drank even at breakfast time. During this period Fernando also became increasingly involved in *candomblé*, the only captain-owner to do so. He eventually became one of the main ceremonial assistants of Crispim, the spirit father in Caraúnas.

On my return to Arembepe in 1980 I was pleasantly surprised to find that Fernando's behavior had stabilized. In fact, he seemed as much at ease with himself and his life style as he had been in the mid-1960s. He was no longer active in *candomblé*, and he was clearly not an alcoholic. His drinking was limited to beer on Sunday, now customary for most Arembepeiros. However, Fernando had dropped a few notches in covillagers' estimation. Some ridiculed his nonintensive fishing strategy, which usually produced small catches. Yet Fernando and his family enjoyed a pleasant life style supported by boat ownership and fishing, the Tibrás salary of a son who still lived at home, and year-round rental from a brick house behind theirs, constructed during the early 1970s to take advantage of the tourist and hippie trade.

By 1980 the modest but wise investments that Fernando and Ivone had made in different areas of Arembepe's changing economy had enabled Fernando to withdraw from the rat race that had threatened his mental health in 1973. He and the two ordinary fishermen in his crew drew unspectacular profits from a leisurely fishing schedule of eight hours at sea (eight to four) weekdays only. Fernando now had time to spend with his wife, children, and grandchildren. His active hostility toward outsiders had turned into ambivalence. One step in his acceptance of change was his acquisition, through the baptism of his six-year-old son, of middle-class *compadres*—a man and his daughter, who resided in Salvador. Fernando and Ivone had gotten to know the boy's godparents when they rented the house next-door for weekend use. The godfather, a middle-aged man whose job in a chemical concern entailed international travel, offered Fernando the security of a kinlike link to a representative of the outside world, and it brought him information that made the rest of the world seem less mysterious and threatening than it once had.

At first I found it curious that Fernando and Ivone had asked the man's daughter, rather than his wife, to stand as *comadre*. But on reflection, I realized that the choice of a younger woman ensured that the link between the families would last longer.

Fernando continued to perceive his lack of actual kin ties to other Arembepeiros as a problem; he complained that he had been unable to finance a well to bring running water to his house, since the ground underneath was very rocky. "If only I had relatives living nearby," he suggested, "we could split the costs." Nevertheless, Fernando had expanded his ritual kinship network through baptism of his ten children, and he had himself been asked to stand as godfather for a dozen others.

Despite his ritual kinship web and his economic comfort, Fernando's resentment and insecurity about outsiders had merely abated rather than disappeared completely. Illustrating this was the explanation he offered me for Tomé's economic decline (see next section). Fernando told me that the bank had seized Tomé's family home when he had been unable to meet a debt. In fact, as Alberto reported accurately, and Tomé later confirmed, Tomé had made the decision to sell his house and buy a smaller one in order to repay debts and finance boat repairs. The result was the same, but Fernando's interpretation showed a feeling of being directly victimized by outside forces.

Another of Fernando's tendencies was inaccuracy. Prior to 1980 I had concluded that Fernando was a less valuable informant than Alberto, but I never stopped to consider why.

A *Community of Outsiders* 275

In 1980 I asked Fernando, Alberto, and others some of the same factual questions. Alberto was almost always right, and Fernando frequently wrong, even about matters on which he should have been the expert—for example, the cost of diesel fuel. Fernando, the boat owner, was 20 percent off, while Alberto, the bartender, was on target. Fernando's inaccuracy can be seen as part of an overall personality that viewed the world more unrealistically and suspiciously than was usually the case in Arembepe.

Fernando's attraction to us can be seen as yet another expression of his ambivalence toward outsiders: although he was fearful, he was also fascinated. As we saw in the cases of Alberto and Dora, Fernando's mental health rebounded as he grew more accustomed to change, and as he enjoyed a stream of modest but steady improvements in his life style. By 1980, though still suspicious, he was no longer irrationally afraid of the outside world, which on the basis of recent experience had generally been good to him.

As an anthropologist rather than a psychologist, I can only speculate about the reasons for Fernando's extreme reaction to outsiders. Was he obsessed with the fear that some of the people and deeds he thought to have left behind would follow him to Arembepe? Perhaps, like us—other strangers who had discovered Arembepe in the old days—Fernando was particularly possessive about the pleasant community where he had established a place for himself. Or did he, as an immigrant, attribute to other outsiders the worst of intentions, as an expression of his own envious and resentful feelings toward his host community? His exaggeration of dangers to us in 1973 may also have disguised a possible (unconscious) wish to seize our wealth and life style for himself. Or was he equating us, as old-time, familiar outsiders, with himself? Did he imagine that people were eager to do to us what he feared they wanted to do to him?

No doubt, multiple psychological factors worked in Fernando's mind during the early and mid-1970s, as he attempted to deal with rapid economic and social change. Fortunately, Fernando did eventually manage to adjust. As in many cases, in many cultures, he used a drug (alcohol) and a new religion (*candomblé*) as temporary crutches. By 1980, however, this stranger had grown more independent and trustful. The outside world and its denizens, though still strange, were no longer overwhelming.

The Innovator

From 1964 through 1973, Tomé was Arembepe's most successful fisherman. He had returned in 1961 from a long period of outside commercial fishing—a brief stay in Salvador and seven years in Rio de Janeiro. In 1964 Tomé still shared his boat with a nonfishing owner, a successful storekeeper who was his neighbor; but by 1965 he had dissolved this relationship and owned his own vessel. In 1964, on the basis of our survey of all Arembepe households, Tomé had the highest fisherman's income. His success rested on a bundle of factors discussed in Chapter 4. More than any other captain-owner, Tomé worked hard, took calculated risks, maintained the loyalty of his (mainly kin-based) crew, and experimented with new fishing strategies. During the mid-1960s, his success was recognized in his election as president of the Fishermen's Society.

Like most successful fishermen during the 1960s, Tomé supplemented his fishing income with agricultural produce from a small farm in one of the nearby agricultural estates. His plot, purchased early in 1964, included over 300 coconut seedlings, which he anticipated would start yielding in seven years. It also provided a variety of fruits and vegetables, mostly used to feed his growing family.

By 1973, Tomé's family had expanded to five sons and one daughter (exactly as in his own sibling set), and Tomé's success relative to other fishermen was even more obvious. He had been among the first to accept a motorization loan from the cooperative. His example spurred other villagers to join and to begin motorized fishing. Once Tomé determined that he could make more money by marketing his own fish than by delivering them to the cooperative, he became the first Arembepeiro to withdraw. He was soon followed by his younger brother Dinho, who, however, remained angry at Tomé for undermining the cooperative.

As Tomé was phasing out his involvement in the cooperative, he also bought a *barco* (large boat) at about the same time as did two nonfishing owners. Tomé's efforts, however, fully launched the pattern of "ice-fishing" that had come to dominate Arembepe's fishing industry by 1980. Tomé's tendency had always been to seek new banks and travel to more distant spots than other captains. The bigger boat permitted him to explore fishing zones even farther north. The (paid) captains of the two other *barcos* followed Tomé to offshore Sauipe and Subaúma, as the new pattern became established.

By July 1973, Tomé had become an entrepreneur *extraordinaire*. He had acquired a van to take his fish to market in Itapoan, raising his per-kilogram profit by half. He let his two youngest brothers use his small motorboat (a modified sailboat) to fish and to set his trammel nets—widely used for lobstering during my 1973 visit. Another of Tomé's innovative investments was in his children's education. The oldest boy was already studying outside.

As a result of intelligence, innovation, income, and plans for education, it seemed likely that Tomé, raised in poverty, might see at least some of his children rise to the middle class. During a long conversation in August 1973, on a Sunday, when Tomé was able to take time out to talk with me, I determined that his annual earnings surpassed my own (unspectacular) salary then as associate professor at the University of Michigan. Tomé's rise, from an annual income worth $1,000 in 1964 to over $14,000 in 1973, had been dramatic.

During that interview, Tomé discussed his motivations and aspirations eloquently and poignantly. His fundamental goal was success for himself and his family. He wanted his own children to escape the poverty he remembered from his childhood. His father, with whom Tomé, the oldest son, began fishing at the age of fourteen, was never more than an ordinary fisherman. Tomé's parents eventually separated, the father moving in with their *comadre*. (This was a nonsexual arrangement. There is a strong taboo against sexual relations between coparents.) The mother lived alone, eventually becoming an alcoholic beggar. Tomé and his four brothers and one sister had grown up, he stated, in one of a poor village's most destitute households. Determined to create a different fate, Tomé had set off for Rio in 1954 at the age of twenty-one. On a brief visit home, he had married a woman of his own age in civil and religious ceremonies. During his lonely years in Rio, he sent money to his wife, his mother, and his brothers. One important goal in 1973 was to build a good brick house for his mother, who had never previously owned more than a wattle-and-daub shack. Responding to the demand for rental housing, Tomé had also nearly finished expansion of his own home; there would be two houses—the new one to rent in the rear, the old one in front for Tomé's family.

On my earlier trips to Arembepe, Tomé and I had talked of his experiences in Rio de Janeiro. He had considered the years of loneliness and strangeness worthwhile, since his earnings eventually financed his house and boat. In 1973 he was pleased that his oldest son had begun formal study; he also seemed happy with his brothers' success. Two owned boats and trammel nets, and the other two had use of Tomé's old but still seaworthy vessel. His brothers were all strong, worked hard, and helped each other, he told me. "I don't much care what other people think of me because I have my brothers and sons to count on."

On the basis of what I saw in 1973 I would not have been surprised to find on my next visit that Tomé and his brothers owned most of Arembepe. My biggest shock in 1980 was to discover Tomé's actual fate. Looking out the seaview window of Claudia's Restaurant on the first day of my return, I recognized (by name) Tomé's large boat, beached alongside a half-dozen others. The restaurant owner told me that it and two of the other large beached boats belonged to Tomé. "Aha!" I thought. "My prediction has come true. Tomé owns an entire fleet."

Assuming that he was out fishing that day in a newer vessel, I dismissed Tomé from my mind until two evenings later, when I encountered him on the beach, returning from a day's fishing in Valter's boat (Valter, Dora's brother, is the common-law husband of Tomé's sister). I greeted Tomé and asked him about his own boats, which, he told me, needed repairs. Only later did I learn that Tomé had sold the most dilapidated of the three boats; another had been beached for nine months, while the third had stopped fishing in early April of 1980. Why, I wondered, had Tomé not repaired at least one of his vessels, and why was he working as an ordinary fisherman? The more I learned about the gap between owners' and ordinary fishermen's earnings in Arembepe's new economy, the more intrigued I became with Tomé's actions.

From as far back as 1962 I remembered Tomé's house in the northern rectangle as one of Arembepe's nicest. Even then it had been made of brick and cement, with a tile roof and decorative Portuguese tiles adorning the front façade. Tomé had even added an uncommonly spacious kitchen and a toilet, one of a half-dozen in Arembepe then. From 1973 I recalled the tour he had proudly given me of his new rental house behind his own. "You'll be able to rent it," he assured me, "the next time you come to Arembepe." I was therefore shocked to learn in 1980 that Tomé no longer lived in his old house. I later discovered that he had sold it to a summer person to repay debts and meet boat expenses. His family had moved to the smaller rental house behind. A few doors up, facing the northern rectangle, was the house Tomé had built for his mother. Unfortunately, her actual stay there had been brief. Again to satisfy debtors, Tomé had made a long-term rental agreement whereby a family from Salvador had year-round use of the dwelling until mid-1981.

As I was discovering evidence of Tomé's economic decline in 1980, I was also being told about Arembepe's new elite—the nonfishing owners of large boats, including Tomé's brother Dinho, who now owned five active boats and was widely considered to be the richest man in town—the role I had imagined for Tomé. Tomé's other brothers were also doing well. One owned a boat; another owned one boat plus a half-share of another; the youngest brother was still a teenager. All told, Tomé and his brothers owned nine and one-half of the twenty-seven boats (active and inactive) registered in Arembepe's fleet. If my predictions about the family had been correct, why had I been wrong about Tomé?

The story unraveled slowly. Fernando, who believed that a Salvador bank had seized Tomé's house, said that Tomé's situation was worsening and blamed Tomé himself for his plight: "He doesn't repair his boats because he doesn't have the means, and the reason for that is that he overextended himself. He took too many loans from banks and couldn't pay them back."

Whereas Fernando saw Tomé's plight as self-inflicted, Alberto talked of Tomé's bad luck; he contrasted the uncertainty of fishing with salaried employment on the land. "Even the most successful captain-owner can fail if he has a run of bad luck." Although Alberto was thinking of motor failures and loss of ice, bait, provisions, and time at sea, he still considered the main reason for Tomé's fall to be that "his luck had left him." Tomé himself dwelt on the overwhelming demands he faced as a fishing owner, the contradiction between maintaining crew loyalty and productive fishing through the captain's role, and the on-land demands of industrial technology and marketing fish. "I simply never got any rest."

I discovered the missing element in Tomé's story during my visit to the hippie Aldeia. Hippie João told me that he rented his house from Sonia, a hippie who lived in Arembepe with a fisherman, Tomé. Did I know him?

As we walked back to Arembepe along the beach, I pestered Alberto, never prone to idle gossip, for details. I learned that Tomé was *not* still living in the northern rectangle with his wife and children, as Fernando had told me, but in rental quarters in Street Down There, with the *ippa*. They had been living together for two years. She had been pregnant with his child but had miscarried. Sonia was a reformed alcoholic who had almost died as a result of illness caused by her drinking; she still looked sick and required expensive medicines, which she could afford, said one man, because she was rich.

Sonia later told us, almost boastfully, that she came from a wealthy Paulista family. Her mother disapproved of her hippie life style and had come to Arembepe to try to break up her living arrangement with Tomé. Sonia had inherited money from a grandparent, but her mother had cut off her access to these funds when Sonia became a hippie. Still, Sonia did receive money from her parents from time to time, and she also collected rent from two hippies. Sonia had told many villagers about her wealth, and she complained to us that she had problems adjusting to Tomé's life style. For example, she found it hard to walk and take buses in the city as he did. "I'm accustomed to cabs." Tomé had been offended by Sonia's mother, who scolded her daughter for living with "a mere fisherman." Yet a similar disdain showed up in Sonia's own statements about Arembepeiros.

Some villagers linked Tomé's economic decline to his association with Sonia, but others told me that his troubles had preceded their union, established in 1978. Still, Tomé's troubles had mounted during the past year, when he, unable to afford repairs, had withdrawn both boats from fishing. He was waiting to hear about his application for a loan from a government-sponsored rural-credit program. He had asked for $6,700 to buy new Japanese-made motors for both his boats; the motors cost $2,700 each; he would use the rest of the loan to repay some of his outstanding debts. Tomé had kept his loan request below the maximum amount for which signature loans were available (about $8,000). He did not want to risk either of his two remaining houses, worth about $11,000 and $13,000, respectively, or either of his boats, which he valued at $4,200 and $5,800. Tomé pointed out to me that despite his current problems, he still owned property worth more than 2 million cruzeiros ($33,300)—not bad for someone who had earned a mere $1000 a year plus the food he had obtained from fishing and farming in 1964.

What would he do, I asked Tomé, if he were denied the loan? He supposed he would sell one of the boats. Both Alberto, with whom I discussed Tomé's plight, and I thought this a better idea than contracting another debt, given the limitations on the captain-owner's time. Tomé, however, although approaching fifty and complaining about getting insufficient rest, still regarded himself as a vigorous man. He was the oldest member of Arembepe's soccer team. He told of a time when his motor had failed offshore. "I tried to get one of the younger men in the crew to swim to shore for help, but no one would. Finally, I put on a life preserver and swam to shore myself in forty-five minutes." When Sonia expressed concern about his taking the rural-credit loan, Tomé asserted "I fear nothing." In traditional Arembepe, men of Tomé's age were planning retirement from the captain's role. Tomé, however, still believed that he could fulfill the demands of the captain-fisherman's role, while owning two boats and marketing their fish.

He had not yet made a realistic plan, given the nature of

the new economy, to extricate himself from debt and to limit demands on his time. To me, the most logical solution was to sell one boat and use the money to buy a motor for the other. Tomé could then work in it as captain-owner until his debts were repaid. Eventually, of course, Tomé would have to retire from fishing, as his brother Dinho had done. Thereafter he might be able to employ an immigrant captain. At first Alberto said that there was no way that Tomé could reverse his luck, but when I suggested the sale of one boat, Alberto thought that it could indeed bring enough cash for a new motor. Tomé himself was keeping this option in mind in case he didn't get the loan.

Tomé's reaction to the outside world contrasted sharply with Fernando's. Tomé "had no fear" of using external resources. He had easily repaid the small loan (about $1,700) he had taken from a Salvador bank for his first big boat. He had just obtained this loan when we talked in 1973. A bank official, impressed with Tomé and his collateral, had also encouraged him to apply for financing of a van to transport his fish. Tomé's downfall was linked to excessive borrowing between 1973 and 1980. He *had* overextended himself, as Fernando contended, and he had also had some "bad luck," including exploitation of this lower-class, poorly educated man by unscrupulous outsiders. As Sonia remarked, "Arembepeiros don't read contracts." Tomé's credit rating had plunged after an experience with dishonest loan-agency officials, who had pocketed his payments, then contended that he had defaulted on his loan. The men were eventually caught, since they were doing the same thing to several other rural people, and Tomé believed that the matter had been set right. He hoped that he would receive his loan despite this incident. Locally, however, Tomé had acquired a damaging reputation as one who reneged on his debts, and storekeepers now denied him credit.

Nor did his brothers offer help. I asked Tomé and several other villagers about this. Tomé was especially bitter about Dinho, who, he said, still resented him for his early withdrawal from the cooperative. Tomé insisted that he had done his duty as eldest brother for all his siblings. Before coming home from Rio, he had arranged a good job in fishing there for Dinho. "It was even better than the one I had." When

Dinho and a younger brother had seen a sailboat they wanted to buy in a fishing village north of Arembepe, Tomé had accompanied them there to look it over, and when they found the price more than they could afford, had written a check for the difference. "Dinho could afford to help me. He has only one child, and plenty of money." He expected less of his three youngest brothers, since one had a large family and the other two were still getting established. Tomé recounted that Dinho, acting through an intermediary, had even tried to buy one of his boats, for far less than it was worth, adding insult to injury.

What did others think of Tomé's claim? Shouldn't brothers help each other out? Alberto suggested that since none of Tomé's four brothers was willing to help him, the fault must lie with Tomé. Dora even questioned Tomé's contention that he had helped his brothers when they were younger. At first I found these responses surprising, since, from previous visits, I knew for a fact that Tomé had helped his brothers.

I finally figured out that something more was going on in villagers' heads—a reaction, based on Arembepe's traditions, to a perceived threat against the local social system. Tomé, who had always deviated positively, excelling as an entrepreneur, was now deviating negatively. His common-law union with a hippie was testing the limits of villagers' tolerance. Although rarely used in 1980, the *rapariga* label was applied to Sonia. Pointing to Sonia's house I asked a woman to tell me who lived there.

"Sonia, a hippie."

"What kind of work does she do," I inquired.

"I don't see her doing anything, except living off other women's men."

Another village woman, who had herself once been classified as a *rapariga* because of a similar involvement with a legally married fisherman, still lambasted Tomé and Sonia: "Tomé's wife can't help being sad that he is living with Sonia. Sonia rules in that house. Tomé stays home except when he's fishing, and he doesn't fish like he used to, because he's inside doing all the work that Sonia should be doing, like washing the dishes and other housework. Tomé only wants his 'little Sonia,' " she mimicked. "She calls him 'my little Tomé,' and then yells at him not to spit on the floor. I don't see what he sees in his wife or Sonia. His wife isn't right in the head, and besides she's ugly, as Sonia is. It looks like Tomé could have found a better woman. Neither of those two is worth much."

Given the surplus of males generally and hippie males in particular, in 1980, villagers viewed Sonia's behavior as particularly selfish. "Always bragging about being rich, she doesn't need Tomé like his family does." In villagers' estimation, Tomé was wrong to abandon his wife and family, particularly for a member of a fringe social category. Tomé's father had left his mother, but not for a sexual liaison. Tomé's behavior was considered much worse.

Expectably, Tomé offered a different view. He portrayed his wife as washed out, listless, mentally and physically sick. His description might have been that of a middle-aged man in the United States, complaining that his marriage lacked excitement, that his wife was no longer vital, attractive, or experimental. "She'd never let me sit on the floor like this." (In Sonia's "hippie pad" we were sitting on a mattress that was covered with bright material; we inclined against the wall on several throw pillows.) "My wife would tell me that being on the floor gives you a cold. Here I have peace. At home, I'd never get any rest."

Tomé was particularly resentful about abuses by his wife's two brothers—both mentally ill. "They'd always come and drink all my whiskey." Although Tomé showed no signs of incipient alcoholism, he, like Fernando, drank more than in the past. He told me that although he enjoyed beer and whiskey, he had trouble affording even the former nowadays. Tomé said that he had been particularly bothered by fights and yelling involving his wife and brothers-in-law. "When I came home from several days in a cramped boat on a cold sea, I just wanted to rest. I didn't want to have people yelling all the time and drinking my whiskey."

Tomé's hopes for his children's future were fading. His oldest son, in whose education Tomé had invested a fortune, wasn't a good student; he had failed the vestibular exam and was looking for work. The next son had mental problems, "which the doctor called a family thing, from the mother's side," remembered Tomé bitterly.

The recurrent "I need to rest" was Tomé's summary of an

overdose of social obligations that went along with being successful. Leading to his plight, Arembepe's traditional leveling mechanisms had combined with the time demands of the new economy and Tomé's own overreliance on external resources. "Nowadays I usually stay inside when I'm not working, because every time I walk in the streets someone asks me for money. People still expect me to buy them beer, when they should be buying for me. When a hippie in the Aldeia asked me for money the other day I told him that he should be making loans to me now." Tomé resented villagers' continued expectations of generosity, their failure to recognize his lack of funds, and their lack of concern and help with his current problems.

Tomé sought refuge from marriage, family, in-laws, covillagers, and unbearable responsibility in a common-law relationship, where enduring obligations were absent. Furthermore, in choosing a hippie consort, he made one of the most total and dramatic breaks possible. (When I first heard about Tomé and Sonia, I remarked to my American co-workers that my surprise would hardly have been greater had I learned that Tomé had gone to Paris to study structuralism.) Tomé sought escape with someone on the fringes of the Arembepe social system, an *ippa* who had lived in Arembepe long enough to qualify as a permanent resident. Sonia's reputation would have been better had she not chosen a married man. Their union thus pushed both Sonia and Tomé further toward the social fringes.

No doubt Sonia chose Tomé because he was strong, intelligent, relatively well-off, and ambitious. And in choosing Sonia, Tomé picked not the strangest hippie but someone sufficiently like himself for a comfortable association. Tomé had middle-class aspirations, and Sonia belonged to the middle class. Their skin color was similar. She looked younger than his wife, as did he.

For the study of family structure and patterns, it is also significant that Tomé found a woman like his mother. Sonia had been an alcoholic, like his mother, who, as an extremely poor woman and a twin, had also been somewhat socially isolated. Several times during our conversation he identified himself with patterns in his parental family, comparing, for example, his children with his siblings (five older boys and a girl), and his own marital breakup with his parents' separation. He also told us, with irony, that Sonia's father had recently left his wife for a younger woman; he made the analogy with himself explicit.

Tomé's relationship with Sonia also illustrates his willingness to experiment with the outside world. By living with a middle-class hippie from southern urban Brazil, Tomé was innovating again, forging a link with a different social world. I think, however, that he had made a bad choice this time, as he had when his wish to increase his stake in the fishing industry led him to contract too many debts. Sonia's statements that villagers didn't read contracts and that she feared Tomé's accepting a large rural-credit loan showed her awareness of the dangers that Arembepeiros faced in dealing with the outside world. If Tomé was to make the best of external resources, he could definitely have used the help of a knowledgeable, sympathetic, trustworthy outsider. But this was certainly not Sonia. When we asked her why she didn't advise Tomé about the implications of the contracts he signed, she said that she chose to have nothing to do with his business affairs. Besides, she asserted, "Tomé is always very certain about what he wants to do, and it's hard to change his mind once he makes a decision."

Sonia seemed to have a poor grasp both of Tomé's business affairs and of his place in the Arembepe social system. What Tomé needed was someone with better knowledge than she of how things worked in the outside world. Paradoxically, the very thing that made a member of the middle class available as Tomé's mistress (her desire through a hippie life style to remove herself from her background and the outside connections) also made her a poor choice to be Tomé's mediator with external institutions. Tomé needed someone with the desire and ability to help him manage his external affairs, not someone who had withdrawn from Brazilian national culture. More bluntly, Arembepeiros needed outsiders to teach them how to use knives and forks, not how to enjoy bean sprouts and macrobiotic foods.

In August 1980, Tomé was biding his time, waiting to hear about a loan that might lead either to the restoration of his old preeminence or the liquidation of his estate. Failing the loan, Tomé would have to make the hard decision to sell one boat to permit his economic survival through the other. In telling me of the meager rewards of ordinary fishing, compared to boat ownership, Tomé clung to his accustomed captain-owner's perspective. This was not unrealistic; there were still ways for Tomé to right himself.

He and Sonia hoped to move to new rental quarters once his boats were operating again. Their current apartment was too small for a freezer—necessary if he was going to market his own fish. They had been trying unsuccessfully to find something for less than $125 per month. Perhaps he might even move back into the house registered in his and his mother's name, once his rental agreement with the Salvadorian expired.

What Tomé's story, through August 1980, tells us is that Arembepe's past haunted its present and its near future. The leveling mechanisms discussed in Chapters 3 and 4 were still there. Mired in the social obligations that accompanied success, Tomé sought escape in deviance. Through behavior perceived as antisocial, he cut himself off from the kin-based support and assistance that might otherwise have been offered. And in the final analysis, good *was* limited—not just in people's minds but in fact—in Tomé's victimization by outsiders and in his lack of education, power, and other middle-class advantages. Poverty had proved to be the most durable legacy of traditional Arembepe. And poverty, now fully contextualized within the national class structure, was a generations-old malady that neither a double dose of achievement motivation nor a liaison with a middle-class dropout could do much to cure.

Epilogue

"It was better then, wasn't it, Conrado?" observed a native woman my age, now principal of the junior high school, about my early times in Arembepe. For her family things had indeed been better. In 1962 her father had run the town's main store, co-owned a productive sailboat, and extended credit to virtually everyone in Arembepe. Over the years his business had fallen off, as Arembepeiros bought groceries in Salvador, Itapoan, or from the traveling supermarket bus that now came once a week. A dozen bars, restaurants, and small stores also offered competition.

By 1980 differences in Arembepeiros' perspectives on change were obvious. Some, like Alberto, had only good things to say about the new Arembepe. For most villagers, however, novelty no longer excited and tantalized as it had on my previous visit. In 1973 it had seemed as though Arembepeiros were so fascinated by new people, new technology, and new opportunities that they had little time for us—familiar, unexciting outsiders. But in 1980 many villagers spoke of the old days nostalgically. Several people made a point of telling us that they remembered the automobile rides we had given them during the 1960s. A fishing captain mentioned that he would be forever grateful to field team leader Marvin Harris for driving his wife to a Salvador hospital. Villagers would never forget that a baby girl had been born in the field team vehicle in 1963, as assistant field leader Shepard Forman rushed the mother to the hospital. Aunt Dalia's son remembered that I had once given him a ride from Portão to Arembepe, as I did for Dinho, now Arembepe's biggest capitalist, the day he returned from two years of commercial fishing in Rio de Janeiro.

"You don't forget Arembepe," said a villager to Betty.

"You and Conrado always come back." Many villagers seemed genuinely moved by our 1980 return. I think that they saw us as a kind of complex symbol of the confrontation that has been the subject of this book. We were not just a simple reminder of the preasphalt, prehippie, pretourist, prefactory past. We simultaneously symbolized tradition and change, past and present. Middle-class and alien, we had been unknowing scouts in a coming invasion; but we had been early and special enough to be captured and assimilated by the hosts, and because of this we had been fused into their deeper social history. To be sure, in 1980 we were still outsiders, but long-familiar ones who had witnessed and been part of Arembepe as it used to be.

After my pleasant 1980 stay, I was particularly sorry to leave. I had arranged to work with Alberto the Saturday afternoon before my Sunday departure, clearing up some points and asking final questions. But when I entered his house, expecting to be able to sit on his balcony and con-

Conrad Kottak does field work in Street Down There in 1980. This time villagers seemed genuinely moved by our return. We had become a kind of representation of the confrontation that has been the subject of this book, simultaneously symbolizing tradition and change, past and present. (Courtesy Jerald T. Milanich)

verse as we had often done, I was irritated to find a crew of boisterous weekend drinkers in the place I had planned for us. Alberto and I got in my rental car and I drove us far south, beyond the last summer house and the neighborhood where I had lived in 1973.

We sat and talked on the beach, constantly forced back as the rising tide threatened the field notes I was holding in my lap. After the late August squall the sea was still strong, and yellower than I had ever seen it. There was a powerful scent of rotten eggs in the air. Currents disturbed by the storm were bringing Tibrás residues closer to shore than usual. How long, I wondered, could Arembepe's tourist appeal and its fishing industry last? Was the marine biologist I had talked with in Salvador right? Would pollution, as she contended, eventually destroy this place that held such importance in my life? What would Arembepe be like on my next visit? Would the boat owners stay as rich? Would Dora build her dream house? Could Tomé strike back? These were among the questions I pondered as, filtered through Tibrás fumes, the orange rays of the tropical setting sun shone on the sulfuric sea, turning waters once aqua to the color of blood.

Appendix 1. Ranking of Household Budgets, Arembepe, 1964

Rank	Occupations in Household*	Total Annual Budget (in 1,000 cruzeiros)†
118	Female earner	58
117	Ordinary fisherman	72
116	Female earner	73
115	Female earner	86
114	Female earner	87
113	Female earner	98
112	Female earner	108
111	2 female earners	161
110	Agricultural worker, 2 female earners	166
109	Fisherman, female earner	169
108	Female earner	180
107	Captain, female earner	184
106	Fisherman, female earner	195
105	Retired fisherman, supported	197
104	Mason, 3 female earners	218
103	Female earner, supported	219
102	Mason, midwife	221
101	Female earner	221
100	Fisherman	234
99	2 fishermen	236
98	Supported	239
97	Female earner	252
96	Captain, fisherman, female earner	254
95	Dragnet owner	268
94	Fisherman	278
93	Fisherman, female earner	282
92	Barber-businessman, 2 female earners	286
91	Fisherman	295
90	Fisherman, female earner	300
89	Captain–half-owner, fisherman, occasional fisherman	309
88	Captain–half-owner, stevedore, 2 female earners	312
87	Fisherman	316
86	Captain–half-owner, fisherman	317
85	Fisherman, female earner	322

Appendix 1 (Cont.)

84	Fisherman-owner, 3 female earners	333
83	Captain–half-owner, female earner	335
82	Captain–half-owner	336
81	2 fishermen	342
80	Fisherman, female earner	343
79	Fisherman, agriculturalist	348
78	Fisherman, female earner	359
77	Captain–half-owner	362
76	2 fishermen, caulker	372
75	2 fishermen, 2 female earners	373
74	Fisherman	374
73	Barber, store worker	375
72	2 female earners, landowner	377
71	Fisherman, female earner	394
70	Storekeeper, female earner, cattle owner	404
69	Fisherman, female earner	405
68	Fisherman, 2 female earners	418
67	3 female earners, supported	418
66	Fisherman, female earner	418
65	Storekeeper	420
64	Captain, female earner	420
63	Fisherman	421
62	Fisherman, female earner	423
61	Fisherman	430
60	Fisherman–occasional captain	431
59	Fisherman, agricultural worker	435
58	Storekeeper	435
57	Fisherman, female earner	440
56	Mason, 2 fishermen, 2 female earners	441
55	Fisherman	446
54	Captain–half-owner, 3 female earners	452
53	Fisherman	453
52	Fisherman, 2 occasional fishermen, female earner	457
51	Captain–half-owner, fisherman	461
50	Fisherman, female earner	462
49	Captain–half-owner–agriculturalist, female earner	465
48	2 fishermen	470
47	2 fishermen, caulker, female earner	478

Appendix 1 (Cont.)

46	2 fishermen, schoolteacher, mason	484
45	Fish marketer–farmer, female earner	489
44	Captain	495
43	Fisherman, storekeeper	496
42	3 fishermen, mason	498
41	Fisherman–coconut picker	502
40	Captain-owner, nonfishing boat owner–carpenter–coconut marketer–fish marketer	503
39	Captain–half-owner	503
38	Captain–owner	503
37	Captain–half-owner, agriculturalist	515
36	3 fishermen, occasional fisherman	520
35	Captain, 2 female earners	529
34	2 fishermen	533
33	Fish marketer–landowner, supported	544
32	Fisherman, female earner	547
31	Captain–half-owner–agriculturalist	553
30	Fisherman–half-owner–coconut marketer	555
29	Captain–half-owner	560
28	Fisherman–sometimes captain, fisherman	562
27	Captain–half-owner, fisherman-half-owner	564
26	2 fishermen, carpenter	570
25	3 fishermen	573
24	Fisherman	577
23	Farmer-businessman	580
22	Fish marketer–nonfishing boat owner	582
21	Storekeeper	597
20	Fisherman, 2 female earners, supported	603
19	Captain–half-owner	605
18	Petrobrás worker	606
17	Fisherman	608
16	Storekeeper–farmer	640
15	Fish marketer, boat owner, female earner	650
14	Fisherman–half-owner–barber	664
13	Captain, storekeeper, cowboy, fisherman	665
12	Captain–half-owner–cowboy–farmer	673
11	Petrobrás worker–boat owner	680
10	2 Petrobrás workers, carpenter, fisherman	697
9	Captain–half-owner–farmer	708
8	Boat carpenter–boat owner	713

Appendix 1 (Cont.)

7	Fisherman–half-owner, farmer, storekeeper	783
6	Port captain, fisherman	792
5	Fisherman, businessman–land owner–fish marketer	846
4	Captain, fish marketer, landowner	884
3	Storekeeper, boat owner, landowner	1049
2	Storekeeper, boat owner, landowner	1125
1	Storekeeper, boat owner–landowner–farmer–marketer of coconuts, fish, and cereals	1201
	Mean budget	435
	Median budget	439

Occupations joined by hyphens indicate a single individual with plural occupations. Occupations separated by commas indicate different individuals living in the same household.

†*Figures are for August 1964. 1,500 (old) cruzeiros = $1.*

Appendix 1 (Cont.)

Appendix 2. Primary Occupations of Arembepe Males in 1964, 1973, and 1980, by Percentage

Type of Occupation	1964 N = 173*	1973 N = 231*	1980 N = 230†
Fishing-related	74.0	53.2	40.4
Building, lotting	5.2	14.7	16.1
Odd jobber	2.8	2.6	3.0
Business, food, bar	11.0	8.7	13.5
Hippie work	0.0	2.6	2.6
Factory employment	1.7	11.3	17.0
Municipal, external work	1.7	3.9	4.3
Local service	1.2	1.7	2.6
Agriculture	2.3	1.3	0.0
Total	99.9	100.0	99.9

Based on complete census, by household, of adult males' occupations.

†*The 1980 percentages are based on averages of data from two samples obtained that year: (1) an occupational survey of the 61 inhabited houses in southern Arembepe; and (2) information on the current occupations of 157 men from the 1973 sample who are still alive, employed, and living in Arembepe.*

Appendix 3. Fish Marketing by Ten Crews Through Arembepe's Fishermen's Cooperative During 1972

Month	Kilograms Sold	Price Received per kg. (new cruzeiros)*	Percentage of Monthly Average Caught This Month
1	3,550	2.2	77
2	8,750	2.6	190
3	3,575	2.8	78
4	5,600	2.7	121
5	6,575	2.5	142
6	4,375	2.6	95
7	5,725	3.2	124
8	3,550	3.1	77
9	2,600	3.5	56
10	2,700	3.5	59
11	2,400	3.3	52
12	5,950	3.3	129
Total	55,350		
Monthly Average	4,600	2.9	

*2.2 new cruzeiros = 2,200 old cruzeiros. In July 1973, 6.1 new cruzeiros = $1.

Appendix 4. 1980 Occupations of Men Who Had Fished in 1973*

	Number	% of Active Men	% of All 1973 Fishermen
Active			
Fishing-related	51	71.8	48.6
Building, lotting	2	2.8	1.9
Odd jobber	1	1.4	1.0
Business, food, bar	8	11.3	7.6
Factory employment	7	9.9	6.7
External, municipal work	1	1.4	1.0
Local service	1	1.4	1.0
Agriculture	0	0.0	0.0
Subtotal	71	100.0	67.6
Inactive			
Pensioned, disabled	14		13.3
Sick, alcoholic	5		4.8
Moved away	3		2.9
Dead	12		11.4
Total	105		100.2

*Based on household census, Arembepe and Caraúnas.

Appendix 5. Types of Marital Union in Arembepe and Caraúnas in 1980, According to Main Occupations, Compared with Arembepe in 1964 and Caraúnas in 1973

	Common-law		Formal		Total No.
	No.	%	No.	%	
Arembepe and Caraúnas 1980					
Ordinary fishermen	39	76.5	12	23.5	51
Captains	11	57.9	8	42.1	19
Tibrás workers*	18	60.0	12	40.0	30
Nonfishing boat owners	7	46.7	8	53.3	15
Total	75	65.2	40	34.8[†]	115
Arembepe 1964					
Wealthier half	22	37.9	36	62.1	58
Poorer half	36	69.2	16	30.8	52
Total	58	52.7	52	47.3[‡]	110
Caraúnas 1973					
All residents	33	91.7	3	8.3	36

*Because Tibrás workers were younger in 1980 than the average captain, their percentage of formal marriage can be expected eventually to surpass that of captains.

†Correlation coefficient (θ) for association of wealth and formal marriage in 1980 was .25. Average wealth increases from ordinary fishermen to captains to Tibrás workers to boat owners.

‡Correlation coefficient (θ) for association between wealth and formal marriage in 1964 was .31.

Appendix 6. Male and Female Employment in Arembepe by Percentage, 1973 and 1980

	Male	1973* Female	Total	Male	1980† Female	Total
Fishing-related	53.2	0.0	41.6	37.1	0.0	26.5
Building, lotting	14.7	1.5	11.8	20.5	0.0	14.7
Odd jobber	2.6	49.2	12.8	4.1	51.7	17.6
Business, food, bar	8.7	24.6	12.2	16.4	31.0	20.6
Hippie work	2.6	3.1	2.7	8.2	10.3	8.8
Factory employment	11.3	0.0	8.8	8.2	0.0	5.9
Municipal, external work	3.9	6.2	4.4	2.7	6.9	3.9
Local service	1.7	4.6	2.4	2.7	0.0	2.0
Agriculture	1.3	10.8	3.4	0.0	0.0	0.0
Total	100.0	100.0	100.1	99.9	99.9	100.0
Sample size	231	65	296	73	29	102

*Based on occupational census of all households in Arembepe and Caraúnas.
†Includes only surveyed area in southern Arembepe; for fuller sample of adult male employment in 1980, see Appendix 2.

Chapter Notes

Chapter 1

[1]Arembepe is too well-known to be disguised by giving it another name in this book. However, names of Arembepeiros and certain details about them have been changed to protect their privacy.

Chapter 3

[1]Correlation coefficients (Pearson's r: all variables were treated as equal interval for association between coconut tree ownership and light skin color, and between boat ownership and light skin color) were .124 and −.044, respectively. Neither coefficient is significant at the 95 percent confidence level.

Chapter 4

[1]As noted previously, even technologically advanced open-sea fishing remains a form of foraging—the appropriation of natural or wild, rather than domesticated, resources. Even the most sophisticated fisheries do little to increase the resources of the sea. Fish farming can proceed in restricted areas of water, e.g., ponds and rice paddies, but is virtually impossible on the open sea. Fishermen, of course, can attempt to increase catches by avoiding overfished areas until fish have returned and reproduced. And electronic instruments such as radar, radio telephone, direction finders, and echo-sounders may help to locate fish. However, these devices, which of course were not used in Arembepe, are just better ways to conserve or track game.

[2]The surest way to catch more fish is to do more fishing. Here we find one of the main differences between open-sea fishing and other forms of foraging. In most hunting-gathering societies the primary danger in intensifying production is that strategic resources—particularly game—may be threatened if people take too much of what nature has to offer. For this reason hunter-gatherers have been characterized by Marshall Sahlins (1972) as the original leisured or "affluent" society. A reduced work load helps to conserve game and vegetation by keeping use of the environment below its actual capacity to support its human population.

With rudimentary technology, marine fishing offers a contrast. Given the vastness of their marine environment, fishermen such as those of Arembepe *could* intensify production without endangering the species they depended on. Among fishing peoples not living in modern nations—such as the native populations of the North Pacific coast of North America—the potlatch (a system of competitive feasting) stimulated production, as people stepped up production of fish and other resources that were consumed and given away in monumental feasts (see Harris, 1974). In Arembepe, as in other modern-day fishing villages, increases in production could instead be funneled into an outside market. Indeed, because fish are so perishable, if there is to be increased production, it must always be accompanied by appropriate opportunities for distribution.

Chapter 5

[1]Shepard Forman (1975, pp. 112–115; originally in Forman and Riegelhaupt, 1970) has identified five stages in the development of the regional marketing system in northeastern Brazil. By 1965 Arembepe was moving from Stage 3 to Stage 4—from a system in which several middlemen went to producers (fishermen) to buy for resale in the marketplace or to wholesalers, to one in which wholesalers had begun to bypass the middlemen, going directly to rural producers. An aspect of the transition noted by Forman is that sale for credit (paid in cash only after resale) is replaced by sale to wholesalers for cash. Although this shift from credit to cash sales had occurred in Arembepe by 1965, Forman's observation that when producers receive immediate cash they often sell for less did *not* apply to Arembepe, where as previously noted, the price of fish had continued to rise. The increasing value of Arembepe's fish reflected the village's progressively easier access to Salvador and the ever-present shortage of sufficient food to feed the capital's rapidly growing population (Forman, 1975, pp. 88–89). Arembepe's subsequent evolution toward Forman's Stage 5, in which wholesalers deal directly with large-scale producers at a central delivery point, was an aspect of change in Arembepe after 1965 that is examined later in this chapter.

Nor, by 1965, had Arembepeiros replaced their regular arrangement of selling to particular agents with sale on a first-come, first-served basis, which Forman (1975, p. 114) found to be usual when wholesalers bought directly from producers. No doubt this was because of fish's perishability. Producers had to be sure that someone would take their fish to market, even if this meant selling for less (which it did *not* in Arembepe's case).

In contrast to fish marketing, however, Arembepeiros maintained no regular sales agreements with the buyers of their coconuts, the village's second major export, which local middlemen transported to market in Salvador. The price that Arembepeiros received for their coconuts, which were sold in Salvador for later resale, varied with supply and demand, and Arembepeiros had to compete on an open market with other rural Bahians. In 1965 Arembepeiros were drawing a total annual income of about $6,000 from the fruits of 16,000 coconut trees owned by 77 villagers. Arembepe's coconut marketing, as practiced in the mid-1960s, remained in the second stage of Forman's (1975, p. 112) model of the development of the northeast Brazilian rural marketing system. That is, rural people sold to middlemen locally or in distribution fairs, i.e., the markets in Salvador just mentioned.

[2]Through education and by offering benefits of patronage, Jorge and a few others were exceptions and received special respect, if not the outright deference that native Arembepeiros knew so little about giving.

Chapter 6

[1]Annual marketed catches averaged 5,500 kilograms at 3.4 cruzeiros per kilogram, or about $3,050.

Chapter 7

[1]Characterization of Arembepe as "the land of dreams" is taken from hippie wall graffiti noted by Maxine Margolis.

[2]I censused 313 people in the 130 houses in the sampled area of southern Arembepe. This gives an average of 5.1 inhabitants in the (61) inhabited houses, and 2.4 on the average for the 130. Multiplying 2.4 by 617, the number of houses in the government census of Arembepe in 1980, gives 1,481 people, not far off the official census figure of 1,561.

Chapter 8

[1]Historian E. Bradford Burns (1980, pp. 534–535) notes that the poor were experiencing something similar throughout Brazil. The working class had to work harder just to maintain a precarious living standard. The work-time cost of a monthly subsistence ration (same amount of same supplies) increased from 87 hours in 1965 to 187 hours in 1976.

[2]Since some members had withdrawn before repaying their debts, SUDEPE apparently cut its losses by dipping into the cooperative's remaining general funds, including payments due to fishermen for the previous month's catches. No legal action was ever taken in connection with the cooperative's collapse.

[3]Since 1976 SUDEPE has employed F., a fairly well educated Arembepeiro, to note the weights of all fish brought to shore in Arembepe. Whenever fish are unloaded, he visits the fish stores to record weights.

I am grateful to Maria Gomes Pereira, a marine biologist employed by SUDEPE in Salvador, for making available to me unpublished data on fishing productivity in Arembepe and Bahia generally. Her figures for Arembepe, which show total annual marketed catches to have been 140,000, 125,000, and 130,000 kilograms in 1977, 1978, and 1979, respectively, are based on F.'s notes, which he delivers monthly to SUDEPE headquarters in Salvador. SUDEPE has hired similar recorders in all Bahian fishing communities. F.'s own estimates of Arembepe's productivity were higher; he thought that the fleet produced between 15,000 and 20,000 kilograms per month, which would give an annual production of between 180,000 and 240,000 kilograms. Assuming fifteen to twenty vessels active for twelve months, the average annual production per boat would then be 12,000 kilograms. To arrive at a (lower) estimate of proceeds from Arembepe's fishing industry, I have averaged three years of SUDEPE figures, arriving at 132,000 kilograms annually, about 9,000 per boat, assuming that fifteen boats fished regularly during the entire year. This is still quite a jump over the 1972 figures given in Appendix 3.

[4]Only four boats of the nineteen active in Arembepe in 1980 had close kin connections among crew members, including captain. Significantly, in three of these, the captain was also the boat owner. Profit taking was less mercenary in these boats than in others. For example, the owner and true captain of one boat gave his aging uncle the captain's (double) share, maintaining the fiction that the old man still held that position. Of the fifteen other active boats, ten with nonfishing owners, two crews included only distant kin (beyond first cousins); the other thirteen crews lacked *any kin ties at all*, another measure of the extent to which most crews had become purely economic units.

[5]The total number of fishermen (counting captains) had also shrunk, from 128 in 1964 to 90 in 1980, supplying five-man crews for most of the nineteen active boats.

[6]In 1973, 113 men fished out of Arembepe. 105 lived in Arembepe and Caraúnas. The others came from nearby settlements, including agricultural estates to the west.

[7]In sharp contrast to the past, when fishermen had received no retirement benefits and needed to rely on kin, coconut trees, and other investments made during their active years, about 13 percent of the 1973 fishermen were receiving government pensions in 1980. Equivalent to $40 monthly, these benefits were a welcome supplement, particularly since a man's obligation to support others decreased with age and he and his wife could still draw on the informal fund of kin-based social security built up before retirement. Twelve (19 percent) of the 1973 fishermen had died, moved away, or become alcoholics or pensionless invalids. Of the seventy-one

still active men, fifty-one (72 percent) still fished, seven had entered business, and eight worked for Tibrás. The other five had turned to other occupations. The contrast with the past was clear. Among still employed men more occupational shifting had occurred between 1973 and 1980 than between 1964 and 1973. Furthermore, given deaths and retirement, less than half the 105 men who had fished in 1973 were still fishing in 1980.

[8]Fishermen get to sell fewer fish today than in 1965, despite the fact that their individual productivity increased from 850 kilograms per year in 1965 to 1,450 in 1980. Ninety fishermen in 1980 outproduced 127 in 1964, catching about 130,000 kilograms annually, versus 108,000 kilograms when thirty-one boats had limited their fishing to offshore Arembepe.

Chapter 9

[1]I thank Nelson Pinheiro, the Director of Statistical Services in Camaçari, for sending me the results of the 1980 census.

[2]The correlation coefficient (θ) for the association of wealth and formal marriage in Arembepe in 1964 was .31. This computation is based on the figures given in Appendix 5. Other figures in that appendix show that the correlation was weaker in 1980.

[3]However, 54 percent of the population between ages ten and forty-nine was female, intensifying the scarcity of husbands.

References Cited

Barry, H., M. K. Bacon, and I. L. Child
    1959   "Relation of Child Training to Subsistence Economy." *American Anthropologist* 61:51–63.

Becker, Howard S.
    1963   *Outsiders*. New York: Free Press.

Brown, Diana
    1979   "Umbanda and Class Relations in Brazil." In *Brazil: Anthropological Perspectives*, ed. Maxine L. Margolis and William E. Carter. New York: Columbia University Press, pp. 270–304.

Burns, E. Bradford
    1980   *A History of Brazil*, 2nd ed. New York: Columbia University Press.

Chagnon, Napoleon
    1977   *Yanomamo: The Fierce People*, 2nd ed. New York: Holt, Rinehart and Winston.

Comitas, Lambros
    1962   "Fishermen and Cooperation in Rural Jamaica." Ph.D. dissertation, Columbia University. Ann Arbor, Michigan: Xerox University Microfilm.

Economist, The (London)
    1979   "Oh! Brazil: A Survey." August 4, 1979.

Eldredge, Niles
    1963   "Some Technological Aspects of the Fishing Industry of a Town on the Northeast Coast of Brazil." New York: Columbia-Cornell-Harvard-Illinois Summer Field Studies Program in Anthropology. (Program Files, Columbia University.)

Farrell, Ronald A., and Victoria Lynn Swigert, eds.
    1975   *Social Deviance*. Philadelphia: Lippincott.

Forman, Shepard
    1967   "Cognition and the Catch: The Location of Fishing Spots in a Brazilian Coastal Village." *Ethnology* 6:417–426.
    1970   *The Raft Fishermen: Tradition and Change in the Brazilian Peasant Economy*. Bloomington: Indiana University Press.
    1975   *The Brazilian Peasantry*. New York: Columbia University Press.

Forman, Shepard, and Joyce Riegelhaupt
    1970   "Market Place and Marketing System: Toward a Theory of Peasant Economic Integration." *Comparative Studies in Society and History* 12(2):188–212.

Foster, George M.
    1965   "Peasant Society and the Image of Limited Good." *American Anthropologist* 67:293–315.

Freeman, Linton
    1965   *Elementary Applied Statistics for Students in the Behavioral Sciences*. New York: Wiley.

Fried, Morton
    1960   "On the Evolution of Social Stratification and the State." In *Culture in History*, ed. S. Diamond. New York: Columbia University Press, pp. 713–731.

Gross, Daniel R.
    1973   "Factionalism and Local Level Politics in Rural Brazil." *Journal of Anthropological Research* 29:123–144.

Gross, Rose Lee
    1964   "Local Politics and Administration: Camaçari, Bahia, Brazil." New York: Columbia-Cornell-Harvard-Illinois Summer Field Studies Program in Anthropology. (Program Files, Columbia University).

Harding, Susan
    1975   "Women and Words in a Spanish Village." In *Toward an Anthropology of Women*, ed. Rayna Reiter. New York: Monthly Review Press, pp. 283–308.

Harris, Marvin
    1974   *Cows, Pigs, Wars, and Witches.* New York: Random House.

Harris, Marvin, and Conrad Kottak
    1963   "The Structural Significance of Brazilian Racial Categories." *Sociologia* 25:203–209.

Hausmann, F., and J. Haar
    1978   *Education in Brazil.* Hamden, Conn.: Archon.

Havinghurst, Robert, and J. Roberto Moreira
    1965   *Society and Education in Brazil.* Pittsburgh: University of Pittsburgh Press.

Hewlett, Sylvia Ann
    1980   *The Cruel Dilemmas of Development: Twentieth-Century Brazil.* New York: Basic Books.

Johnson, Allen
    1971   *Sharecroppers of the Sertão: Economics and Dependence on a Brazilian Plantation,* Stanford, Calif.: Stanford University Press.

Kottak, Conrad Phillip
    1966   "The Structure of Equality in a Brazilian Fishing Community." Ph.D. dissertation, Columbia University. Ann Arbor: Xerox University Microfilms.
    1967a   "Kinship and Class in Brazil." *Ethnology* 6:427–443.
    1967b   "Race Relations in a Bahian Fishing Village." *Luso-Brazilian Review* 4:35–52.
    1980   *The Past in the Present: History, Ecology, and Cultural Variation in Highland Madagascar.* Ann Arbor: University of Michigan Press.

Kottak, Isabel Wagley
    1977   "A Village Prostitute in Northeastern Brazil." *Michigan Discussions in Anthropology* 2:245–252.

Labov, William
    1972   *Sociolinguistic Patterns.* Philadelphia: University of Pennsylvania Press.

Lemert, Edwin M.
    1951   *Social Pathology: A Systematic Approach to the Theory of Sociopathic Behavior.* New York: McGraw-Hill.

Lévi-Strauss, Claude
    1967   *Structural Anthropology.* New York: Basic Books.

Malinowski, Bronislaw
    1961   (orig. 1922) *Argonauts of the Western Pacific.* New York: Dutton.

Marshall, Mac
    1979   *Weekend Warriors: Alcohol in a Micronesian Culture.* Palo Alto, Calif.: Mayfield.

Mintz, Sidney, and Eric R. Wolf
    1950   "An Analysis of Ritual Co-parenthood *(Compadrazgo).*" *Southwestern Journal of Anthropology* 6:341–368.

Redfield, Robert
    1948   *The Folk Culture of Yucatan.* Chicago: University of Chicago Press.
    1960   *Peasant Society and Culture and the Little Community.* Chicago: University of Chicago Press.

Reiter, Rayna
    1975   "Men and Women in the South of France: Public and Private Domains." In *Toward an Anthropology of Women,* ed. Rayna Reiter. New York: Monthly Review Press, pp. 252–282.

Robock, Stefan H.
    1975   *Brazil: A Study in Development Progress.* Lexington, Mass.: Heath.

Sahlins, Marshall D.
   1972   *Stone Age Economics*. Chicago: Aldine.
Tolkien, J. R. R.
   1965   *The Lord of the Rings*. Part III: *The Return of the King*. New York: Ballantine.
Wagley, Charles W.
   1963   *Introduction to Brazil*. New York: Columbia University Press.
Wagley, Charles W., ed.
   1952   *Race and Class in Rural Brazil*. Paris: UNESCO.
Weber, Max
   1958   (orig. 1920) *The Protestant Ethic and the Spirit of Capitalism*. New York: Scribner's.
Wolf, Eric R.
   1955   "Types of Latin American Peasantry." *American Anthropologist* 57:452–471.

Index

Abrantes, 4–5

Alberto: and *candomblé*, 250; and case of wife, Carolina, 148–150; family of in 1980, 160–161; and loss of his child, 65–66; in 1964, 19; in 1973, 41; in 1980, 160

Alberto, interactions of: with *ippa*, 181–182; with João, 183–184; with Milton, 168

Alberto, story of: background of in, 256–257; illustration of, 259–263; success of in, 258–259; talents of in, 262, years between 1965 and 1980 in, 257–258

Alcoholism, 236–237

Aldeia: as hippie settlement, 131–133; location of, 41; in 1980, 176–177; separations of, 177–179

Anthropologists: objectivity of, 40–41; as observers, participants, 20; and people worked with, 16; research techniques of, 17

Anthropology, cultural, and contrasts between sociology, 16–17

Arembepe: and avoidance of hippies during visits to, 41–42; blights of, in 1960s, 10; comparison of, with Coqueiral, 116–118; crime in, in 1973, 36 (*see also* Arembepeiros, and fear of robbers); culture shock during visits to, 20–21, 23–24; economy of (*see* Economy; Fishing); education in (*see* Education; Government, and education); establishment of rapport during visits to, 12–14; fate of, 3; festivities in (*see* Chegança; Saint John's night; Saint Francis, ceremony for); ghetto of (*see* Cara-únas); government in (*see* Government); growth of, physical, between 1965 and 1973, 38,

127; health of (*see* Health Services); hippie invasion of (*see* Hippies); history of, between 1973 and 1980, 206; household budgets in, in 1964, 52; housing in (*see* Housing); life in, 24–25, 78–79 (*see also* Arembepeiros; Government; Health services; Social system); location of, 3, 8; lotting in, results of, 162–163; marketing opportunities of, 101; and mass media, 131; medical posts in, 218 (*see also* Health services, in 1980s); medicine in (*see* Health services); and motorized transportation (*see* Fishing; Motorized fishing agents); in 1962, 7–8, 10; in 1964, 101–102; in 1973, 31–33; in 1980, 46–47, 187; as open community, 56–58; outsiders in, 167–169 (*see also* Arembepeiros, and outsiders, treatment of); people of (*see* Arembepeiros); pollution in, 29–30, 32, 129 (*see also* Tibrás); population of (*see* Arembepeiros; Population); renters in, 169–170; results of visits to, 27–28; roads to, 31–33, 44–45, 101–102, 187; and Salvador, 4; satellite of (*see* Big Well); social system in (*see* Social system); as sociocultural micro-evolution, 47; tourism in, 29, 128–129, 159; visits to, 3–4, 7–8, 11, 15, 29, 43, 157; visits to, by Conrad Phillip Kottak, 3; weather of, 25–26

Arembepeiros, 3; and alcoholism, 236–238; and bourgeois (burgués), 232–233; and change, perspectives on, 288–289; characteristics of, in 1964, 18–19; co-parenthood of (compadesco), 67, 102, 229; diet of, 65–66; diver-

309

sity of occupations in 1973,
133–134; employment of male,
188; experiences of, with outside
world, 118–122; and fear of robbers, 36, 233–236; and guilt,
engendered by birth and death,
239–240; and hippies, view of,
173–176 (see also Hippies); kinship of, 61–63, 238; marriage of,
63–64, 224–228 (see also Marriage); and mental illness,
238–240; and mule drivers, 102
(see also Fishing, and mule
drivers; nostalgia of, 288–289;
occupations of, in 1960s, 79–80;
occupations in 1980, 204; and
outsiders, treatment of, 70–72,
162–163, 167–169; race relations
of, 73–77, 242–243; rapport of,
with fieldworkers in 1962, 12–
14; religion of (see Candomblé
cult; Catholicism, Roman); sex
discrimination of, 67–70, 72–73,
242–245; sex ratio of, 229–230;
sex roles of, 67–70, 243–245;
sharing system of, 64, 66–67;
social system of (see Social
system); terminology of, racial,
75–76
Argonauts of the Western Pacific, 11
Autoestrada (superhighway), 31

Basic Education Reform Law of
1971, 217. *See also* Government,
and education
Betsileo, 18–19
Bichos (beasts), 23
Big Well, 30, 60
Boat captains: first-class, 91–92;
role of, 87–91; second-class, 92;
successful, 91, 93; third-class,
92; unsuccessful, 91, 93
Bourgeois (burguês), rise of,
232–233
Brandão, Maria, 103
Brazil: classes of society in, according to Robert Havinghurst and
Roberto Moreira, 121; communities in, stratified, study of, 51;

development in, economic, 186–
187; "economic miracle" of, 127;
"Great Tradition" of, 27; inflation in, 55; population of, 203;
race relations in, comparison of,
with United States, 6, 14–15;
and "Revolution of 1964," 127
Bressler, Erica, 32

Cachaça (common run), 24, 26,
27, 46, 57, 159
Camaçari, 61
Camões, Emily, 107
Camões, Jorge: initiation of, to
make Arembepe a tourist attraction, 58; and lotting, 107, 110–
111; as patron of Arembepe,
114, 180; politics of, 112–114;
real estate business of, 163–166
Camões, Miguel, 109
Candomblé cult: ceremonies of,
145–146, 246–253; and change,
means of dealing with, 149–150;
and curing, 249–250; and deviance, 245; as expression, of involvement with external systems,
246; imagery of, reproductive
and kinship, 251; and Maria,
case of, 251–253; in 1973, 144,
146–149; and problems, solution
to unfamiliar, 148; reasons for,
250–251; sex roles in, 253
Caraúnas: as ghetto, 33–34; housing in, 39, 166; in 1980, 45;
prices in, real estate, 170
Catholicism, Roman, 147, 247
Chagnon, Napoleon, 20
Chegança, 26
Coconut Road, 45
Columbia-Cornell-Harvard-Illinois
Summer Field Studies Program
in Anthropology, 4
Comitas, Lambros: review of
fishing literature, 79; seminar
by, 6, 11
Conformity, social, 240
Coqueiral: comparison of, with
Arembepe, 116–118; economy
of, in 1960s, 81; study of, by
Shepard Forman, 79

Crews, fishing boat: distinction of, between the captain and ordinary fishermen, 84: and joint line system, 144; in 1960s, 84; in 1980, 190–191, 199–200
Crispim, 245–246, 248–249
Culture shock, 20

deAzevedo, Thales, 15
Deviance, social, 240–241
Dinho, 193–195
Dora, role of in 1962, 21
Dora, story of: deviation in, 265–266; and kinship in, 268–269; as *rapariga* or village prostitute in, 264–268; rise of, in social status in, 268–270; social rejection of, in, 266; years between mid-1960s until early 1970s in, 264–268

Economy: change in, 47; decreases in, of farming, livestock, and tree ownership, 135–136; diversity of, 127 (*see also* Fishing); hierarchy in, 80–82; increases in, of tourism, business, construction, and factory employment, 134–136; and inflation, 55; isolation of, from national power structure, 58; and link between crew members and captains of fishing boats, 140–142; in 1960s, 58; in 1980, 186–187; and Protestant-capitalist-individualism, 53–56; socioeconomic differentiation within, 140–141
Education: in 1960s, 37; in 1973, 37; in 1980, 217–218. *See also* Government, and education
Eldredge, Niles, 99
Epstein, David, 5
Ethnography: definition of, 4; personal aspect of, 11, 20; scientific and professional, 11; techniques used in, 6

Farofeiros, 128–129
Fernando, story of: alcoholic consumption of in, 272; as captain-

owner in, 271; and change, fear and resistance to in, 271–272; childhood of in, 270; as fisherman in, 271; and kin ties, lack of in, 274; in 1980, 273–276; and outsiders, reactions to in, 275–276; as successful captain in, 150; tendencies of, of inaccuracy in, 274; and use of traditional fishing patterns in, 191
Fishermen's Society, The, 60, 205
Fishing: and bait, access to, 138; changes in allocation profits, 192, 195–197; cooperatives for (*see* SUPEDE); dependence of, on external supplies, 197–199; dependence of, on immigration, 202–203; and failure of cooperative, 192; gas lamps in, 190; and grievances of Arembepeiros, 200–201; hook-and-line, 83; and ice, availability of, 137–138; and "ice fishing," 138, 190; landmarking system of, 95–99; and link, between crew members and captains of fishing boats, 140–142; and lobstering, 152–153; and long-distance fishing, 191; and marketing in, 193–195; and middleman, external, 104; motorization of, 136–138; and motorized fishing agents, 104–105; and mule drivers, 102–104; and natives (Arembepe fishermen), 203–204; new order of, 204–207; in 1960s, 82, 84, 86–93; in 1970s, 140–142; in 1980s, 190–192; 197–203; and overfishing, 151–153; and overnight fishing, 191; patterns, change in, 152, 157, 189, 199–200; and price of fish, 84–85; problems of, 206–207; production, relations, of, 188, 192, 200; productivity of, 151; profit, double for owner, 195–196; and range of fishing industry, expansion of, 138; relationships, social, change in, 152, 201–203; seasons, 83–84; tech-

nology, 84; and time, reduction of to reaching fishing grounds, 137–138; and wholesalers, 104

Fishing boats: in 1960s, 82, 85–87; in 1980s, 189; owners of, and nonfishing, 85. *See also* Boat captains; Crews, fishing boat

Forman, Shepard: generalization of, about fishermen, 101; study by, of Coqueiral, 79, 116; theory of, of "patron-clientship" versus "patron-dependency," 106

Foster, George: and leveling mechanisms, 53; and peasant societies, 94; theory of, 53

Fried, Morton, 96

Fundo Rural, 218, 222

Gorlin, Peter: in 1964, 15; study by, of Jauá, 15, 18, 32; work of, with the interview schedule in Jauá and Arembepe, 18

Government: and education, 217–218 (*see also* Arembepe, education in); effects of pensions, on formal marriage, 225; and health services, 218, 221–222 (*see also* Health services); in 1960s, 58–61; in 1980s, 214–217; pensions, 214–215; role of, in villager's lives, 58–61, 214–217; structure of, internal political, in 1960s, 58–61

Gross, Daniel, 112

Gross, Rose Lee, 61

Harris, Marvin: and *candomblé* house, 146; and Maria Brandão, 103; in 1962, 4–6, 21, 23; seminar by, 6; study by, of race relations in Brazil, 6, 14–15

Havinghurst, Robert, 121

Health services: changes in, in knowledge and customs, 219–220; in 1960s, 10–11; in 1970s, 37–38; in 1980s, 218–220, 223–224; problems of, 219–221

Hewlett, Sylvia, 186

Hippies: acceptance, of, 171–173; characteristics of, 173–176;

culture of, in Aldeia, 176–179; effects of, on marriage in Arembepe, 227–228; end of era of, 184–185; female (*ippas*), 39; invasion of, in Arembepe, 29; male (*ippis*), 39; and population, growth of, 39; settlement of (*see* Aldeia); and transformation of Arembepe, 129, 131–133

Housing: and boxcar apartments, 170–171; in 1960s, 33–34; in 1973, 34–37; in 1980, 166; of summer people, 128

Ice fishing, 138, 190

Identity, social. *See* Label, social identity

INPS (Instituto Nacional de Previdência Social), 222

Interview schedule: in Arembepe, in 1964, 17–20; and questionnaire, contrast with, 16

Itapoan, 31

Jagger, Mick, 39, 132

Jaime, 210–212

Jauá, 15

João, 179–180, 182–184

Joplin, Janis, 39, 132

Julia, 238–239

Kinship, costs and benefits of, 61–67

Label, social identity, 240

Landmark system of fishing: *emic* explanation (native's account) of, 96; *etic* explanation (anthropologist's account) of, 96; exaggeration of significance of, 97–99

Laurentino, 86–87

Leveling mechanism, 52–53; sharing, as, 64, 85

Lord of the Rings, 32

Madagascar, 5

Male-female relations: in 1960s, 67–70; in 1980, 242–245

Malinowski, Bronislaw: and *Argo-*

nauts of the Western Pacific, 11; study by, of fishermen and traders in Melanesia, 11–12

Margolis, Maxine, 43

Marriage: and common-law arrangements, 226–229; formal, causes of reduced, 225–229; and hippies effects of on, 227–228; and inheritance, 226–227; modifications in, between 1960s and 1980, 224–225; in 1980, 225–229; and pensions, government regulations of, 225

Marshall, Mac, 237

Mental illness, 238–239

Milanich, Jerald, 43

Moreira, Roberto, 121

Motorized fishing agents, 104–105; and Roberto, 102

Nora (daughter of Francisca Ricardo's daughter), 107

Patronage system, 106; weakness of, 110. *See also* Ricardo, Francisca; Camões, Jorge; Camões, Emily; Camões, Miguel; Nora; Prudencio

Pesqueiros. *See* Landmark system of fishing

Petrobrás, 56, 80, 121–122

Polanski, Roman, 39

Pollution scandal of Tibrás, 131, 213

Population: of Brazil, 203; and hippies, effects of on, 39; in 1977, 166–167; in 1980, 167; of renters, 169–170

Population growth: between 1964 and 1973, 38–39, 127; between 1964 and 1980, 203

Protestant Ethic and the Spirit of Capitalism, The, 52

Prudencio: politics of, 112, 114–116; as representative of landlords, 57; work of, 109–110

Questionnaire, in contrast with interview schedule, 16

Race relations: in 1960s, 73–77; in 1980, 242–243; social differentiation in, 242

Ranked social system, versus stratified social system, 51–52, 197–199

Rapaport, Raymond, 41, 46

Rapport, establishing, 12

Redfield, Robert, 27, 241

Ricardo, Francisca, 107

Roberto, 102, 104–105

Role personality, 240

Saint Francis, ceremony for, 26, 60, 147

Saint John's night, 26–27, 60, 147

Salvador, 4

Sampling techniques, 17

Social identity, 240

Social system: and bourgeois (*burguês*), rise of, 232–233; change in, 231–232; conversion of, from ranked to stratified, 197–199; differences of, ranked versus stratified, 51–52; and features of open community, 56; and immigrants, 70–73; and kinship, 61–63; and leveling mechanisms (*see* Leveling mechanism); and male-female relation (*see* Male-female relations); and marriage, 63–64; in 1960s, 53–56; in 1973, 30; and outsiders, 167–169; and Protestant-capitalist-individualism, 53–56; and race relations (*see* Race relations); research of, on conformity and deviance, 240–242; and sharing, 64–65; social differentiation in, 241, 242; stratification in, 141–144

Sociologists: and people worked with, 16; research techniques of, 17

Sociology, and contrasts between cultural anthropology, 16–17

Stratification, 141–144; process of, in Arembepe, 197–199

SUDEPE (Superintendência do

Desenvolvimento da Pesca),
136–137
Summer people, 35–36

Thompson, Elizabeth, 32
Tibrás (Titanium of Brazil): effects
of, on tourism, 130–131; and
fate of Arembepe, 213; in-
fluences of, on Arembepe,
212–213; manufacturing at, of
titanium dioxide, 129; and mass
media, 130–131; in 1973, 32; in
1980, 44; pollution scandal of,
131, 213; and road to Arembepe, 187; services provided by,
209–210; and transformation of
Arembepe, 129; work at, 208
Titanium dioxide, 129
Tomé: as example of Arembepeiros' lack of risk taking, 55;
and The Fishermen's Society, 60;
and fishing, 193 (see also
Dinho); income of, 80; in 1964,
19; in 1973, 42; and 1973 interview, 139; multiple occupations
of, 81
Tomé, story of: deviation of in,
283– 285; economic decline of,

278–282; as entrepreneur in,
277; as fisherman in, 276–277;
illustration of, 287; marriage of
in, 277–278; and outsiders, reactions to, in, 282, 286; in Rio de
Janeiro in, 277–278; and Sonia
in, 280–281, 286–287

Volta do Robalo, 45, 166

Wagley, Betty (Mrs. Conrad
Phillip Kottak): and Dora, 263;
and "Great Tradition" of Brazil,
27; in 1962, 5, 23; in 1980, 43
Wagley, Charles: description of, of
rural Brazilian community, 60;
in 1962, 4; theory of, on kinship,
62
Wattle-and-daub huts, in
Arembepe, 34
Weber, Max: and Protestant-
capitalists, and successful boat
captains, 93–94; and Protestant
ethic of early capitalism, 91, 94;
and The Protestant Ethic and
the Spirit of Capitalism, 52;
theory of, 52
Withers, Carl, 210
Wolf, Eric, 56

About the Author

Conrad Phillip Kottak is Professor of Anthropology and Chairman of the Graduate Program in Anthropology at the University of Michigan, Ann Arbor, where he has taught since 1968. He received his Ph.D. from Columbia University in 1966, and immediately thereafter set out for Madagascar to do field work among the Betsileo in 1966 and 1967. Professor Kottak's doctoral research (1962, 1964, 1965) was in an Atlantic fishing community, Arembepe, in northeastern Brazil. He returned to Arembepe in 1973 and 1980 to investigate the social impact of "modernization" in this rapidly changing area. Professor Kottak's last research involved a brief visit to Madagascar in 1981.

Conrad Kottak's recent books include *The Past in the Present: History, Ecology, and Cultural Variation in Highland Madagascar* (1980) and *Researching American Culture: A Guide for Student Anthropologists* (1982). Both are published by the University of Michigan Press in Ann Arbor. The third editions of Kottak's general anthropology texts, *Anthropology: The Exploration of Human Diversity* and *Cultural Anthropology*, were published by Random House in spring 1982.

Professor Kottak has contributed articles to many journals, including *American Anthropologist, American Ethnologist, Comparative Studies in Society and History, Ethnology, Journal of Anthropological Research, Natural History*, and *Psychology Today*. He belongs to several professional associations, including the American Anthropological Association, Society for Applied Anthropology, American Ethnological Society, Society for Medical Anthropology, and Central States Anthropological Association.

At the University of Michigan Conrad Kottak has taught courses on anthropology and economic development, field methods, cultural ecology, anthropological theory, Africa, Brazil, and the contemporary United States. Most regularly, however, he teaches introductory anthropology to 600 students per semester.